Teaching Children who are Deafblind

CONTACT, COMMUNICATION AND LEARNING

EDITED BY

STUART AITKEN • MARIANNA BUULTJENS
CATHERINE CLARK • JANE T. EYRE • LAURA PEASE

David Fulton Publishers
London

David Fulton Publishers Ltd
Ormond House, 26–27 Boswell Street, London WC1N 3JD
Web site: http://www.fultonbooks.co.uk

First published in Great Britain by David Fulton Publishers 2000

Note: The rights of Stuart Aitken, Marianna Buultjens, Catherine Clark, Jane T. Eyre and Laura Pease to be identified as the editors of this work has been asserted by them in accordance with the Copyright, Designs and Patents Act 1988.

Copyright © David Fulton Publishers 2000

British Library Cataloguing in Publication Data

A catalogue record for this book is available from the British Library

ISBN 1–85346–674–3

Typeset by FiSH Books, London
Printed by The Cromwell Press Ltd, Trowbridge, Wilts.

Contents

Acknowledgements

The editors and authors would like to acknowledge the original work done by Ailish Massey and Elizabeth Bryson, the main authors of the package which inspired this book: *Contact: a resource for staff working with children who are deafblind.*

Thanks are due to the Scottish Office Education and Industry Department (now the Scottish Executive Education Department) for contributing financially to the evaluation of *Contact* and the writing of this book.

For advice and contribution throughout, thanks to Joyce Wilson of Sense Scotland and also to Eileen Boothroyd and David Brown of Sense UK.

We would like to recognise the contribution of colleagues in the Scottish Sensory Centre (SSC), Sense Scotland and of staff and pupils of Carnbooth School, Glasgow and Whitefield Schools and Centre, Walthamstow, London.

Our special thanks to Ruth Simpson, SSC Administrator, who kept us in order during the three years of the evaluation exercise and writing of the book and prepared the text for sending to the publishers.

Finally, our gratitude goes to family and friends who patiently supported our efforts.

Foreword

Resources and training material about children who are deafblind are all too rare, so it is therefore a great privilege to have been asked to write the foreword to this work. I have been involved in deafblindness personally and professionally for twenty-five years. It is an area that has enriched and challenged me.

I am also proud to know the contributors and consider them as respected colleagues. It is without doubt that their individual and collective knowledge is extensive. Moreover, their wisdom is rooted in both practice and research which brings great authority to this work.

The principles of contact, communication and learning are fundamental; they apply to us all. The process of putting these same principles into practice with children who are deafblind can be complex, incremental and challenging. This book rewards the reader by identifying what contact, communication and learning can mean for a deafblind child. At the same time it sets out detailed guidance on practice.

Throughout, information is given with a rare insight and compassion for children with these very special needs. The reader will come to understand that the child is first and the condition of deafblindness is secondary.

The educator will be taken on a journey that outlines deafblindness and the early importance of assessment. This is set in a context of understanding the impact of the environment through to a clear and tested approach. Further, the work acknowledges the importance of the relationship between the educator and the child. Thus an overarching framework is created which is informed by all aspects of a child's life.

The reader will gain an understanding of children who are deafblind and will find their educational skills much enhanced by this work. The children and families will be reassured by the dedication, commitment and growing knowledge to which this book undoubtedly contributes.

Gillian Morbey OBE
Sense Scotland
April 2000

Preface

Teaching Children who are Deafblind: Contact, Communication and Learning has its roots in *Contact: A resource for staff working with children who are deafblind*, a staff development package whose main authors were Ailish Massey, then head teacher of Carnbooth School for Deafblind Children, and Elizabeth Bryson, an educational psychologist who worked closely with the school.

Following its publication in 1993, detailed feedback was sought from all who used *Contact*. The majority acknowledged it as a valuable teaching resource. At the same time many respondents noted that deafblindness may be accompanied by additional, often complex, physical, communication and learning difficulties, and that teaching resources could reflect this changing population. With post-school transition a prime concern to parents and practitioners, advice on the 16+ age group was requested. Finally, major developments have taken place in both the curricular and legislative context of education and child care since *Contact* was published.

The Scottish Office Education and Industry Department (now Scottish Executive Education Department) agreed to fund the updating and expansion of a resource on deafblindness that would encompass a wider range of educational support needs, address issues of transition and reflect the new legislative and curricular context. This book is the outcome.

The authors are delighted that a well-respected educational publisher, David Fulton, agreed to take on the title. We hope that *Teaching Children who are Deafblind: Contact, Communication and Learning* will take forward the education of deafblind children in the twenty-first century, just as much as *Contact: A resource for staff working with children who are deafblind* did in the twentieth.

Stuart Aitken and Marianna Buultjens
April 2000

Contributors

Stuart Aitken is Principal Officer (Research and Practice) with Sense Scotland, and Senior Research Fellow with the CALL Centre, which is located in the Faculty of Education, University of Edinburgh. He has contributed to several publications on the education, learning and communication of children and young people with a range of special educational needs, including visual impairment, deafblindness and multiple disability.

Marianna Buultjens is the Coordinator of the Scottish Sensory Centre at Moray House Institute of Education, University of Edinburgh. As a member of the team which produced the original *Contact* staff development package she has been committed to ensuring that this material for people working with deafblind children should be extended and updated. The present book is the outcome of this process.

Catherine Clark is the head teacher of Carnbooth School. A Glasgow City Council school, Carnbooth is the only provision for pupils with a dual sensory impairment in Scotland. As a teacher appointed to the newly opened Carnbooth School in 1985, her work, along with that of other staff members, was incorporated into the *Contact* package. Over the years she has worked to expand the provision for children and young people with this low incidence impairment by increasing the understanding of the impairment among colleagues through staff development and training.

Jane T. Eyre is assistant head teacher at Carnbooth School. She has been involved with deafblind education for approximately fourteen years, mostly working hands on with deafblind students of all ages and abilities. More recently, in her capacity as assistant head teacher, she has been involved substantially with curricular development activities, work on assessment and, in particular, staff development training. She is committed to raising awareness of deafblindness and to developing and enhancing the education provision on offer to deafblind pupils.

Liz Hodges is an advisory teacher for deafblind children, a training coordinator and a tutor on the Whitefield Schools/Kingston MSI diploma course. She has been teaching deafblind children and adults since 1988 in a variety of settings. She has contributed to published staff training packages for the RNIB and Birmingham University, and has been involved in revising the *Contact* package since 1997.

Marion McLarty is Senior Lecturer in the Department of Special Educational Needs at the University of Strathclyde in Glasgow. As a past head teacher of Carnbooth School she has practical experience of the issues involved in the education of children who are deafblind. Her research and publishing over the past five years has built upon and developed this experience.

Olga Miller is currently RNIB's National Development Officer for Services for Children and Young People with Visual Impairment and Multiple Disabilities. She is also a Research Fellow at London University, Institute of Education.

Laura Pease is Head of the School for Children with Sensory Impairment and Learning Difficulties at Whitefield Schools and Centre in London. She has eighteen years' experience teaching deafblind children, young people and other pupils with complex needs including sensory impairment. Her present role includes curriculum development and staff training and she has also contributed to many training courses, including those leading to the mandatory qualification for teachers of MSI pupils. She has a particular interest in early communication, seeing it as the key to all effective teaching and learning.

CHAPTER 1

Understanding deafblindness

Stuart Aitken

Who is deafblind?

Born with severe hearing and visual impairments, Leah is now four years old and school placement is being considered. She is described as being withdrawn into herself, avoiding communicating with others whom she does not know well. She is unwilling to explore her surroundings and is reported to have severe behaviour difficulties.

Sean goes into a shop to buy groceries. He is totally deaf and blind. Although he can use his fingers to spell words on other people's hands, and understands when words are spelled on his hands, the shopkeeper does not know this system. He leaves the shop without provisions.

As President of a North American University for deaf students, Chuck is presenting the keynote speech at a major international conference. Via a speaking interpreter he presents his message: that there is no reason why a deafblind person cannot become President of the United States of America. Chuck was born deaf and became blind in adulthood.

Hugh is 13 years old and attends a school for deaf children at which the main means of communication is through sign. He has just been diagnosed as having a visual impairment which will deteriorate, although at this stage it is not known how fast or to what extent. His parents do not want him to know, his teachers feel he should know so that he can start to learn braille to prepare for the world of employment.

As a result of a car accident Dipalah has severe brain damage. She is now blind, has a severe hearing loss and uses a wheelchair. She is learning to use a computer and hopes to return to employment.

Susan was born deafblind. In addition to impaired sight and hearing, she has complex health needs. These include a heart defect, severe cerebral palsy and breathing difficulties.

Jeannie is 75 years old and over the past ten years has gradually lost much of her sight and hearing. She now finds it difficult to communicate with her relatives, friends and neighbours and can no longer read the newspapers. She has lost confidence and no longer feels able to shop or go out on her own.

What is deafblindness?

Each of these people is deafblind, having impaired vision and hearing. These senses are often known as our two major distance senses, because they provide us with most of the information that is beyond what we can reach out and touch.

People who have severely impaired vision often come to depend more on their hearing, for example listening intently for traffic while crossing the road. Similarly, people whose hearing is severely impaired often compensate by using their sight, for example using lip-reading or sign language to communicate with others. People who are deafblind cannot easily compensate. They may not be able to use their hearing or vision at all. (This is rare: most people who are deafblind have some level of either hearing, vision or both.)

Why use the term 'deafblind'?

Over the years a number of different terms have been used to describe dual impairment to hearing and sight. In 1993, the term 'deafblind' came to be used in place of 'deaf/blind', or 'deaf-blind'. The reason for using a single word is that some people felt that combining the words deaf and blind to create the one word, deafblind, suggested a unique impairment, in which deafblindness is more than just deafness plus blindness. Others argued that it is not normal in English to combine words in this way and, especially in the USA, the term 'deaf-blind' is still widely used. We will return to the debate over what term to use later in this chapter. We will though for the most part use the term 'deafblind' throughout.

The effects of deafblindness

If you are not deafblind, it is not possible to say exactly what it is like to have both sight and hearing impairments. The profiles at the beginning of the chapter begin to tell us what it is like to be deafblind. You may have noticed at least three themes that the profiles have in common. These themes show that people who are deafblind experience difficulties in:

- finding out information;
- communicating with others;
- moving around the environment.

Difficulties in finding out information

Take a minute or two to think about what is meant by 'information'. You probably thought about newspapers, books, radio, television. Certainly these are sources of information. Each of these sources is often inaccessible to someone who is deafblind. However, information also includes the contents of a recipe book, a pub menu, a job application form, the electricity bill and a host of other trivia that most people take for granted.

Someone who is deafblind also faces a more subtle difficulty in finding out information. All of our everyday ordinary experiences – seeing the face of a familiar person, the angry expression of someone crossed, the shape of any object bigger than one's hand can hold, any object beyond one's reach – each of these depends on our use of information. Information is central to our lives.

The consequence of not being able to access information is that life experiences are reduced. Lack of everyday ordinary experiences – how to make a sandwich, knowing that water comes from a tap – makes it more difficult for the person who is deafblind to build up a store of world knowledge. Without that store of world knowledge what is there to communicate about?

Difficulties in communicating

This is perhaps the most obvious challenge to a person who is deafblind and for people who want to communicate with the person. Some people who are deafblind may use a form of sign language, for instance they might draw with their finger the shapes of the letters of a word on another person's hand. Another form of signing uses different positions on the person's fingers and palm to correspond to different letters of the alphabet. The communication partner then taps that position. Later you will be introduced to a range of ways of communicating with the person who is deafblind. Some of these are based on knowing and using language, others use simple gestures, facial expressions or movements of the body.

Each person who is deafblind has individual communication needs. The obvious difficulty for the person who is deafblind in trying to communicate is that very few people will know how to do this successfully. Faced with so many unsuccessful attempts at communicating with others it is perhaps not surprising that the person who is deafblind finds it difficult to learn to communicate.

Difficulties in moving around

We rely on our sight to move around, not just to avoid bumping into obstacles or to avoid falling down stairs. Our sight helps us to navigate, to pick out familiar buildings as landmarks. Someone who is blind will often be able to compensate for lack of sight by using navigational cues such as traffic noises in the street to know the road is nearby, that cars are coming from the right and that the bleeping sound means it is safe to cross at the pelican crossing. The distinctive sounds coming from refrigerators or televisions in the house help the person to know which room is off to the right, where the table is and how to get to the bathroom.

The person who is deafblind, not being able to compensate for vision with hearing, or for hearing with vision, is vulnerable, especially in unfamiliar surroundings. Often it is easier to shut oneself off from the world, to withdraw into a private world.

As we have seen, accessing information, communicating with others and moving around the environment are central to daily living and learning. All three of these depend on each other. People who are deafblind experience difficulties in their daily living and learning, affecting how they access, learn and remember information, communicate with other people and move around their environment.

Causes of deafblindness

Deafblindness is not caused by a single medical condition. People can be born deafblind, possibly as a result of infection, a genetic syndrome or birth defect. This is often referred to as congenital or early onset deafblindness. Acquired[1] deafblindness refers to occasions where a person becomes deafblind later in life, for example through infection, as a result of a genetic syndrome, a road traffic accident or due to the process of ageing. (For note 1 and other notes, see end of chapter.)

It may seem puzzling that a genetic syndrome can result in deafblindness at birth or later in life. This is because a gene might have an immediate effect on a developing foetus or its effects may not be apparent until later in life.

Congenital or early onset deafblindness

1. Infections as a cause of deafblindness
Deafblindness can arise as a result of infection – transmitted by parasite, bacteria or virus. Historically, one of the most common infectious causes was the rubella virus[2] commonly known as German measles. (For a comprehensive discussion of rubella see Sidle 1985.) The number of children who became deafblind as a result of the mother's infection during pregnancy peaked in the 1960s in the UK. As a result of immunisation programmes, the number of new cases of congenital rubella has declined. Note though that the decline may be reversed unless people continue to be immunised. To be effective in stopping the spread of rubella in the community both males and females need to be immunised.

Other infectious agents such as cytomegalovirus (CMV) or toxoplasmosis, can affect the developing foetus. Meningitis is an example of an infection which can cause impairments at any time in life, depending on the strain and severity of the infection. Some particular types of meningitis affect young babies more than other groups.

2. Genetic or chromosomal syndromes as a cause of deafblindness
Goldenhaar syndrome, or Oculo-Articulo-Vertebral syndrome (or OAV syndrome) is one example of a condition present at birth with a likely genetic cause. The syndrome may affect a range of functions, for example malformation of parts of the skeleton, as well as visual and hearing impairment.

3. Congenital birth trauma as a cause of deafblindness
Vision and hearing impairment can arise as a result of problems at birth or soon after. However, the cause of congenital birth defects is often unknown. These problems might be due to:

- prematurity;
- low birth weight (usually associated with prematurity);
- anoxia (lack of oxygen);
- other trauma or birth injury.

Children who are deafblind as a result of one of these causes often have additional, or multiple, impairments. They may have severe physical impairment, learning disabilities and communication difficulties. An example of this type of deafblindness is CHARGE association. Although there is speculation that CHARGE association has a genetic cause, at the time of writing this has not been confirmed.

Acquired deafblindness

1. Genetic syndromes as a cause of deafblindness
A number of genetically inherited syndromes can give rise to deafblindness, for example Usher syndrome. Usher syndrome is due to a gene defect which, although present from birth, its *effects* appear over the course of development. Hearing loss, usually present from birth or soon after, can range from moderate to profound. Visual impairment, the onset of which can often vary from late childhood to early adolescence or even adulthood, is progressive. It is not possible to predict how much sight will be lost. Usher syndrome is thought to affect three to six per cent of congenitally deaf people.

2. Accidents or other trauma as a cause of deafblindness
People can become deafblind as a result of an accident. Often a road traffic accident can result in injury to parts of the brain that deal with how we process information

through sight and hearing and the injury can have many different effects that are difficult to understand.

Some kinds of trauma can result in deafblindness, for instance a stroke (a cerebral haemorrhage). Again parts of the brain that deal with sight and hearing may be affected.

3. Deafblindness associated with ageing

The most common cause of being deafblind is simply age. After the age of around 50 years hearing and vision impairments become more common. The prevalence of sensory impairment increases with age.

Deafblindness and multi-sensory impairment

Recall the people you were introduced to at the beginning of this chapter. Four-year-old Leah was born deafblind; Sean was also born deafblind but was older when we met him on a shopping trip. Chuck was not satisfied with Presidency of a university and wanted to go for the big job. He was born deaf and became blind in adulthood. Hugh's medical diagnosis was the same as Chuck's but we met him as a teenager. Dipalah's deafblindness arose as a result of a car accident. Susan was born deafblind with additional impairments. Jeannie lost her sight and hearing when 75 years old.

Individual support needs

These people have in common certain difficulties – in accessing information, in communicating with other people and moving around the environment – that are associated with deafblindness. However, the impact of each of these difficulties will differ for each person. Even though the descriptions given about Dipalah, Sean and the others are brief, close inspection reveals some of these differences (you might like to look at the descriptions given to refresh your memory). To some extent differences in the effects of deafblindness are explained by the age at which deafblindness occurs, and on whether the first impairment was to hearing or to sight. So, while each person's experience of deafblindness will differ, some common patterns do emerge, depending on whether deafblindness is due to:

1. Congenital or early onset hearing and visual impairment.
2. Congenital or early onset hearing impairment with acquired visual impairment.
3. Congenital or early onset visual impairment with acquired hearing impairment.
4. Late onset hearing and visual impairment.

We will consider each in a little more detail.

1. Congenital or early onset hearing and visual impairment
The greatest needs of children and young people like four-year-old Leah (and Sean who is older) who are born deafblind are to: acquire and develop communication, perhaps using specialised signing; develop skills in mobility; access information – for instance learning to read can be a long and difficult process, and for some this may not be possible.

In the preschool and school period it is not only the deafblind child who is affected – the whole family will be. Time spent doing ordinary activities with deafblind children can be very demanding, in addition to having to do all the extraordinary things: offering consistent, continuous communication and perhaps assisting with mobility and personal care. This makes demands on all of the family's time, including brothers and sisters. Parents may need a break from caring, just as brothers and sisters may need some time on their own with their parents. No two families will share exactly the same experiences, nor will they have exactly the same needs.

A family may wish someone to take the time to listen, provide information by which they can make choices, offer respite, develop and take part in play activities and so on. Schooling will be a major concern for some families and getting to know the complexities of special educational needs arrangements can be quite daunting. Opportunities for deafblind adults may also be a major worry for some, and as the young person leaves school, his or her needs will change and there may be a shift in emphasis towards securing forms of housing. Support may also be needed for continuing education and the development of communication skills.

As can be seen, even within this notional 'group' different kinds of support needs, educational and other, will emerge.

2. Congenital or early onset hearing impairment with acquired visual impairment
The most common example of this form of deafblindness is that of Usher syndrome. People like Chuck, who has one type of Usher syndrome (there are two other types), may be born with a moderate to profound hearing loss. Later, perhaps during early adolescence, sight becomes progressively impaired. If the hearing loss is profound, sign language may have been learned prior to the onset of visual impairment. A moderate hearing loss may allow lip-reading to be used to understand people's communication. With sign or other language already developed, the support needs of this group are very different from those born with both hearing and visual impairment.

The unexpected onset of visual impairment in early adolescence may present major problems of emotional adjustment and this can be seen with Hugh. Sign language may have already been learned, perhaps in a special school for deaf pupils. The sign language may now need to be adapted because of impaired vision and specialised interpreter services may be required. Other means may be required to access information – helped by specialised aids and computer technology. Usually, the person will benefit from help in mobility training. Housing, family support and employment may all be important services that need to be accessed by the person.

3. Congenital or early onset visual impairment with acquired hearing impairment

Unlike the previous 'category' of deafblindness this group has no well-known syndrome associated with it, although children with Norrie syndrome may be born blind and later develop hearing impairment. The difficulties encountered are to a large extent the opposite of those in the second group. Congenital visual impairment or blindness may have meant early education being tailored towards learning braille, mobility and other skills associated with the education of blind children. Because speech and hearing is usually intact early on, reading and writing in braille is generally taken up. For otherwise intellectually able people the foundations are then laid for deafblind fingerspelling, keyboarding skills, braille, mobility and other skills.

The onset of hearing impairment often results in problems of emotional adjustment for both the client and family, and possibly requires the use of specialised interpreter services. On leaving school some form of supported housing and employment may be of benefit.

4. Late onset hearing and visual impairments

Dipalah and Jeannie became deafblind later in life, Dipalah through brain damage caused by an accident, Jeannie as a result of ageing. By far the majority of deafblindness is acquired late in life, and most of that after the age of 60 years. People's well-established abilities to access information, communicate and move around their surroundings may be affected. Reading personal mail, going to the shops, communicating with family and friends may all be helped by offering systems of social support, perhaps through friendship clubs, good neighbour schemes and the like.

Voluntary agencies such as Deafblind UK offer support to people who become deafblind late in life. Other agencies such as Sense, the Royal National Institute for the Blind (RNIB) and Royal National Institute for the Deaf (RNID) also provide services.

The only feature common to the four groups of people who are described as deafblind is that they all have some degree of impairment in their use of vision and hearing. Other than that the groups differ. The degree of visual and hearing impairments will differ. The onset of the visual and hearing loss may have occurred before birth or at any age. Hearing and vision may have been impaired or lost at the same time, or at different times. Other impairments may accompany impairments to sight and hearing. Even within each so-called group the effects of deafblindness on each person will be very different.

Deafblindness: educational support needs

Each of the groups described above could certainly be considered as having support needs associated with deafblindness. From an educational perspective, however, the people described seem to have little in common.

With so many possible differences it appears that what was once a difficult challenge – understanding how to educate a child or young person who is deafblind – has become almost intractable. We need some way of identifying which children and young people might benefit from educational approaches that are tailored to deafblindness. A definition of deafblindness would help.

Deafblindness: towards a definition

You may be interested to know that many different definitions of deafblindness have been tried over the years and the search for a definition has exercised the minds of many different groups across the world. To date, a universally accepted definition still seems some way off. In part, difficulty in reaching agreement over an acceptable definition reflects an ongoing controversy. And in part, that controversy is about the methods of education that are most appropriate to use with people who are deafblind.

At this stage we do not propose to detail all of this controversy. However, it is helpful to have a general understanding of the issues involved. Three positions are represented in the controversy.

1. Some argue that the term 'deafblindness' should, for the purposes of education, be limited to a very small group of pupils. Such children would have to be born with impairment of both sight and hearing. The children would have no other impairments.

   In this view only some of the first group of people – those with congenital or early onset hearing and visual impairment – would be considered as benefiting from specialised deafblind teaching methods. People in the other three groups: who are born blind and become deaf; who are born deaf and become blind; or who become deaf and blind late in life, would still be considered as deafblind. It is just that the methods and approaches used with them would often be very different.

   Those taking this position also argue that children with impairments in addition to hearing and sight will not benefit from specialised methods for teaching deafblind children. They believe that including children with additional impairments has significant detrimental effects, for example:

   • specialised approaches to teaching deafblind children are diluted;
   • children who should receive specialised deafblind teaching methods are placed in inappropriate schools;

- fewer skilled practitioners become available to meet the needs of the small group of children who should be considered as deafblind.

2. Others take the position that the term 'deafblindness' should embrace a wider group of children. In addition to those in 1, it would include children born with impairments to both sight and hearing, who may have additional, often multiple, impairments.

   The argument made here is that lack of hearing and sight causes severe problems of lack of information, and only by understanding these effects can significant progress be made in understanding and tackling difficulties caused by their other impairments.

   For this group, deafblindness could be defined as '... not having sufficient vision to compensate for loss of hearing and not having sufficient hearing to compensate for the loss of vision' (McInnes and Treffry 1982).

3. A third position taken is that the term 'deafblindness' might include, in addition to those in 2, children who have an impairment to only one of the distance senses (vision or hearing) as well as additional, often multiple, impairments.

   People who take this position are essentially adopting a practical approach, asking the question 'Who would benefit from being taught as deafblind?' (Meshcheryakov 1979). There are three main reasons for adopting this essentially practical position:

   (a) It can be difficult to identify how much of a person's difficulties in daily living and learning can be explained by severely impaired sight or hearing, and how much by other difficulties in learning or communicating. This is particularly problematic with young children.
   (b) Approaches to communication and learning that have been successful with people who are deafblind have often been successful when tried with people who have impairment to one sense, when additional impairments occur.
   (c) Families may have had very similar experiences and may request very similar services from education, health and other agencies.

Our own view is that the techniques and methods used with children and young people who are deafblind often can be of benefit to others. We align ourselves most closely with 3 above.

Deafblindness and multi-sensory impairment

To recap, so far we have outlined four groups of people who, *in terms of their impairments*, would be considered as deafblind. These were people with:

1. congenital or early onset hearing and visual impairment;
2. congenital or early onset hearing impairment with acquired visual impairment;
3. congenital or early onset visual impairment with acquired hearing impairment;
4. late onset hearing and visual impairment.

We pointed out that quite different teaching approaches and methods may be required for each of the different groups. Because of the educational focus taken in this book, its contents will have most application to the first group of people. For the most part it will have less application to groups 2, 3 and 4.

However, by taking this educational perspective, much of what we say may also be useful when working with children and young people who have:

5. congenital or early onset visual impairment plus additional disabilities, for example severe learning, communication and physical disabilities;
6. congenital or early onset hearing impairment plus additional disabilities, for example severe learning and physical disabilities.

Often these two groups, *as well as those children who at birth have impairments in addition to those of sight and hearing*, are known as multi-sensory impaired (this term is not in common use in Scotland). Others prefer terms such as people who are multiply disabled and visually impaired (MDVI) or, multiply disabled and hearing impaired (MDHI), respectively. In England and Wales, the term Profound and Multiple Learning Difficulties (PMLD) is used in education. In Scotland the term Complex Learning Difficulties (CLD) is in common use.

Although the authors are aware of the many different terms in use, in order to keep things simple we will use the term 'deafblind' throughout the book unless we want to refer specifically to one or other of the terms.

5. Congenital visual impairment plus additional disabilities

This group is increasing in number. Often there is a degree of intellectual impairment associated with profound or complex learning difficulty. Physical impairment is often present.

Specialised health care may be required from the neonatal period right through to young childhood. Many will require continued access to a range of health care services. Throughout their lives they will require assistance with accessing information.

In early childhood access to education may require specialised communication and technical aids to be made available. House adaptations and extensions are often required – mostly in the age group four years and upwards.

Throughout childhood and into young adulthood there may be a need for respite care and leisure breaks. These ways of providing breaks in caring are of most benefit when they are flexible enough to accommodate different needs and different circumstances, and are easily accessible.

In the post-school period and on into adulthood the focus shifts to community living and provision of day services. High staffing ratios with investment in specialised forms of training will be necessary. Quality of inter-agency cooperation among housing agencies, voluntary sector and statutory agencies such as social work departments and health providers, is a key factor in success.

6. Congenital hearing impairment plus additional disabilities

This group tends to be less prevalent than those in 5 above but the issues involved are almost exactly the same.[3]

In an analysis of the patterns of children referred to a Sense Family Centre in London, David Brown showed that while one of the commonest causes of deafblindness, congenital rubella syndrome, has been reduced through immunisation, other causes are taking its place (Brown 1997). Most of these causes of deafblindness result in children being born with multiple impairments.

Observing the child

Observation is something we all do during most of our waking life. Because it is something that is automatic, we assume it is relatively straightforward. But we only need to consider how difficult it is for people to identify criminals on identity parades, and for two witnesses to pick out the same person, for us to realise that there is more to observation than meets the eyes – and ears, touch, smell and taste!

Note that when discussing observation we draw heavily on the text of the original *Contact* resource pack (Bryson 1993). We do this for two main reasons. First, the description of what to observe, how to do it and how to interpret from these observations provides an excellent account of what is needed. The second reason for referring to this material, now eight years old, is that it shows how timeless the skill of observation can be.

What is observation?

Observation is a skill and when applied to children and young people who are deafblind it is even more of a skill. With the majority of children, it is usually fairly easy to find out what they have learned and what they should learn next. We often make assumptions about what the average two-year-old can do or what the average five-year-old will know. However, it is more difficult to apply such expectations to a child who is deafblind. His or her experience of the world will be very different from other children.

Figure 1.1 Experimenting with paper and paint – and with each other

Learn from colleagues

Like all skills observation can be learned. With practice most people can become skilled observers. This topic provides a framework within which to develop observation skills. It also assumes that there will be substantial opportunities for gaining practical experience in observing pupils. In other words, what you *read* about observation will be of help. But to become a skilled observer you need to *practise* these skills.

Note that the various exercises should be carried out under the guidance of an experienced colleague. If you cannot manage all the activities it may be helpful to discuss with others, such as senior staff, which ones to focus on and in which situations to practise observation.

Arrange for time to discuss findings with a colleague. The direct observation exercises can be an ongoing process and need not hold up progress through the subsequent topics.

Observation means looking *carefully* to note significant types of behaviour. In this way important information can be gathered about a pupil. Observation should be for a specific purpose, not just 'watching'. Also, results of observations should separate statements of fact from how you interpret the observations. There are therefore two steps. First, describe what the pupil did, what you saw and heard. Next, record what you took this behaviour to mean.

Observation is a skill for everyone. Kitchen staff, minibus driver, gardener as well as teachers, classroom assistants, care staff all have something to offer. Never disregard what they might have to offer about their observations of a child. Be prepared to revise opinions on the basis of a chance observation, provided that arrangements can be made to have it confirmed.

Learn from parents

To educate children who are deafblind, as much information as possible is needed about the individual child. Parents can usually supply a great many details about their child. Never underestimate the observational skills of parents and what parents have to say about their child. They can often provide background information which, once you are aware of it, helps to inform why a child does or does not do something.

For the most part, the contact a deafblind child has with any one educator, social worker, speech and language therapist or other practitioner will be relatively short. It is the family who will provide the child with continuity of love, care and nurturing. They will be there for the child long after any one person's involvement has ended.

It is easy to forget that only twenty years ago many parents of children and young people with severe and complex learning difficulties were encouraged to leave their children in long-stay hospitals. Today the vital role of the family is recognised and increasingly valued.

A sobering thought to bear in mind is that parents, not the medical profession, are often the first to diagnose if their child has a visual or hearing impairment. An unpublished study carried out in the early 1980s found that, even after their child had been referred to an ophthalmologist (an eye doctor), and having then been told that their child's sight was fine and not to worry, parental concerns about their children's sight were often found, later, to have been correct.

When considering the early diagnosis of hearing impairment, there are many parents whose children were only diagnosed as having a hearing impairment at the age of two, three and even four years of age, even though parents had first expressed concerns about their child's hearing when the child was a few months of age.

Parents' specialist knowledge of their own child comes from having seen the child in every situation, when happy or sad, when tired or full of energy, when getting up or when going to bed. Parents do not always recognise the skills they possess and may not be able to put a name to what they know. For this reason the way practitioners ask questions of parents should aim to value the knowledge they possess, avoiding the use of jargon or theorising.

Times and places for observation

It is important that observation is not just carried out on 'special occasions'. Instead, everyone should develop an 'observational attitude', ready to observe at all times – travelling on the bus, meeting someone, going for a walk. Often it is when least expected that the child says or does something that reveals an unexpected ability, an area of strength to be harnessed in new activities.

Equally, it is often helpful to identify a specific time or location in order to observe how the child or young person responds to a new activity, with a new person, in a strange environment. We will have more to say about these more specific types of observation in the discussion on assessment in Chapter 4.

The focus of observation[4]

The focus for observation will depend on its purpose, that is what will be done with the recorded observations. The purpose to which the results of observations are put might include the following:

- to obtain an overall picture of a pupil in a new situation, such as when the pupil starts school;
- to find out a pupil's reaction to various sounds in the environment.

Before starting to observe the pupil it is worth remembering that children do change, so be open to having your conclusions challenged through later observation. The following are some of the broad areas for which careful observation may prove useful. All of these suggestions will need to be followed up before firm conclusions are drawn.

(a) What skills does the pupil have (in relation to curriculum objectives)?
(b) What skills have progressed, remained the same, or possibly deteriorated?
(c) What skills does the pupil appear to learn most easily?
(d) What skills does the pupil appear to find most difficult to learn?
(e) What does the pupil like and dislike? (This information may be helpful in motivating the pupil.)
(f) Does the pupil use his or her skills constructively?
(g) Can the pupil use skills learned in one situation and apply these in other settings? If so, the learning and skills acquired are said to have been generalised.

In addition it is helpful to try to discover what other factors seem to affect the pupil's learning and responses to people. These other factors might include:

- factors in the pupil (e.g. vision; hearing; attention or concentration);
- factors in the environment (e.g. level of lighting; familiar/strange surroundings);
- factors in the task (e.g. what benefit it is to the pupil; how clear is the desired outcome to the pupil; how it relates to activities that have been successful);

- factors in the resources available (e.g. what skills the teacher or parent brings to help the pupil's learning, or otherwise; whether and how technology is being used).

Taken together observations such as these begin to offer clues about how the world appears to each child who is deafblind. They help to identify the skills he or she has mastered or is developing and suggest what is significant to them.

Over the next two or three weeks observe one of the pupils with whom you work. Under each of the following headings: use of sight; use of hearing; mobility skills; communication by the pupil; responding to others communicating; fine motor skills; dressing skills; likes/dislikes, note any findings you feel are important to that area of observation. For example, if the pupil you are observing is totally blind, record 'totally blind' under 'Use of sight'.

Having done this, record the effects you think this might have on how the pupil:

- finds out information;
- communicates with other people;
- moves around the environment.

You might like to share findings with colleagues. This should help to confirm your observations.

Other areas in which observation could be made would include the pupil's responses to people, what sort of play is enjoyed, whether the pupil seems to be aware of time and routine, their skills in eating, bathing, how well they recognise everyday objects.

Earlier we introduced three broad areas in which people who are deafblind experience difficulty. To recap, difficulties were noted in:

- finding out information;
- communicating with others;
- moving around the environment.

Although it would be possible through observation to discover more about the ways in which these difficulties are experienced, it is helpful to have more background information. Above, we suggest a few areas in which to make observations of one or two children who are deafblind. We then invite you to state how the sort of difficulty you observed might affect:

Figure 1.2 Letting the wind blow grass from his hand

- how the pupil finds out information, what kind of information he or she might be able to find out and what information it might be difficult for him or her to access;
- how he or she might understand what others are trying to communicate, and how his or her own attempts to 'get the message across' might be affected;
- in what ways opportunities to move around the environment might be affected, and how any restrictions imposed might affect the pupil, e.g. what it might do to motivation.

When working closely with a pupil who is deafblind, a great deal of information will be collated. It is time-consuming to take note of every single behaviour such as nod of the head, slight arm or finger movement. With experience, you will come to know those behaviours that are of particular significance and should be taken note of. In this process of sifting out what is important, be aware that each person brings attitudes, beliefs, preconceptions and prejudices to any observation. The best way of dealing with any bias is to discuss observations and conclusions with other colleagues and parents. They may disagree with your conclusions and they may be right. Encourage open discussion of areas of difference.

If the information collected from observing the pupil is significant it will need to be shared with others. There are many ways of sharing information. These might include holding a case conference, discussing observations at staff meetings or at shift change-overs, writing a report, writing in a daily diary, or some combination of these.

The method that is likely to have the greatest impact is when observations are written down. In writing down information it is important that it is objective. This means information should be:

(a) based on what you have *seen*;
(b) able to be *confirmed* by other staff or parents;
(c) put in *context*, i.e. whether it is typical of the pupil in all situations or specific to one situation or person;
(d) stated as *precisely* as possible to avoid misunderstanding and uncertainty by others reading it at a later date.

Methods for recording observations

Various methods are available for recording observations. Some of these can become quite complex and are not easy either to use or to interpret later. We shall focus on some of the most practical approaches, but you may be asked (by an educational psychologist for example) to collaborate in the use of alternative methods. Below, we describe some common ways of recording your observations. Other options will be described in Chapter 4 on assessment.

Diary
Some people find it easiest to keep anecdotal 'diary' type records. Often a home–school liaison diary records staff and parents' informal observations about the child. These are very useful for day to day purposes but often a more structured approach is required in order to obtain a more complete picture.

Total observation record
This is a 'catch-all' approach to try to record the pupil's total repertoire of behaviours.

Often with very young children or children with additional learning difficulties, behaviour has to be recorded in fairly minute detail, e.g. the different hand grasps used for different objects.

A total observation record can help to get to know a new pupil, but later it is necessary to concentrate on specific behaviours which seem most important for learning.

Always distinguish between *fact* ('child did not hold toy') and *impression* or interpretation ('child did not like the toy'). Only once sufficient information is collected to back up inferences ('that the child does not like the toy') should the conclusion be drawn.

It is very important to compare behaviours in different situations.

Behaviour Log

This is the most straightforward type of observation and is quite common. It can be used:

- to see if there is any pattern of behaviour;
- to show a change in the frequency of occurrence of behaviours at a later date.

A common example of a Behaviour Log could be a continence management chart (formerly referred to as a 'toileting chart'). This is frequently used to note if there is any pattern to wetting and soiling as a preliminary to introducing a programme to assist toileting. It is useful in situations where there are several members of staff involved with the child.

Specific observation record

This would refer to the observation of previously specified behaviour(s), e.g.

- the child's attempts to communicate;
- mobility in unfamiliar surroundings.

It is necessary to plan beforehand. A useful observation record will ensure that no relevant information is omitted. Commercial checklists can be useful here, but are not always appropriate for those who are deafblind.

Video recordings

When working closely with a pupil, it is not always easy to 'stand back' and observe objectively. Each of us tends to see what we want to see. It can therefore be very helpful if another colleague observes the pupil. This will of course depend on resources available. Video recording allows several people to observe the same situation and 'observer-bias' is reduced. Other advantages of video include:

- it allows limitless replay for closer inspection;
- it allows observation of all the people participating in an interaction, e.g. both pupil and teacher;
- it provides a visual record of progress to demonstrate change over time.

A video record is often of great interest to parents and it will be helpful to discuss with them beforehand the sorts of things they too might like to have a record of.

Points of caution are:

- Video can be misleading, especially if a short clip is taken out of context. It is easy to read things into video recordings especially if you were not present at the time.
- Always check against your own knowledge of the child. Is this typical behaviour? How would I go about confirming it?

Finding out about the world

We receive a constant flow of information about our world. It influences our every action, every decision, how we interpret what others are doing. We use information to anticipate coming events, to interact socially with other people, to understand and manipulate objects, to communicate, to learn a new skill and to use that newly acquired skill. We select from this constant array of information to learn about people, places, the norms of society and so on. We do not consciously have to be aware of absorbing any information. Instead, learning is incidental to whatever we are doing.

For people who are deafblind, this incidental learning is made much more difficult because the information on which learning is based is much reduced or distorted. Instead of seeing someone's face, their dark hair, a smiling expression, a child who is deafblind may see only the outline of the face with little understanding of hair colour and none of facial expression. Activities will need to be designed or structured to help the process of learning as well as 'what' is learned. The things we learn incidentally, by watching brothers and sisters playing, living in a family and growing up in the community are not easily acquired. If they are acquired, it is often in a distorted form.

Limited experience leads to limited understanding. Limited understanding leads to limited communication – for what is there for the pupil to communicate about?

Reduced information, reduced learning

Before reading on, try the little quiz below.

John McInnes draws a parallel to show the importance of incidental learning. Without referring to other people, or to other resources, and working quickly, use a piece of paper, and:

1. List 12 inuit words for snow.
2. Give the location of your house to the nearest minute and second.
3. Describe what a 'Calabogie' is.
4. To the nearest half degree give the surface temperature of lava.
5. Describe in detail why the ink in your ballpoint pen does not run out.

(McInnes 1998, personal communication)

How well did you do? McInnes points out that these questions might seem esoteric, but only because you have not yet acquired the information needed to answer these questions. If you do not know all of the answers, does that mean you have learning disabilities? Or it is just that you simply lack the information needed to respond to these questions? Now think of the child who is deafblind. He or she may not know what a newspaper is for, or that a cup is to drink from, or that grass is green and soft. Does this lack of experience mean that he or she has a learning disability? Not necessarily. It could mean that the incidental learning experiences needed for that knowledge have so far not taken place.

Incidental learning experiences provide the person who is deafblind with cues about what is taking place in the environment; they offer the chance to anticipate what is about to happen next; they provide meaningful information on which to make choices.

Loss of environmental cues

Lack of, or reduced visual and auditory information deprives the person from being able to use cues in the environment that help to identify and recognise familiar events. A mother entering the room can signify comfort, food, or cuddling but only if the child knows someone has entered the room and that it is 'mummy'. For a deafblind pupil the teacher's entry into the classroom cannot signal that it is time to work, if the child does not know teacher has entered the room. The inability to recognise change in one's surroundings leads to each experience being a new, puzzling or frightening one.

Less able to anticipate events

Not being able to perceive or understand the environment accurately prevents the child from knowing the results of his or her actions or the actions of others. People who are totally blind and profoundly deaf receive little or no information about their surroundings. For those with some remaining vision or hearing, two added difficulties will have to be overcome:

- the information they receive may be distorted and be misinterpreted;
- people whom they contact, even familiar people, may assume that what they see, hear and understand is the same as what the pupil sees, hears and understands; as a result, they expect the pupil to respond in a way that is consistent with that information.

Less able to make choices

People who are deafblind are given few opportunities to make choices in or about their lives. Difficulties in communicating, being rushed, tight schedules, all reduce the number of opportunities to communicate. In the short term it may be faster and more convenient for staff to pour breakfast cereal into a plate rather than encourage a choice of several different ones, or to choose what clothing the child will wear on a particular day than spend time introducing choice. Lack of opportunities to make choices about everyday activities has a negative effect over the long term. Once someone has learned that there are few occasions in which choice is allowed, it becomes more difficult on subsequent occasions for that person to recognise that choice is being offered.

For one pupil, choice might be of the clothing to wear that morning. While one person may recognise clothing by colour, to a blind person colour may be meaningless and real choice may require choice to be made from different textures. For another pupil it may mean pointing to pictures of places to visit – that same pupil might eye point rather than finger point. Others still may only be able to cry to show their displeasure, but may have different cries for different events in their lives.

Observation skills help to identify opportunities for encouraging choice. Having given the choice, make sure that it is meaningful; that is, the pupil achieves what is chosen. This can be hard to put into practice. For instance, a pupil may just have made a choice but another member of staff asks a question before there is a chance to carry through the choice. If it were you, and you had been given a choice, made your choice and then were not given what you chose, how would you feel?

Having identified what the pupil is likely to choose, and/or how he or she makes this choice, share this information. Communicate the information to colleagues and parents, and, where appropriate, other professionals in contact with the pupil.

There are, of course, limits to making choices: a pupil may not like to have medication but it may be necessary for survival that it is given.

Structuring information for learning

We develop certain routines or rhythms in order to save us thinking about everything we do all of the time. These routines become more or less automatic. Through ordinary everyday experiences a routine is developed. The child who is deafblind, with limited sensory information, finds it much more difficult to understand the patterns involved in developing a routine. Order and structure depend on being able to see, hear and, to a lesser extent touch, smell and taste the many impressions which life offers. Learning from experience becomes a major task. The pupil who is deafblind may:

- not know the desired outcome of an activity or have a concept of the final product;
- not be aware of the parts that make up an activity because it is difficult to compare that activity with past experiences of that activity;
- only understand each element of an event in isolation, and have no association with the whole or final outcome;
- have difficulty organising the stages or steps needed to complete an activity.

How then can the pupil be helped to make use of experiences and to organise his or her physical and social world? How can opportunities for incidental learning be given? One important way of giving opportunities for incidental learning is, as we outlined above, to offer the pupil choices. Secondly, we can provide structured opportunities within which to interact with people, the physical environment, objects, places and activities. Later, in Chapter 6, we describe in more detail how to structure opportunities for learning.

Communication: an introduction

What is communication?

A nine-month-old girl looks to a toy out of reach, looks to her mother and back to the toy. Her mother brings the toy over for her to play with. Her father fetches her bath towel and baby shampoo and holds it in front of her. She looks at him and across to the baby bath beside the fire. He says 'Yes, it is bath time', perhaps in a soft, slightly modulated voice to increase emphasis.

A 12-month-old girl is playing with her toys. Her father looks over to her. She reaches for a car, holds it up for him to see and continues to look at him. As soon as her father says 'Yes, that's the car you like', she puts it down and carries on playing.

A 16-month-old walks into the kitchen, looks over at the tap, then at his mother, and makes a drinking gesture (curved hand to mouth). She pours a glass of water. Later on the same child points to his father's jacket hanging in the hallway and says 'Daddy'. His mother responds, saying 'Yes, Daddy's gone out to work.'

These examples illustrate several things. First, they show the power of communication: it makes things happen, you only need to point a finger or look at someone for that person to do things for you. Second, that power gives someone as young as a few months of age increasingly precise control over other people and their surroundings. The third point raised by these everyday examples is that the early communicator benefits from having a willing listener who shares some past history. The last child's mother knew her son did not think the jacket was his father, but that the jacket was something he wore: to him it represented his father. The final point raised by these examples that we will mention is that communication is different for different people, and the same person will use different methods of communicating for different purposes. The 12-month-old could not speak; instead she shows the car to her father, and he acknowledges. The older child uses a gesture in his first exchange and a single word in his second exchange.

Many other points are raised by these simple exchanges, some of which we will return to later. For now, though, they illustrate the essence of communication. Communication is a sharing of information. It requires:

- someone to communicate with (a giver and receiver);
- something about which to communicate;
- a reason or intention to communicate;
- some means of communicating.

Notice that this definition does not mention language, speech or any type of sign language. Communication can certainly include each or all of these as well as printed words, symbols and a host of others.

These foundations to communication can be observed not only in the exchanges of a baby girl not yet able to speak. As skilled communicators we all use these foundations to communication. We use them countless times each and every day – when out with friends, at work, on the telephone and out shopping. But because these skills are so commonplace we generally do not stop to think about them.

An important point to note therefore is that when meeting a pupil who is deafblind for the first time, you will build on communication skills that you already have. You already use these skills all the time. The difference lies in trying to think through how to apply them with a child who is deafblind. In order to equip you with these skills a good place to begin is to try to understand how deafblindness affects communication.

Communication and deafblindness

How does deafblindness affect a child's communication? Consider infants who are deafblind and the same ages as those introduced above.

Discuss with colleagues how deafblindness may affect the following:

- **Obtaining a toy that is out of the child's reach.**
- **Understanding the link between a bath towel and having a bath.**
- **Commenting on an activity.**
- **Requesting a drink.**
- **Commenting on something or someone (Daddy) who is absent.**

You may have identified some of the following difficulties (we assume throughout that the child is female):

Information questions
If she cannot see, how will she know that a toy is beyond her reach?

If she happens to come across the toy, how will she know what it is?

Suppose her mother brings her the toy by chance, how will she know where it came from? Will she expect her mother to bring the toy next time she comes to her?

If she doesn't bring it to her, how can she show her mother she wants it?

How will she know her father has the bath towel?

How will she know it is a bath towel and not just any towel?

How will she show she does or does not want a bath?

Communication questions

If she cannot see the toy, she cannot look at it and then to her mother. So how will she show her she wants the toy that is out of reach?

If she cannot see the bath beside the fire, how will she show that she knows the bath towel means she is to have a bath?

If she cannot hear, how will she link the words to the activity of bathing?

Movement questions

If she is deafblind, what motivation will she have to move around?

If her movement is restricted by physical impairment, how will she reach for objects, crawl, stand or walk?

How will she happen across objects, people and places to then explore?

These are a few of the areas that need to be considered if we are to approach even quite simple activities with a child who is deafblind – getting a toy to play with and telling her it is bath time. They show clearly the link between major areas of difficulty caused by deafblindness and how these impact on the key foundations of communication.

Difficulties in finding out information mean it is not easy for the child who is deafblind to know if the person approaching is someone to communicate with. These difficulties also make it hard to find something to communicate about. Because of this it is often hard to find a reason to communicate. On a more subtle level, difficulties in finding out information also present obstacles to finding a means of communicating with the child.

Communicating with a child who is deafblind

Throughout this book we emphasise the differences that exist between one deafblind child and another. There is no such thing as *the* deafblind child. Equally, there is no such thing as *the* way to communicate with a child who is deafblind. Each will require what might be called a different communication package, one that is tailored to individual communication support needs.

One child may be able to learn to use one or other form of sign language – for example British Sign Language, Paget Gorman, Signed English. Another child, while unable to use a formal system of sign language, might still be able to use a limited range of natural gestures. A third may be able to read whole words (for example the sign for lavatory) but be unable to recognise individual parts of words, so cannot read unfamiliar words. A fourth child may express herself only by using her own gross body movements, e.g. pushing the upper body forward and back might mean 'I want a swing.'

But if there are so many different ways of communicating with a child who is deafblind, how can they all be learned and where should one begin?

Having someone to communicate with

At the beginning of this section we described a few young children to illustrate communication in action. One of the points raised by the examples was that it helps to have someone with a deep knowledge of the child, someone who knows his or her interests, likes, dislikes and how to interpret feelings.

All of this stems from a close relationship having been established with the infants described. Communicating with a deafblind person is no different, it depends on you making a conscious decision and effort to begin a relationship with the pupil who is deafblind. The first priority, a priority that continues at all times, should be *to establish and improve your social contact with the pupil*.

Notice that the focus is not on any particular activity or activities but on the relationship or interactions between people: you and the pupil. Relationships take time to develop and they depend on someone making a conscious effort to establish trust. That conscious effort has to come from you; after all, the pupil who is deafblind has no way of knowing that the person who is trying to make contact with him or her (i.e. you) is someone to trust. Perhaps that person could do them harm. Establishing trust does, as we have said, take time. However, there are some things you can do that will develop trust sooner and make it more likely to last. These include:

- treat children (and young people) who are deafblind like ordinary children at all times, with feelings, likes and dislikes;
- show them you are happy to be with them;
- speak whenever you are with them (even if they cannot hear you); talk about what you are doing, but do not overdo the chat;
- ensure the child recognises you before you begin or resume an activity;
- join in an activity that the person shows preference for, perhaps by copying their body movement;
- share space in a non-threatening way, e.g. sit alongside them without directing the child into an activity.

Having something to communicate about

Read through the examples given of young infants communicating. For one or two examples consider what the child is communicating about. Each instance depends on the child having prior information of the objects, people or places about which he or she is communicating. The bath towel, jacket, tap and so on are familiar objects related to familiar and enjoyable activities. Often the child who is deafblind does not have sufficient information to have something to communicate about. The world ends at the end of their outstretched fingertips. If past experience of trying to explore beyond their reach has resulted in burnt fingers, falling down a flight of stairs or being lost, it is understandable that they might prefer to stay in one place.

Your task is to help build the child's physical and social world, and offer information about, and experiences with, the people, objects, events and places in the physical and social world. Through this the child will have things about which to communicate. You can help by:

- encouraging the pupil to take the lead on what he or she wants to explore, rather than directing their interests (to someone who can see and hear, a red, yellow and blue plastic squeaky toy may be highly attractive, interesting and distinctive; to a child who is deafblind it may be a lump of plastic just like a dozen others);
- giving time and patience to explore objects and not thrusting them into the hands or forcing their hands onto the objects;
- offering the chance to experience where things come from and are stored (the juice in a cup of juice does not magically disappear after drinking and re-appear ready for the next drink; instead, that juice may come from a carton made of cardboard, kept in a fridge, which is cold inside and warm outside and vibrates . . . and so on).

The information and experiences from which most people learn about the world are incidental and not fashioned as structured learning experiences. In contrast deafblindness presents challenges as to how these experiences and that information can be offered in ways that maintain interest and avoid threats. Children who are deafblind have great difficulty acquiring often the most basic knowledge for themselves. Always consider how you can *structure experiences for the pupil to discover himself or herself*. By doing so the child who is deafblind will begin to acquire the information and experiences which will be the basis for wanting to communicate.

Having a reason and intention to communicate

Imagine you live in a world in which there is no choice, everyone gets the same food at the same time of day, and it is brought to the table. Your day follows the same routine with almost no deviation. Would there be much point in communicating? If there was, what would you communicate about?

While we are not saying that this is the reality for children who are deafblind, it is important to recognise that this scenario can become the norm for some. If choice is limited to a very narrow range and, possibly, choice is given about things they have no particular wish to have or to do, the child will have little reason to communicate. Aim to create an environment (people, places and objects) that is responsive. To do this:

- encourage choice in whatever form the pupil can manage;
- offer real choices in context throughout the person's day;
- value the choice made;
- set up situations where the pupil *needs* to communicate.

Communication is not a specific skill, it is part of being human. Communication is not done in isolation – it will change depending on the situation and the people around at the time. If people and situations seem to give out the message that communication is too difficult or takes too much time then the child is unlikely to be motivated to communicate. The pupil needs to feel the environment is one that encourages and values communication. Communication should not be left to specific times and circumstances while following a timetabled activity. Communication should be part of everyday activities. That way it will be useful and fun.

Responsibility for helping someone to communicate effectively should never be a job assigned to a single 'communicator', but be a part of everyone around that pupil.

Having a means to communicate

Receptive and expressive communication
It is useful to distinguish between what a pupil understands in communication (receptive) and the same pupil's ability to use communication (expressive). Often children might understand some of what others are communicating but be unable to express himself or herself.

A pupil may well use a different means of communication for understanding than for expression. For example, a pupil may be able to understand some of what is spoken to him but prefer to use sign to express needs.

It can be easy to overestimate a pupil's understanding on the basis of what we know the pupil understands. For example, if a pupil responds to the statement 'The butter is in the fridge', by going to the fridge and bringing out the butter, he or she may not understand the entire statement. He may only understand the words 'butter' and 'fridge' and, because he is asked to do this every day around lunch-time, may assume that he is being invited to get the butter from the fridge.

A variety of methods are available to enhance communication, some of which will be explored in later chapters. At this stage it is important to appreciate that many of these means of communication were designed to be used with people who became deafblind later in life. At the time they became deafblind most will already have had a well-established language system. For example, if someone is born blind and becomes deaf at 15 years of age, that person may very well be competent at reading and writing braille as well as having developed language and speech.

Most children born deafblind in recent years have additional, often multiple impairments. Methods of communicating with them might include the following.

Speech

Short sentences, spoken clearly, are generally much easier to understand than single words and should be included in all programmes of learning and curriculum. Very often speech will have to be supported by other means of communicating but it should not be excluded.

Body language and natural gesture

Especially for children with some vision remaining (often called residual vision), these are important ways of communicating. They help to signal intention and can be a useful way for a pupil with hearing impairment to discriminate what you are saying. For best effect when working with a pupil with visual impairment make sure you make best use of available light. Position yourself so that the light falls on your face and hands.

Understandably, if a pupil has no vision it may seem rather pointless to emphasise your own body language and natural gesture, if it cannot be seen. But there are two reasons for continuing to do so. First, it is easier for you to get your message across if you use body language in a natural way. Second, body language and natural gesture can be included when sitting next to the child, when parts of your body are in contact.

Use of everyday objects

Recall the nine-month-old girl at the start of this section. Her father brought the bath towel and shampoo. She understood it was bath time. Objects that are associated or refer to an activity can have an important role to play in communication, especially when the child has very limited vision and hearing.

Objects can be used to represent activities that will take place each day. We will have much more to say about the use of objects as a means of communication in later chapters.

Movement, orientation and mobility

Think of very young children as they play – with their toys, with their playmates, and with their parents. Much of what they talk about is in their immediate surroundings – what they are doing right at that moment. Much of what they learn involves moving around. New ideas are tested out through action. As they move they explore. These simple observations help to explain why babies spend so much effort in learning to crawl, stand and walk. The rewards of mobility are tangible, and immediate. Successful mobility gives power and self-esteem.

Now think of a young child who is deafblind. What can she play with? Who can she play with? What about exploring and becoming independent, approaching people to make friends, and generally becoming part of society? If successful mobility motivates the person to take the next challenge, what about the self-esteem of someone whose opportunities to move around safely are restricted? Restricted movement means that for the deafblind child there is much less to talk about.

Restricted mobility: restricted learning

For the ambulant child, most learning experiences that occur in a typical day are incidental. A leaf in a paddling pool provides concrete examples of how light bends between solid and liquid; climbing stairs allows the child to investigate her sister's room, discover that she is out and, perhaps, follow it up with a discussion about school.

Mobility provides a wide range of opportunities to learn about the world. Barbara Tizard and Martin Hughes argued that most of a child's learning takes place outwith formal teaching settings: learning is incidental or intrinsic to day to day life and depends on personal freedom to enjoy it. Tizard and Hughes (1984) point out that when a child follows a parent around vacuuming the carpet, this affords a discussion point about electricity, reinforced understanding of object permanence and provided openings to many other topics. One crucial feature of this incidental, or intrinsic, learning is having the opportunity to explore. An ambulant child creates his or her own learning opportunities, giving many opportunities for learning through discovery.

A non-ambulant child's learning opportunities are created for, and given to, her. The order of learning is outwith her control. The speed of that learning is outwith her control. And the content of that learning is outwith her control. For the non-ambulant child, learning is much more akin to that which takes place in a formal setting: it has to be taught.

Over the past three decades a wealth of evidence has accrued to show the positive effects which come when children, even young infants, have the chance to gain control over their environment, and how that control is severely impaired in the non-ambulant child.

Even though they have fewer chances to decide and control their experiences, non-ambulant children still learn by them. However, those experiences are much more likely to be of frustration and failure. At this point, a second difficulty arises, because experiences gained in one setting can carry over to other settings.

Expectations of failure learned in one setting make the learning of new activities much more difficult. The person who is non-ambulant may therefore be 'turned off' the learning of new tasks and activities. Rather than learning that they can be successful they have learned that there is little point even in trying.

Starting out

Establishing the child's trust is a crucial first stage in encouraging movement and mobility with a child who is deafblind. It is easy to understand why it is important to try to gain the child's trust early on. Unless there is trust why would the child want to put her life in your hands? That first step with you could result in a fall down stairs or stepping onto something rough and uneven. Staying put is less risky. At least in the early stages all movement work should be carried out by someone who knows the pupil well.

Rather than commencing with any formal activities, play situations should be looked for. These early play sessions should emphasise using gross body movements, perhaps through rhymes, rhythms and songs. Although the child may not hear these rhythms they help you to keep to the rhythm, making it easier for the child to pick up on you moving with her and to anticipate what will happen next. Within these play settings it may be possible to establish basic concepts such as 'up and down', 'in and out', 'in front and behind', and 'right and left' with some children. For others, whose movements are more severely impaired, the focus may be to respond to the child's movement.

The world for the deafblind child is what can be touched (or tasted and smelled) within arm's reach. Beyond that the world does not exist. So before trying to locate objects out in that 'world beyond reach' the child needs to begin to feel secure about reaching out to and moving towards objects and people that are just beyond reach.

A 'resonance board' can be a helpful tool to motivate the child to explore the area both within and beyond her own body space. This simple plywood board provides a resonating platform when objects are dropped on it. The resonating surface of the board makes it easier to find the thing that has dropped or is causing the vibrations.

Motivation to explore and to succeed in that exploration can be promoted by placing a box containing a few different items beside the child, who is then encouraged by the teacher to explore and empty the items from the box and to retrieve them. Lilli Nielsen (1990) has for many years advocated the use of a 'Little room', a box made of a wooden frame which can be adapted to suit many different purposes. As a very poor alternative, a large cardboard box can be used. The child along with a few familiar objects is placed lying comfortably inside. The box can be fitted with contrasting textures and hanging objects for the child to enjoy and explore.

Even leaning to the side, or stretching, while lying can be a distressing experience. A quiet room offering few distractions can help the child to focus more on the activity of locating the object. On the first few occasions the child may have to be shown how to stretch to the side, in front, or behind without losing her balance. For example, if the object is on the right, just out of reach, she may need to be shown how to lean and stretch or how to support herself with her right hand.

It may be several years, and for some children it may not be possible, before the child can stand and walk to a desired object. For those who can make that leap, independent movement can be supported at first if the child is given a pram or trolley to push around. Aside from being safer from hazards, the child begins to learn the boundaries of the environment.

Children who reject contact with prams, trolleys and the like but do tolerate human contact can be encouraged to depend less and less on being guided by contact. Letting the child follow your voice, a fan, or interesting smell are possible ways of moving towards independent walking. Or the child may be prompted to walk in unfamiliar surroundings by gently touching her each step she takes. As confidence grows the number of contacts made is reduced. All the time the child is assured that comfort and security from the adult is available and within reach.

Usually formal mobility training will at some point require the person to be introduced to the technique of trailing. In this method the hand contacting the wall trails in front of the blind person, using two or three knuckles or fingers to find out about the wall. Because this does not give enough information for the child to be confident in moving along the child may need to be encouraged to have as much of their body in contact with the surface as possible.

Further encouragement can be given by using different textures placed on a wall. 'Bubble-wrap' is often preferred because the bubbles can be popped before moving on to a different texture such as polystyrene, egg cartons, velvet. In this way the focus is less on the movement rather than on the purpose of that movement. There is every point in moving if there is something of interest to be found along the way.

Unless the pupil explores the environment, even if that environment is restricted, he or she cannot be expected to develop the idea of what is out there, where it is or how to get there. By moving around the environment the deafblind child gains information which can be generalised, for example that:

- soft and warm carpets are different from hard and cold tiles or stone floors;
- wet, spongy grass is easier on the feet than hard roads and gravel paths;
- hard walls, sharp edges, unstable pieces of furniture exist and care needs to be taken when moving around them.

From movement to communication

Many of the points mentioned above assume that the child's physical abilities to move are fairly good and that any mobility and orientation difficulties are a result of deafblindness. However, for an increasing number of children who are deafblind, physical impairment restricts the type and range of movements to be made. Given the clear link established between communication and movement, does this mean that communication is destined to be as restricted as movement?

There are many examples that demonstrate how a child's movement can be used to support communication. One well-developed example is the 'Movement, Gesture and Sign' communication programme described by Lee and MacWilliam (1995). They describe how:

> The aim of the movement session is to approach the child on his own terms, focusing on what he can do, rather than on what we want him to do . . . The adult may then engage the child in simple and quite natural movement play. The aim is to form a bond of mutual trust.

Through a process of making reciprocal actions, responding to what the child does without deciding beforehand what the child is expected to do or to follow, the child is encouraged to learn that he can influence the other person: interaction has begun. To the child, trust and participation is what is important, and not being expected to learn patterns of movement such as learning individual signs.

Lee and MacWilliam go on to describe the need to keep an open mind, so as to support his efforts to communicate, and that movement sessions like these encourage the child to learn that 'communication is fun and he wants to participate in the social world' and 'movement and gesture have meaning'.

Chapters 2 and 6 develop these and similar approaches which can facilitate the link between encouraging the child to move to find out information about their world about which they can then communicate.

Summary

Each of the seven people introduced at the beginning of this chapter is described as deafblind, although the effects of that deafblindness vary from person to person. What they had in common was that deafblindness affected how they obtain information and gain experiences, how they communicate with people and how they move around in their environment.

Other than that, the people were different individuals. They illustrate differences in the effects of deafblindness. The degree of visual and hearing impairments may differ. The age at which hearing and/or vision is impaired or lost may differ. Other impairments may or may not accompany impairments to sight and hearing.

Not surprisingly, different medical causes of deafblindness give rise to different effects and in turn to different support needs. Some are associated with additional, often multiple impairments to those of impaired vision and hearing. Some causes are associated with deafblindness being present at or soon after birth. Other causes are associated with deafblindness being acquired later in life.

For practical reasons – difficulties in assessment, transfer of good practice and families having shared experiences – pupils with visual plus multiple impairment, and those with hearing plus multiple impairment are often considered to be potential beneficiaries of methods of working with deafblind pupils.

Notes

[1] The word 'adventitious' is often used in place of 'acquired'.

[2] The rubella virus causes deafblindness because it affects the foetus at an early stage of development when many of the important functions of the brain are just forming.

[3] This category is less prevalent. If congenital impairments to the brain are severe enough to affect hearing and learning abilities they will usually also affect vision. This is because foetal development of the visual system is completed after development of the auditory system.

[4] Discussion of the focus of observation builds on Bryson's writings on this topic, presented in Module 1 of *Contact* (Bryson 1993).

References

Brown, D. (1997) 'Trends in the population of children with multi-sensory impairment', *Talking Sense* 43(2), 12–14.

Bryson, E. (1993) 'Introduction to Observation', in Blythman, M. and Diniz, F. A. (eds) *Contact: A resource for staff working with children who are deafblind*. Module 1, Topic 3, Sensory Series 3. Edinburgh: Moray House Publications.

Lee, M. and MacWilliam, L. (1995) *Movement, Gesture and Sign. An interactive approach to sign communication for children who are visually impaired with additional disabilities*. London: Royal National Institute for the Blind (book and video to accompany).

McInnes, J. (1998) Personal Communication.

McInnes, J. M. and Treffry, J. A. (1982) *Deaf-Blind Infants and Children: A Developmental Guide*. Toronto: University of Toronto Press.

Meshcheryakov, A. (1979) *Awakening to Life*. Moscow: Progress Publishers.

Nielsen, L. (1990) *Are You Blind? Promotion of the development of children who are especially developmentally threatened*. Denmark: Sikon.

Sidle, N. (1985) *Rubella in Pregnancy: A review of rubella as an infection in pregnancy, its consequences and prevention*. London: Sense.

Tizard, B. and Hughes, M. (1984) *Young Children Learning: Talking at Home and at School*. London: Fontana.

CHAPTER 2

Creating a communicating environment

Laura Pease

Deafblind children communicating

The subtitle of this book stresses the importance of communication in any attempt to educate deafblind children. Long before the child can have access to a formal curriculum, the adults around him must establish contact and begin to develop a means of communication through which the child can be enabled to understand events around him and, in time, to exert some control.

When the present author took up her post as a classroom teacher in a unit for children with dual sensory impairment, the main aim of the communication curriculum was to teach the children to use sign language. Activities were carefully structured to give the children the opportunity to experience a basic sign vocabulary and to motivate them to use their first signs. For some children this was undoubtedly successful and one of the pupils from that era, now in her twenties, is able to visit her teacher and chat in BSL about her memories of school. For many of our pupils, however, signing was not an appropriate strategy. Some were prevented from signing by physical limitations. Some lacked the detailed vision to develop an extensive sign vocabulary. Some were not intellectually 'ready' to sign. Others lacked the confidence or self-awareness to express their wishes. Rather than a curriculum designed to teach a complex code, they needed strategies designed to encourage them to use the small signals they already had which told us what they wanted.

For these groups of children, an overwhelming emphasis on sign led to a great deal of confusion and frustration. It was all too common, for example, to see members of staff holding biscuits a foot or so above a child's head while waiting for that precious moment when the child managed to hit his elbow in an approximation of the 'biscuit' sign! If the child could not or would not produce that simple movement, the adult was faced with a dilemma. Should we use a physical prompt, reinforcing the idea that communication was something very difficult which relied on adult support? Should we give the child the biscuit anyway, nullifying the previous five minutes' effort? Should we put the biscuit back in the tin, risking a major temper tantrum and reinforcing the idea that communication was a clever trick known only to clever and powerful adults?

Fortunately for us and our pupils, we learnt instead to value and reinforce a whole range of communication strategies which will be considered in more detail later in the chapter. This acknowledgement of a range of strategies became more important as the profile of deafblind pupils changed, with more children having profound or complex needs.

Today at snack time, in our school and in other centres where deafblind children are educated, the following scenes are more common:

- Mark uses a mixture of speech and BSL to tell his teacher about the video he watched the previous evening, breaking off to ask for more toast and to complain that his friend has burnt it again.
- Janice uses a 'Lightwriter' to spell out, letter by letter, 'More biscuit please' and to say 'Janice have blackcurrant now'.
- David, who is totally blind, searches the table in front of him with his hands. A classroom assistant who knows him well wonders whether he is anticipating the snack routine. She finger spells to him 'David want drink?' and shows him, by moving his hand to the tray, that preparations are well in hand.
- Zahra turns the pages of a thick communication book until she finds the 'food and drink' page. She taps her classroom assistant's hand before indicating 'want tea (and) sugar' and helping herself to three large spoonfuls.
- Martin's teacher holds a cup in front of his mouth. When Martin is ready for another sip of juice, he will pull her hand towards him and open his mouth wide.
- Louise takes a toy cup from the bag at the side of her wheelchair and waves it in the air before banging it energetically on her tray as a request for a drink.

These children are confident communicators. They have each learnt to use a means of communication that meets their needs. Equally important, they know that the people around them are ready to take an interest in what they have to say and to respond to their message.

Communication development in deafblind children

Chapter 1 looked at the impact of deafblindness on a child's development. Nowhere are the devastating effects of deafblindness more evident than in the area of communication.

From an early age, young children with intact hearing and vision will chat as they play. Language seems continual and forms a 'running commentary' on the activities of their daily lives. Whether playing with other children, sharing time with their family, or spending time in the local community, children comment on the things they see and do and make any shared experience a focus of communication. Indeed, even before speech develops, children will use pre-linguistic skills to engage other people in a shared activity, by pointing at an interesting object, holding out a toy to be admired or making eye contact to start off a game of peekaboo. As language develops, it is used, apparently 'naturally', to make a link between the here and now and previous or future experience ('me got one at home'), to plan ('we go park tomorrow'), to persuade ('not go home now, one more swing') or to explain ('push the button, Lala say Eh-oh').

For deafblind children, none of these processes happens naturally. They lack the basic strategies which are open to their peers and also seem to lack the will to make relationships or to interact with other people.

> David, who is almost totally deaf and blind, takes little interest in the other children in his class but he has learnt to communicate with his teacher, Meg. At first sight there may seem to be little communication going on. David can neither speak nor sign, he cannot make eye contact to show interest and he does not smile to show pleasure or frown when he is annoyed. When things are not as he would like them he is likely to push the adult away or remove himself from the activity. David doesn't comment on events around him, nor does he show any awareness of the other children's contributions. The communication which does exist between Meg and David is in some ways peculiar to themselves, born of their shared experience over the past two years. Meg knows that when David taps the side of his head he is mildly distressed and that a tantrum may follow if she cannot identify the source of his distress fairly quickly. When David reaches out his hand in the middle of a familiar activity, Meg can guess what he is looking for and place it within his reach. In any event, there is much that David and Meg cannot say to each other. They cannot discuss what happened yesterday or what may happen tomorrow. Meg recognises many of David's preferences and can anticipate things he will not like (for example when the school cook produces yoghurt rather than a proper pudding) but they do not share a language which will allow her to reassure him or show that she understands.

Why do even relatively able youngsters with multi-sensory impairment (MSI) show such limited communication and why does a young man like David rely on very basic ways of getting a message across?

Babies who develop normally interact with the important people in their lives from their first moments together. When a new mother holds her baby close, speaks soothingly and establishes eye contact, they begin the process of bonding and communicating which will lead to the baby's first words in about a year's time. Throughout games, routines and the simple experiences of daily life, early communication develops as the important people in a child's world talk to him and respond to his actions. By making and holding eye contact and by enthusiastic noises, movements and facial expressions, the baby keeps a game going and keeps mother near at hand.

For a baby who is born deafblind, the normal process of communication development begins to go wrong literally from the moment of birth. Assuming that the baby has not been whisked away for medical intervention but remains close to his mother, he may not be able to make and sustain eye contact or to respond to a soothing voice. His mother's face may be invisible or only a blur and her speech only a low sound which he cannot pick out from the background of other noises. The deafblind baby may register little of the world around him, or may find it a frightening place full of half-registered shapes and sounds. He will not hold his mother's attention with a ready gaze and will not be able to play the games of sight, sound and movement which other babies enjoy. If his vision and hearing are so seriously damaged that he cannot use visual or auditory cues to warn him that someone is coming to pick him up, or that a particular activity is about to happen, contact with other people may even become threatening.

As time goes on, the deafblind baby's difficulties will be compounded. Depending on the severity of the impairments, visual and hearing impairments in combination will:

- Limit interaction – the baby has fewer ways of interacting with others or perceiving their attempts to interact with him. Speech and vocalisation, shared glances and smiles will be of limited value for him. He has fewer opportunities to interact as he needs to be in very close contact with other people to do so.
- Limit information – the baby has access only to objects, people and events very near him. Until his hand movements are more fully developed (and this in itself takes longer than normal for babies with visual impairments) he has limited ability to learn through exploration by touch. Thus his understanding of the world will be piecemeal and he will have fewer concepts and experiences to shape his communication.
- Limit shared attention – the baby who is reliant on touch or is able to use only vision or hearing for attention will find it very difficult to attend to a toy or an event and *at the same time* engage in communication with another person. So, for example, he will not be able to point at an object and attend to its name in sign or speech.

So the deafblind baby will develop only a limited repertoire of communicative behaviours and responses. Instead of crowing and holding out his hands in response to a toy, he may quieten, or hold his hands still for a second when they are placed on something of interest to him. He may not show any obvious response to events beyond the immediate sensations of his own body, or he may show fear and anger when brought into contact with a wider world. He will be less aware of other people and their responses to him. He will have fewer opportunities to interact with people or objects in a positive way.

For the typical baby, success in communication builds on success. As he establishes a measure of control over the people around him through sounds and gestures, his communication becomes more deliberate and more specific. Before his first recognisable word, he learns to ask by pointing for a biscuit or a specific toy, to keep a game going by his delighted response. He and his mother attend together to a picture book or a toy and his continuing interest encourages his mother to turn the page or to make Jack jump out of his box for the twentieth time! His mother assumes that the sounds he makes have meaning and interprets them to him, 'Oh, you want Jack to jump up again! Here he comes!' The baby becomes an increasingly sociable being with favourite people and games.

For the deafblind child, the initial failure to communicate effectively may set up a downward spiral. His communication is unclear and his ability to respond to communication from other people is poorly developed. Shared attention to toys and games will be very difficult. Thus he may become less motivated to communicate and may withdraw markedly from social contact. He may resort to aggressive or otherwise unacceptable behaviour in order to exert some control over a threatening and unpredictable world.

It is also, unfortunately, the case that those around the deafblind child may unwittingly contribute to his communication difficulties by their responses to him. Parents are likely to find their deafblind baby's 'signals' difficult to read and may become discouraged, especially if the child seems to reject them or show little interest. Parents and carers may find it easier to do things for the child without waiting for his response so that activities which for the typical child are full of fun and communication become a quiet routine for the deafblind infant. With little encouragement to interact or to exert control within activities, the child may become a passive recipient of care as 'learned helplessness' develops.

As we have already seen, many deafblind children have other difficulties in addition to their sensory impairments. These additional problems may hinder communication further. For example:

- the child with severe epilepsy will find it difficult to link cause and effect if frequent absences or the effects of medication fragment events and interactions;
- the child who is ill or in pain will have less energy to interact and less opportunity to experience the world around them;
- the child with physical impairments will be limited in his ability to explore the world and to communicate by movement, sign and gesture.

This is a gloomy scenario and it is likely that even an able deafblind young person will have language which is restricted and to some degree impoverished.

Nevertheless, it is also true that parents and educators can make a significant difference by the quality of our intervention, particularly if we are committed to giving the deafblind child a degree of autonomy and control. The sections that follow attempt to outline possible approaches to this challenging task.

Summary

Factors which impede communication in deafblind children:

- direct effects of sensory impairment;
- effects of motor impairment;
- effects of ill health and medication;
- lack of opportunities to interact;
- lack of interactive strategies;
- lack of information;
- lack of knowledge about the world;
- poor self-image;
- impaired communication from other people;
- 'doing for' the child.

Learning from typical language development

Nind and Hewett (1994), whose work on intensive interaction grew from their teaching experience with deafblind adults, say that:

> It seems logical that in order to help someone learn something as complicated, subtle and yet as little understood as communication, then we should carefully examine the way that it is learnt naturally and use those processes wherever possible.

This does seem to be a logical argument and it led to the development of an approach which has been enormously successful in helping severely handicapped people develop the skills and the motivation to communicate with others. How far, though, can it be applied to the children with whom we are concerned? As already discussed, the development of communication in deafblind people can be very far from 'natural' and we might want to argue that if we simply behave 'naturally', deafblind children will develop only the most basic communication and will become extremely frustrated and withdrawn. To take an extreme example, most adults interacting with normally developing babies will 'chat' to them as they engage in basic care such as changing nappies or enjoying a bath. The profoundly deaf baby will make little sense of chat and the baby with multiple handicaps including a visual impairment may screen it out as meaningless noise without obvious relevance to the sensations he is experiencing. This 'natural' interaction will contribute little to these babies' language development.

Current approaches to encourage children with complex needs to communicate attempt to steer a middle path between 'natural' behaviour and careful planning. We do need to understand and learn from the process of typical language development. But we also need to adapt the strategies used with typical babies when working with children and young people with special needs. Deafblind children will only access the typical process if great care is taken to create a communicative environment which they can understand and to design individual programmes to help them communicate with others in appropriate ways. Teachers and carers will need to adapt their approach to communication, making conscious and explicit what appears to happen instinctively between mothers and typical children and looking carefully at the value of specific strategies for individual deafblind children.

Stages in language development

Typical children's language develops along a number of parameters:

- from direct action to formal language;
- from reflexive behaviours to intentional communication;
- from single elements to combinations;
- from context bound to context free;
- from a limited to an extensive vocabulary.

From direct action to formal language

In the early stages of development, babies act directly on their environment. They grab hold of the things they want or shut their mouths firmly at the sight of lovingly prepared vegetables! Later they will use gestures or sounds to indicate their wishes – pointing at a favourite toy or making a characteristic noise when they want more dinner – or to show interest in things around them, and later still they develop an understanding of a formal code by using words, singly at first and then in combination. So language becomes more complex and conventional, and less idiosyncratic as the child learns to use more abstract means of expression.

From reflexive behaviours to intentional communication

Three stages have been identified in this process.

1. At first babies respond reflexively to stimuli such as hunger or environmental sounds by crying or startling. Babies have no control over these actions, but, although a degree of trial and error may be involved, the adults around them can often interpret these reflexive behaviours and respond appropriately with milk, a soothing cuddle or a dry nappy.
2. Early in the first year of life, babies gain control over their responses. They may still to listen to an interesting sound, reach out for a toy or kick their legs

with excitement when they enjoy a particular game. There is no deliberate attempt to communicate as yet, but again adults interpret the child's behaviour and aim to make an appropriate response. As more controlled vocalisations and giggles begin to replace crying the adults will treat these sounds as one half of a conversation and fit their actions to the supposed meaning of the sounds the baby makes.

3. The outcome of the conversations between adult and child is that, later in the first year, babies use similar vocalisations and movements with clear communicative intent. They begin to wait for an adult's attention, or deliberately to attract it, before gesturing towards the biscuit cupboard or vocalising to call attention to the ducks on the pond. They make excited noises while leaning towards the swings and show their disgust if the adult with them does not share their interest or accede to their request.

Thus, by the time the first words are uttered, the typical baby is using words to achieve greater precision in a communicative exchange, the basics of which have already been practised. The baby in the last example who eventually says 'swing' somewhere around his or her first birthday will already have been able to draw mother's attention to the swing in a clear and intentional way.

From single elements to combinations

First words and gestures are used singly – the baby will point towards an object, make a sound or speak a single word to comment on 'dog', 'ball' and so on. As the child's conceptual understanding grows, so he is able to relate two or more words to express increasingly complicated ideas – 'dog run', 'Mummy ball', 'me give dog a ball' – until full sentences appear.

From context bound to context free

Early communication makes sense only in context. A gesture or an excited movement in response to some object or event has meaning only for the people present at the time, who are able to use all available cues to interpret what the child is 'saying'.

As the child learns to use a more complex abstract code, so his utterances begin to make sense outside the immediate context. At first they may only be intelligible to people who share the child's immediate history, as the child may refer back to a previous event or conversation without filling in the details. 'Big car' may be an attempt to talk about a new toy, a television programme or the taxi that will shortly take him to visit Grandma. Later the child's utterances will truly stand alone. 'I like Teletubbies' can be understood, if not shared, by anyone who is aware of the television programme concerned; 'I got new shoes at the shop' is universally intelligible.

However, children remain dependent on context to some extent for several years as they may continue to assume a shared understanding where none exists. The present writer was concerned to hear 'I did maths in the shed with Miss Clarke today', given that her five year old's school was housed in a beautiful new building. On parents evening the teacher removed the confusion which arose from Simon's East London vowels and his assumption that Mum was familiar with the school layout by explaining that she often asked the classroom assistant to work with a small group in the 'shared area' between the classrooms in the Reception unit!

From a limited to an extensive vocabulary

The growth in a young child's vocabulary in the second year of life amazes those around him. The child's vocabulary expands in nature as well as in size, with early nouns joined by verbs and adjectives and the gradual inclusion of more abstract words and words expressing more complex concepts.

The context of language development

Research in the 1980s highlighted some key features in the way that normally developing babies learn language. The research showed that children learn language:

- through interaction with familiar adults;
- in the context of normally-occurring activities;
- in secure settings;
- with adult support.

Interaction

Children learn language through engaging with other people. From the way that the adult responds to them the child learns that his movements and sounds can have an effect on other people and he is encouraged to develop meaning further.

Through interaction a child learns that language is a two-way process. Videos of children less than three months old interacting with their mothers show that mother and child respond to each other constantly in a 'conversation' well before spoken language emerges.

Through shared attention to toys, other people and the dozens of objects and events encountered in daily life the child develops his understanding of the world and the verbal labels given to important events. Shared games and small routines allow the child to exert control and to practise using simple language.

Normal activities

The routine activities of a baby's life – eating, dressing, changing, playing – form a natural context for developing language. They carry an intrinsic meaning for the child and their regular structure helps the child to anticipate the next step and to learn the appropriate vocabulary.

Security

Effective learning cannot take place in conditions of stress. Language develops best in a setting where the child can feel secure and comfortable and with an adult who is able to give the child a high level of attention and to respond to the child's communication.

With adult support

Adults caring for young children instinctively adapt their behaviour to create a context in which the children can develop language and cognitive skills. Vygotsky, a psychologist who studied this process, uses the term 'scaffolding' to describe how an adult will give a child just enough support by, for example, developing simple routines or helping a child to carry out a practical task, but will leave the child room to make their own contribution, gradually withdrawing over time until the child can carry out the task alone. In language terms, carers initially give babies considerable support by interpreting their sounds and gestures and by structuring activities so that a child's role is clear.

A mother feeding her five month old baby stops as the spoon returns to the bowl, waits as the baby looks at the spoon and moves excitedly and then asks 'Do you want some more? More yummy pudding?' Baby's wide open mouth is easily interpreted! 'Yes you do! More yummy pudding!' Mother has 'scaffolded' the activity by giving it a clear structure and baby is able to control the pace by his waves and open mouth.

Carers also support a child's language by using what has been termed 'motherese' (although there is evidence that all adults and even some older children use similar strategies when talking to babies and young children). Sentences are short and simple, as in the examples above. The adult speaks more slowly and with more emphasis on key words. The adult's facial expression becomes expectant and wide-eyed and the tone of voice rises. All this helps the baby to attend to spoken language and to identify the key elements of speech.

The deafblind learner

Teachers working with deafblind children need to be aware of the ways in which language develops for typical children. They will want to assess the progress of their deafblind pupils against the 'landmarks' of typical development and use this information to set appropriate educational goals. They will want to create some of the conditions in which language typically develops, for example by providing plenty of opportunities for natural interaction within activities which have meaning for the child, by creating situations in which the child feels secure and by paying attention to some of the features of motherese.

But teachers also need to take into account important differences between typical communication development and the way in which deafblind children develop. They will need to work hard to signal opportunities for communication, given that, in the early stages at least, many of the strategies which typical children use to initiate interaction (such as eye contact, or pointing at an interesting object) are not available to the deafblind child and that deafblind children therefore rarely seem to initiate 'conversation'. They will need to identify and then to build on very small responses and quite idiosyncratic behaviours, like David hitting the side of his head when he becomes agitated, or perhaps a specific vocalisation that means hunger or boredom. They will try to replace visual, auditory and vocal signals with signals within the range of the individual child, such as a tap on the shoulder to attract attention or the use of object cues to signal activities. Above all, they need to exploit every possible avenue to help the child develop a sense of agency, the understanding that he can affect his environment and 'make things happen'.

The language environment

From now on we will be considering aspects of programme design and language assessment. The present writer has been extremely fortunate in recent years to have worked with excellent speech and language therapists and to have seen her teaching colleagues work with therapists, classroom assistants and parents to design and implement language and communication programmes. References to 'the teacher' in what follows are made for simplicity and should be seen to refer to the whole multi-disciplinary team as they engage in the fascinating and challenging task of programme design, implementation and evaluation.

In order to communicate successfully, a child needs:

- to want something;
- to know he or she can effect a change;
- to know the 'code', i.e. a way of expressing his or her wish, whether by gesture, direct action or a truly symbolic code such as sign language or speech.

'Real' communication arises from something within the person communicating. This may be a primary need such as food or warmth, a need for comfort, the desire to interact or the wish to respond to a partner. It does not take place within a sterile environment where the child is expected to perform communication 'tasks' with no intrinsic meaning *to the child*.

Effective communication grows from a feeling of competence and confidence. The child needs to know that someone will 'hear' him and respond to his message. As communication with a partner develops and the child experiences success, so his confidence will grow and the frequency of attempts at communication will increase.

Communication also involves learning to behave in different ways depending on the outcome you are seeking. This may involve learning a complicated code such as speech or sign; in the early stages of development it may involve learning that reaching towards a specific toy may lead to it being placed in front of you or that turning your head away from a cup will bring drink time to an end.

These three elements pose real challenges for deafblind children and the people working with them. The children may not appear to want anything. They may seem happy in their own world and vehemently resist new experiences. They are likely to have very low self-esteem, born at least partly out of unsuccessful attempts at communication. They find it hard to learn specific responses and to link them to the desired outcomes.

If we are to help these children develop effective communication we need to create a language environment in the home or classroom which will permeate their whole day, so that no opportunity to give the child an experience of success will be lost. Language is not something that can be taught in separate sessions or left to the language 'expert'. Ideally, every person involved with the child should seek to create the right language setting for them and every activity should be planned with a child's language programme in mind.

Siegel-Causey and Guess (1989) have written a very helpful book called *Enhancing Nonsymbolic Communication Interactions among Learners with Severe Disabilities*. This is well worth reading from cover to cover for its overall approach and its many practical ideas. They advocate five 'instructional guidelines' which should shape the whole language ethos of a classroom and affect every activity in which a child is engaged. These are:

- developing nurturance;
- enhancing sensitivity;
- structuring activities;
- increasing opportunities to communicate;
- utilising movement.

Although their book arises from work with quite severely delayed children, the 'instructional guidelines' are highly relevant to deafblind children at all levels of development

Developing nurturance

This relates to helping children develop a sense of well-being arising directly from their contact with adults.

Increasing numbers of our children are very physically dependent on adult carers. Adult support is needed when the children eat or drink, for all aspects of their physical care, to enable them to move from place to place, to help them be positioned comfortably and so on. It is essential that adults engaged in the physical care of children do so in such a way that the children feel relaxed and cared for. This means paying close attention to:

- pace – working slowly enough to help the child relax and give him time to process the sensations he is experiencing;
- physical surroundings – ensuring that the area is clean and comfortable, that the temperature is appropriate for the activity and the child's medical needs;
- equipment – giving the child adequate physical support and using hoists, etc., to enable both the child and the adult to feel secure;
- body language – looking at the way the child is handled, at facial expression and tone of voice, so that the child receives the appropriate messages;
- level of attention – doing everything possible to give the child full attention during activities by choosing a distraction-free environment, by being well-prepared with all equipment to hand and creating a school ethos which strongly discourages interruptions.

One of the most effective ways of establishing contact with deafblind children and so encouraging a communicative response is to share activities with a high level of physical contact and pleasant sensations. These include:

- massage;
- one to one signing;
- co-active/resonance movement (see below);
- swimming or hydrotherapy;
- 'Tacpac' – a package where taped music is linked to a range of tactile sensations;
- Sherborne movement;
- aromatherapy;
- intensive interaction.

Sharing 'quality time' with an adult in a physically pleasurable activity seems to be a key experience in the development of communication. However, some children initially find close contact very threatening and may need a programme of gradual desensitisation.

As a child outgrows such intensive sessions, activities involving less intensive physical contact but still offering high levels of adult attention can be introduced, for example:

- physical play;
- music therapy;
- play with toys;
- 'beauty' sessions involving make-up and skin care.

The need for informal contact with adults who show pleasure in the child's company and can offer a measure of affection expressed through appropriate physical contact will continue throughout life.

The emphasis placed on physical contact in individual programmes for deafblind children raises some issues in the area of child protection. Children cannot be said to give informed consent to this physical contact and staff may well be anxious that their intervention may be misinterpreted. However the nature of the disability precludes a 'hands-off' approach. Staff and parents will, rightly, expect an educational setting to have a clear published policy on child protection which recognises the needs of this group of children and sets out practical guidelines on classroom practice. This is likely to include guidelines for staff recruitment, a requirement for careful documentation of programme planning, an expectation that only named people who are familiar to the child will carry out activities such as massage and guidelines for informing parents about the details of any programme. See Chapter 7 for a more general discussion of child protection issues.

Nurturance also involves paying attention to a child's emotional comfort. Deafblind children are subject to excessive levels of stress and adults working with them need to make every effort to minimise the stress arising from adult demands. For example, the adult may:

- work at a pace which appears comfortable for the individual child, looking for indications that the child has processed visual or tactile information and is ready to move on to the next step of an activity;
- give children opportunities for free play or self-occupation between adult-led tasks;
- construct the timetable so that there are plenty of activities which the child appears to like or at least is willing to participate in;
- follow the child's lead in structuring some activities;
- continually review the balance between new or challenging activities and consolidation tasks;
- monitor her own communication to ensure the child receives enough positive feedback.

Enhancing sensitivity

All children show some behaviours, such as a vocalisation which suggests pleasure or a movement of the hand which indicates that an activity should continue, which can be identified as communicative. Adults working with deafblind children, like parents with young children, should actively seek to ascribe meaning to such behaviours and to respond to their perceived meaning. It will be far easier to achieve this if a child has significant periods or individual time with a small number of adults who can come to know him well enough to interpret cues which are often subtle or idiosyncratic.

Jonathan, who had only limited physical control, would sometimes very definitely turn his head to the left. The member of staff who helped him at dinner time believed that this behaviour had grown from attempts to eye point his cup when it was kept on a shelf just behind his shoulder during the lunch period and interpreted this particular behaviour in all contexts as a request for a drink.

As cues become clearer and more formal means of communication develop it remains important to establish what has been called a 'reactive environment', where adults seek to respond positively to all attempts at communication. This does not necessarily mean a permissive regime (indeed, deafblind children will generally benefit from clear rules and expectations) but one where a child's requests (explicit or inferred) receive an explicit response.

> For Imran, swimming was the highlight of the week, and he continually went to the cloakroom area, removed his swimming bag from the hook and set off towards the school pool. Whenever a member of staff was able to accompany him, he would be allowed to complete his journey so that she could try to show him that another class was using the pool at that moment. In this way he did at least perceive that an adult had understood his intent and sympathised with him, even if swimming had to wait for the appointed day!

It is equally important that adults are sensitive in their communications *to* children. We need to be careful in pitching our language at the right level of difficulty and using the appropriate means of communication. Adults should be aware that some approaches may be stressful to individual children – some may be wary of too much physical contact, others will resist eye contact and others will be unwilling to focus on signs. Establishing a two-way flow of conversation is no easy task when the child's signals are fleeting or difficult to recognise. Adults may need to exercise restraint in waiting for a response from the child rather than simply pressing on with a flow of adult conversation which in the end risks teaching the child that conversation is a one-way business.

Finally, we should observe children for signs that they are not ready to communicate because of tiredness or because they are concentrating on other things. Carole, for example, is delightfully sociable except at mealtimes. It appears that the physical effort of maintaining a good position, opening her mouth at the right time, chewing and swallowing, plus the fact that she obviously thoroughly enjoys her food, leaves little room for attending to the adult. Whatever the reason, she eats more quickly and seems more relaxed if the adult helping her is quiet for most of the mealtime.

Sequencing experiences

This is a key concept in the education of deafblind children.

When the child's daily life is structured:

- it puts order on the child's experiences, building up expectations and anticipation and thus making life predictable;

- it aids learning because the memory is developed through frequent repetition;
- it develops independence by teaching the sequence of steps needed to achieve a desired goal;
- it develops an awareness of time: past, present and future;
- it leads to tolerance and responsiveness to people and activities by reducing the stress that arises from uncertainty about what may happen next.

From the communication standpoint, structure will:

- promote the understanding of contingencies, i.e. that certain behaviours are likely to be followed by specific responses;
- encourage communicative behaviour by helping the child to anticipate the next step and so to signal appropriately.

Where possible, key activities should be *characterised* by being carried out:

- at a consistent time;
- with a consistent adult;
- with a consistent group of children where appropriate;
- in a consistent place;
- using specific equipment, e.g. one towel is always used for swimming, another for the bath.

Activities should also have a strong and consistent shape with clear features to mark different parts and a definite start and finish point – see the discussion of 'Scripts' later in this chapter.

> Hassan has been taking part in a music therapy group every week for two terms. Throughout this time the session has followed a very consistent pattern and now that Hassan is familiar with the routine he is able to show his anticipation of particular sections and sometimes to initiate the next part of the routine. He makes excited noises when he is seated in his chair by the piano and the music therapist introduces herself by helping Hassan to shake the tambourine which she is holding. As the greeting song begins, Hassan reaches towards the classroom assistant sitting next to him in anticipation of being helped to shake another child's hand. The classroom assistant recognises this signal and pats his hand encouragingly.

As children move beyond the need for such extreme structure the teacher needs to introduce greater variety within each activity, perhaps through offering choices or through introducing different steps within a familiar task. Nevertheless it is difficult to overestimate the value of routine in promoting confidence and reducing stress, even for children who are ready to address an academic curriculum.

A class of deafblind young people recently went out for a meal to celebrate the eighteenth birthday of a class member. Happily full of food and drink, they returned to school for the afternoon. Michael, however, was clearly agitated and presented his picture symbol for 'café'. Despite not wanting anything more to eat, he needed the reassurance of the regular Thursday afternoon activity! Most adults working with deafblind young people can tell a similar story.

An issue arises here relating to medically fragile children who may be subject to fits or may drift between sleeping and waking and so lose the structure of individual routines. It is not easy to address this situation without creating a totally fragmented day full of 'false starts'. Teachers should consider creating short or very repetitive routines or incorporating 'mini routines' within longer activities so that small units exist which a child can gradually come to comprehend.

Increasing opportunities to communicate

Children developing in a typical way have literally hundreds of opportunities to communicate each day; some offered by parents and carers, some arising naturally within their environment, many initiated by the children themselves. Children with special needs, in contrast, may have relatively few communication opportunities; indeed some depressing research carried out in special schools suggests that children with the most severe communication delays are given fewest opportunities to communicate with busy members of staff, while children whose communication was already well developed were given a disproportionate share of staff attention.

Staff working with deafblind children need explicitly to create opportunities for communication by:

- increasing the number of opportunities;
- extending the range of communication;
- ensuring that communication is functional.

Increasing the number of opportunities

Siegel-Causey and Guess (1989) give plenty of practical ideas for bringing communication into an activity – see Figure 2.1 for an example of how an activity can be structured to make it communication-centred, based on their ideas.

A teacher may well find it instructive to ask a trusted observer to 'audit' the communication experience of a deafblind child across a period of time. Is there sufficient time for the children to process events and make a response or do activities proceed at a hurried pace? Do staff pause frequently and wait for a response from the children, or do they surround the children with a flow of adult talk? Are plenty of communicative incidents built into each activity?

Communicative signals used during a cookery lesson. The pupil, Sarah, is 16 years old, profoundly deaf and thought to be totally blind.

Adult's signals	Meaning
Lifts S's hand to her throat and says 'hello'.	It's Laura.
Puts objects of reference on to a board.	Time for cooking.
Puts S's hand onto her walking frame.	Time to walk to the kitchen.
Puts S's hand onto the door handle.	Here's the kitchen.
Puts S's hand onto the chopping board.	Look at the ingredients.
Taps S's hand onto her (S's) chest.	You do it please.
Strokes S's cheek.	Well done.
Puts S's hand on to her (L's) chest.	I'll do this bit.
Taps S's back as she walks past.	I'm still here.
Mimes stirring action with S's hand.	Stir the mixture.
Holds S's hand over the bowl.	Careful, it's hot.
Puts S's hand onto the tissue box.	Do you want a tissue?
Puts hand under S's elbow.	Do you want to stand up?

Pupil's signals	Ascribed meaning
Stands up.	I know where I'm going.
*Pulls L's hand to her shoe.	This shoe's on wrong, put it right.
Sits quietly and cooperates.	I know what I'm doing/I like cooking.
*Pats hand on own chest.	I can (? want to) do this bit.
*Pats hand on own chest.	I did that bit.
Shakes head from side to side.	I'm not happy (onions had made her cry).
*Puts hand out in searching motion.	Are you still there?
*Pulls self to standing.	Time to go and eat this food.

Those marked * are thought by the adult to have communicative intent.

Figure 2.1 Non-symbolic communication in practice

Sarah and Matthew enjoy playing with bubbles and will concentrate on their movements for 5–10 minutes at a time. Their teacher wants to make this play session an opportunity to develop communication skills as well as visual skills and early scientific concepts. Therefore she frequently stops blowing the bubbles in order to sign simple comments or to look for an indication from Sarah that she wants the activity to continue and to encourage her to sign 'bubble' rather than simply pointing. She is also beginning to encourage the two children to communicate with each other by allowing each in turn to take the lead in the game while the other watches.

Extending the range of communication

There are many different reasons for communicating with other people.

Where adults are responsible for structuring and facilitating communication, however, it is possible that the types of language 'on offer' will be restricted. As Rowland and Stramel-Campbell (1987) say, 'All too often learners with sensory impairments use only communicative functions that attract attention, request more (generally food) and protest.'

It is no easy task to give deafblind children the opportunity to experience a range of different types of language. It is important to avoid restricting their language opportunities to simple choices or responding to requests. More able children can and should receive and express the whole range of language functions. Again an 'audit' carried out by a trusted colleague can be a salutary experience.

A teacher in a specialist unit was concerned that a 16 year old pupil, Eric, was only using his very extensive communication book to ask for activities or to request items of food. She and her colleagues decided to make greater efforts to use his book themselves to model a range of ways to communicate, such as commenting on the world or asking questions. After several weeks their efforts were rewarded when, on the way to the local shops, Eric opened his book at the bus stop and indicated 'bus'. This was interpreted as a question and when his teacher indicated 'walk' Eric continued past the bus stop on foot.

Ensuring that communication is functional

Communication is functional if it allows the child some measure of autonomy and influence over aspects of daily life which are important *to the child*. This means that adults who know a child well need to explore the communication opportunities they provide in terms of the *child's* needs and preferences.

For example, it is relatively easy (and common) to provide choices at snack time. An individual child, however, may have no strong preference between orange and blackcurrant drink and for him such a choice will not be particularly motivating. He may however have a strong preference for a particular toy or a particular fragrance of soap and thus functional choices will occur at playtime or in the bathroom.

Sehar caused her teacher concern by her passivity and her failure to make interpretable choices during daily activities. After much experimentation, her teacher found an interactive game which she thoroughly enjoyed and in which she was able to initiate different games by modelling the first step of each. Sehar had an opportunity each day to take part in what came to be known as the 'banana game' because one of the objects was a brightly coloured plastic banana(!) and in this context she became a very active participant, prolonging the game for 15–20 minutes and appearing to realise that the teacher was following her lead.

Utilising movement

In using this phrase, Siegel-Causey and Guess (1989) mean that adults should start from the movements which the child spontaneously produces and ascribe a communicative intent to them. Looking at a broader range of children, we might rather say that adults should aim to use whichever channels are available to children at a given point in their development. For example, a child may have no intelligible speech but may use a range of vocalisations with meaning. Another child may not be ready to sign but may have a great deal to communicate using gestures and eye movements.

The basic principle is to use behaviours which the child spontaneously produces and to respond appropriately. Such behaviours may carry a range of meanings, including:

stop
look
I'm angry
I know what comes next
I want more...
I like this/I don't like this
come here
I'm fed up
this is interesting.

In the early stages, the child's behaviours may be highly idiosyncratic (as with Jonathan in the example above). Later the child may be able to use a system which is more generally accessible, but he should still have the opportunity to choose the system and mode with which he is most comfortable, rather than be expected to fit into the school language policy.

After four years at school, in a signing environment, Peter had shown only very limited use of sign. His teacher and parents felt that his fine motor control, rather than his overall ability, was limiting his progress and were concerned at the growing signs of frustration when Peter could not make adults understand his needs. They set up a programme to teach him to relate pictures to objects and activities. Peter quickly made the required link and within a term was using pictures to make requests and to hold simple conversations about the activities scheduled for that day. Over the next ten years he progressed from large pictures to pictograms and symbols and finally to print. At present he communicates using a 'Lightwriter' or an alphabetic board. He is a keen and eager communicator, with the written language clearly fulfilling a social function for him. He still uses only three or four signs.

The physical environment

This is not discussed in any detail by Siegel-Causey and Guess (1989) but it is of course a vital element in creating a communication environment for deafblind children. Children need to have ready access to communication from other people and they need an environment which will help them to make best use of their residual senses and physical abilities if they are to respond.

The physical environment is fully discussed in Chapter 6. From a communication point of view, adults need to pay particular attention to:

- lighting levels – is lighting good enough to enable the child to see sign, picture or object in sufficient detail?, is the area free from shadow?;
- glare – is the lighting so strong as to cause discomfort?, is it shining directly into the child's eyes? (be particularly careful where children in wheelchairs or standers are placed);
- visual contrast between foreground and background – does the picture or symbol stand out clearly?;
- the auditory environment – are speech and key sounds accessible or lost in a welter of extraneous noise?, could headphones be used when some children are listening to music, to reduce the overall noise level?;
- use of aids – do hearing aids or glasses make a significant difference to the child's ability to access communication?;
- physical clutter – is the environment so busy that the child cannot pick out the main stimulus?;
- 'zoning' the classroom – can particular activities be linked with certain places and equipment to help the child anticipate what is happening and later to request an activity by moving to the appropriate place or selecting the appropriate equipment?

Ways to communicate

Choosing appropriate methods of communication

Anyone working with deafblind children needs to have access to a repertoire of communication methods. Adults may need to use a different method or more likely a different combination of methods with each child we encounter.

In choosing appropriate communication methods the following questions must be borne in mind:

What do we know about the child's functional vision?

- Is he aware of any visual sensations?

- Can he see the kind of detail which will allow him to make sense of signs or pictures?
- Should he wear glasses, and does he?
- Does he have sufficient control of head and eye movements to focus on a series of signs or an array of pictures?
- Is there evidence of cortical visual impairment or other features which may lead to inconsistent use of vision?

What do we know about the child's functional hearing?

- Is he aware of any sounds around him?
- Does he have hearing within the 'speech envelope', i.e. the range of tone and volume which will give him some access to the spoken word?
- Does he attend to speech and other sounds?
- Does he respond to music?
- Can he discriminate sounds to a level which will allow him to make sense of any words?
- Should he wear hearing aids, and does he?
- Is there evidence of a conductive hearing loss and does this fluctuate, e.g. when he has a cold?

What do we know about the child's tactile development?

- Is he happy to move co-actively with an adult? (see below)
- Is he willing to explore by touch?
- Does he spontaneously explore objects and people within reach?
- Can he move his hands and fingers systematically over an array of objects?
- Can he explore objects with sufficient control to make fine distinctions between them?
- Will he tolerate tactile signing or fingerspelling and is there evidence of discrimination between signs or letters?

What do we know about the child's motor development?

- Does he have control over whole-body movements?
- Can he move to a particular place in the room?
- How much control does he have over hands and fingers?
- Can he pick up and handle objects?
- Can he reliably point to, or otherwise indicate, one object or picture from an array?
- Can he explore objects with sufficient control to make fine distinctions between them?
- Can he copy gross and fine movements?

What do we know about the child's use of vocalisation?

- Can he make controlled noises?
- Does he use speech sounds?
- Is he able to copy speech sounds?
- Does he produce specific vocalisations in specific circumstances?
- Can he produce intelligible words?

What do we know about the child's cognitive ability?

- What is his developmental level compared with typical children of the same age?
- What discrimination does he show in other areas?
- What awareness does he have of key concepts such as contingency or cause and effect?
- What routines does he recognise and how much support does he need to participate?
- What level of symbolic understanding does he show?
- How reliable is his short and long term memory?

What do we know about the child's communication?

- What channels does he currently use – visual, auditory or motor?
- How does he currently make his needs known?
- In what circumstances does he communicate spontaneously?
- Does he use the same mode(s) for expressive and receptive communication?
- Can familiar adults generally understand him?
- Does he communicate for a range of reasons?

The answers to these questions will enable the teacher to build up a communication profile of the child and should begin to suggest which avenues of communication are likely to be successful.

Published assessment tools may also be useful – see 'Some tools for assessing communication' towards the end of this chapter. See also Chapter 4 for a general consideration of approaches to assessment.

Peter, whose communication programme was discussed earlier, had poor motor control and little tolerance for activities involving motor imitation. Visually, however, he was very receptive with an emerging interest in books and pictures. As discussed earlier, a change from sign to pictures as a means of communication was extremely successful.

Samira, on the other hand, showed a keen interest in both aural and visual stimuli, making effective use of both residual senses. She also had good fine motor ability. Within the total communication environment of her classroom, speech, sign and pictograms were used with Samira who seemed at first to be helped by the combination of methods. Eventually she dropped the use of pictures but she continues to sign and speak herself and to gain reassurance from the use of sign (Signs Supporting English) by other people.

In the rest of this section a range of communication methods is discussed, with brief notes about each and examples of their use with deafblind children. This list does not, of course, pretend to be exhaustive!

Non-symbolic communication

Non-symbolic communication refers to direct means of communication which do not rely upon symbolic understanding. As many of the children with whom we are concerned will not develop the use of symbolic communication, the teacher's aim will be to extend their use of non-symbolic forms to give them a range of opportunities to exert control and to develop social relationships. In this context the use of terms such as 'pre-formal' (or pre-anything else) appears inappropriate and the more neutral term 'non-symbolic communication' is used throughout this section.

Reflexive responses

These are the most basic forms of response to the environment, or to the sensations of the child's own body, such as hunger or pain, and include:

- startle movements;
- stilling;
- crying;
- relaxing;
- cooing or shouting;
- changes in body tone;
- pulling back.

Apparently instinctive acts of aggressive behaviour such as biting in response to a perceived threat may also be included in this category.

By definition, children have no control over these responses and they cannot be taught. Nevertheless, they help the teacher assess what a child is aware of in his environment and they give important clues about preferences, likes and dislikes. Adults who take note of these cues can create a positive environment for the child by gradually reducing the sources of stress and increasing the number of favoured experiences, to which the child may in time respond more deliberately.

Meg has found that Imran is noticeably more relaxed and more tolerant of physical contact when she sings to him. After the morning greetings each day, Meg and Imran work for 15 minutes in a quiet room. She sings three songs with a clear structure while gently moving with him as he sits across her lap. Each song has its own characteristic movement. At present Meg's main aims are to create a 'special time' for Imran early in the school day, to help him accept physical contact and to develop his listening skills by encouraging him to attend for longer periods. In the longer term she hopes that he will show anticipation of the movements attached to each song by rocking his own body when she sings 'Rock together'.

Signals

These are deliberate responses to the environment made with a specific end in view. Depending on the pupil's level of control they may include:

- whole body movements such as cuddling in or moving away;
- reaching for a stimulus;
- pulling at an adult's hand;
- leading an adult towards the door;
- picking up a desired object;
- hitting an adult or child;
- vocalising in response to pleasure or displeasure;
- spitting out food;
- pushing an object away;
- getting up or rolling to one side to move away from an activity;
- vocalising or waving when a favourite adult is not paying attention.

While these signals often do affect other people's behaviour the child may not realise that they will do so, i.e. they are not always *intentionally* communicative. However, if adults consistently respond to signals, the children will learn that signals produce a desired outcome and the degree of intentionality should increase.

At this stage it is important to encourage the child specifically to approach an adult or attract their attention before making a signal in order to establish the adult as a partner in communication. Unless this is done, not only will many signals be missed, with obvious effects on the child's motivation to use signals, but the child's understanding of the two-way nature of communication will be impaired.

Mary enjoyed her school's sensory room. When the bubble tube was not operative she would vocalise angrily and tap the tube with her fingers. At first her teacher reinforced this behaviour by activating the tube in response to Mary's signal. She considered whether to use a switch so that Mary could operate the bubbles herself or to treat the session as a context for developing communication with an adult. Choosing the latter course, Mary's teacher would gently hold her hand as she made contact with the tube. Over time Mary learnt to seek out her teacher's hand and so actively make contact with her teacher before making her request.

Place or object cues

If a child's routine is closely structured so that a particular place or object is always involved in an activity, it will come to *characterise* that activity for a child. Once this association is established the adult can use the place or object as a signal for the activity concerned, or the child can use the place or object to request the activity. For example:

- going to the door or fetching a coat as a request/cue for playtime;
- putting on an apron as a request/cue for dinner;
- sitting on the mat and removing shoes and socks as a request/cue for using the footspa;
- picking up a swimming bag as a request/cue for swimming.

If this strategy is to provide the child with a means of expressive communication, then the place or object must always be available to the child and the adults must be willing or able to respond. This undoubtedly leads to some dilemmas in classroom organisation.

Teachers usually cannot offer swimming on demand or provide lunch at 10.30 a.m. They may have concerns about allowing a child to use the footspa when the timetabled activity is music. Staffing may not allow a favourite one to one activity if all hands are on deck to organise a cookery session. Nevertheless, for children developing intentional communication there must be sufficient flexibility in the system and enough accessible activities to offer a degree of real choice. When requests cannot be granted, adults must make every effort to show the child that their message has been received.

Tiffany would become distressed at about 11.30 a.m. each morning and when offered a number of possible cues would consistently hold on to her dinner apron. Her teacher wheeled her chair to the hall and helped her to explore the area so she could feel that the tables were still stacked against the wall and that the dinner trolley was not in its accustomed place. He explained in simple language that there was no dinner until the tables were in place. Initially Tiffany interpreted the journey to the hall as a cue that it was dinner time, and was very upset to find that nothing was ready! Gradually however the tables came to function as a cue for dinner time and she appeared to understand that she could not have dinner until they were set out. On a few occasions she 'helped' the midday assistants to prepare the hall.

James used a rather extreme form of object cue on one occasion when he went home for the Christmas holidays. He had a good look around the house and found it bare of Christmas decorations as his family had planned to involve him in the preparation. James took things into his own hands by going into the garden and trying to uproot last year's Christmas tree, presumably in order to bring it into the living room! Despite the damage to the garden, his parents were delighted at this evidence that James was remembering previous Christmas holidays and trying to 'make it Christmas' again.

Symbolic communication

In symbolic communication an object, picture, sign or word symbolises a concept and can be used to discuss that concept in isolation from the actual event. Accessing symbolic communication is a significant step towards independence for a child, since it allows them to request or remember something not physically or temporally present. In the example above, James could only 'ask for' or 'talk about' Christmas by using an object which happened to be to hand. The following year he could use picture symbols and several years later he could type on a communication aid 'It is snowing. James will see Santa.'

Objects of reference

Symbolic understanding often grows from the use of object cues. For example, dinner may initially be signalled by giving a child the apron or spoon they will actually use at dinner time. Later the child will accept a different apron or a piece of apron fabric as a symbol that it is dinner time and later still as a marker on a timetable to show her that dinner will happen, but only after other activities are finished. Once the cue is separated from the real event both in time and by being a different object from that actually used, it has become fully symbolic and can properly be called an 'object of reference' (OR) as opposed to an object cue.

Ingenious parents and teachers can make a plentiful supply of ORs to provide a child with many opportunities to communicate. It is worth noting two dangers, however.

Because an OR provides a clear way of enabling a child to ask for something not actually present, their use may lead to communication being reduced to a kind of 'shopping list' where a child makes demands which are agreed or not by the adult. Adults need to model the use of ORs in the same way as they might model other symbolic forms of communication, so that the child can see ORs being used to:

- recall events;
- name activities, places and people;
- show the different parts of an activity;
- ask questions.

They also need to be sure that children have plenty of opportunities to interact in other ways, perhaps using some of the techniques of intensive interaction (see 'Teaching strategies' below).

Because an OR has to be deliberately created and teachers are busy people it is possible unwittingly to reduce a child's ability to communicate by providing only a restricted vocabulary. It is also possible to use them as a way of controlling what a child can talk about. Just as verbal children may talk about specific activities whether or not they are planned for that day, so children using ORs should have access to their full vocabulary throughout the week.

> James used to sit and hold his swimming OR at different times in the week, long after he understood that swimming would only take place on Thursday mornings. At first his teacher would explain that there was 'no swimming today' and would try to remove the OR, but James resisted. For him the OR had moved beyond a simple request, to become a way of helping him to remember his favourite activity and to anticipate the following Thursday.

In designing ORs, teachers will need to consider the following:

- Meaning for the child. ORs can become very abstract, but in the initial stages it is worth maintaining a clear link with the activity.
- Visual or tactile features – can the child access the OR easily? Can the child discriminate them from other ORs in his repertoire?
- Portability – will the child need to be followed by a large suitcase containing his communication tools, or can smaller objects be used as readily?
- Durability – will the OR withstand repeated handling by adult and child?
- Availability – ORs are inevitably lost or left at the site of an activity. Will it be easy to make a new one when this happens?

See the next section for a discussion of timetable boxes.

Pictures and pictograms

The use of pictures and pictograms may develop from a pupil's use of ORs when the pupil is not ready to move directly to the use of sign or speech. 2D representation is more symbolic than ORs, more portable and far more flexible, since a picture can be produced by anyone with a pen or paper while ORs need to be thought out and created in advance.

Several options exist within this category of symbolic communication:

- 'home-made' pictures;
- photographs;
- Makaton symbols;
- COMPIC symbols.

'Home-made' pictures

However limited your artistic ability, there is a great deal to be said for beginning with home-made pictures. Surprisingly, pupils learn to recognise pictures drawn by the least gifted artist – the present writer remembers with affection a pupil who responded happily to her grossly inadequate drawing of a horse because it was familiar to him! Home-drawn pictures can be closely linked to established ORs, with corresponding shapes and colours.

Pictures can be introduced to the pupil by child and adult drawing a picture, perhaps drawing round an object or familiar OR and colouring it in while the adult stresses the similarity, or looking closely at an object or Object of Reference together before drawing it slowly and step by step, again stressing the correspondence between object and picture. This helps the pupil to understand the nature of pictorial representation and may therefore help in the use of pictures in other areas of the curriculum, such as recording a science project or a piece of mathematics. Later the teacher may prepare a stock of photocopied drawings from which the pupil can select and colour the appropriate picture. As the pupil's understanding of pictorial representation grows, the teacher can judge when the pupil is ready to use pictures without the immediate link to ORs.

Pupils may also demonstrate their growing understanding by attempting their own pictorial representations, for example as a request or to voice a question about plans for the day.

Photographs

Some children are more able to link photographs than drawings to the real object or activity. The link can be reinforced by allowing a child to be involved in taking the photos and, as with drawings, by using photos of familiar objects or ORs before branching out into new photos.

However, many visually impaired people find photographs quite inaccessible. Teachers need to be confident that the photos do make sense to a pupil before investing time and money in a complex system. It is also likely that a matt finish will be more visually accessible than gloss.

The advent of digital cameras will remove some of the delays and inconvenience from using photos as a communication mode by making it possible to produce a photo relatively quickly and to manipulate the image or add text.

Makaton symbols

These symbols correspond to items in the Makaton vocabulary and this is both its strength and weakness. Schools using Makaton as their main signing system will want to give serious consideration to using Makaton symbols as a communication mode. However, not all are easily accessible to children with visual impairment as they require detailed discrimination. Their correspondence with sign may also be difficult for visually impaired children to appreciate. As with all limited vocabularies, teachers will need to produce their own pictures when the one they need is not available. They may find the Makaton style difficult to reproduce and they may not know the appropriate sign on which to base their picture.

COMPIC symbols

This is an Australian system where pictures are supplied on computer disk. Size can be varied and the vocabulary is comprehensive and varied, with several hundred items including many suitable for discussing topics within Personal and Health, Social Education (PHSE), sometimes also known as PSE. Again teachers will need to augment the pictures and again children with severe visual impairment may find it difficult to recognise some of the pictures used.

Many of the points made in the previous section apply equally to pictures as to objects. In addition we need to consider:

- Ways of managing large stocks of pictures – should they be arranged in a book, sorted into boxes or threaded onto a key ring? However the teacher manages the pictures physically, she will also have to classify them in a way which makes sense to adult and pupil alike and allows easy access to key vocabulary. This, of course, will become more challenging once the pupil is able to put two pictures together into a phrase or to understand a phrase or sentence generated by the adult.
- Ensuring that pictures are kept in good condition so that they remain easy to distinguish.
- Ways of assessing the benefits or otherwise of using colour. There is some evidence that children with cortical visual impairment are particularly helped by the use of colour, but teachers need to assess such children's comprehension of form as the use of pictures can only become a long-term strategy if children are able to discriminate form sufficiently well to differentiate a reasonable number of pictures.

Tactile symbols

Children with a visual impairment which prevents the use of pictures who have established an initial vocabulary of ORs need to develop a comprehensive system which can be easily managed as the child moves about the school and between home, school and community. Options for moving on from object cues and ORs include:

(a) using miniature objects;
(b) using parts of objects;
(c) using arbitrary symbols;
(d) using raised outlines.

(a) Using miniature objects, e.g. a doll's cup signifies drink, a toy bus represents an outing. Some children cope with this transition successfully but teachers need to remember that miniature objects are very different in nature from the real-life objects they represent – a plastic horse bears no tactile resemblance to the real animal a child will meet at the riding stables; the overall shape of a toy bus will not correspond to the parts of the school bus with which the child has contact – and to assess carefully what meaning the miniature object carries for the child. Careful introduction of individual objects is likely to be the key to success in this area. Miniature objects are most likely to be successful if a child has well-established representative play with small objects and/or sufficient receptive language to follow an explanation of what they represent.

(b) Using parts of objects, e.g. a cup handle for drink, a section of a seat belt for an outing, a rein for horse-riding. This approach has a more obvious link with experience for totally blind children, especially if the adult selecting the objects knows the child's experience well enough to pick out critical features *for the individual* – in this area, as in many other areas of communication development, individual planning is crucial. A central bank of tactile symbols, while tempting from the organisational point of view, is unlikely to be helpful in the development of individual programmes.

(c) Making arbitrary symbols, e.g. a different texture for each day of the week, different shapes for timetabled activities. This places a large load on the child's memory (not to mention the teacher's ingenuity) and is more appropriate for children beyond the early stages of developing symbolic language. At this stage, however, it may well allow the representation of more abstract concepts and may perhaps serve as a bridge to reading in the same way that COMPICs or BLISS symbols may help a sighted child develop literacy skills.

(d) Using raised outlines, perhaps produced on a Thermoform machine or made with less impressive technology such as string or Hi-mark. This approach is recommended by some teachers working with the MOON script and like arbitrary symbols its strength is probably its function as a bridge to more formal literacy – for example, a tactile representation of a folded mobility cane bears enough resemblance to the MOON letter M to smooth the transition from representation to letter.

At earlier stages, however, the issue of links to the real object arises again: a bus outline is very difficult to perceive with the fingers and still more difficult to link to the feel of the real bus.

Sign language

There are real advantages to the use of sign. It is a full language shared by a real community and by increasing numbers of adults and children who have attended classes. Where deafblind children are placed in hearing-impaired, or to a lesser extent SLD/PMLD provision, their peers will also be using some form of signing. Many deafblind children will benefit from being exposed to sign as a cue to the spoken work and others will come to use sign as a primary language.

However it would be unrealistic to see the use of a full sign language as the inevitable goal of a language programme for the current deafblind population as it makes enormous demands on physical control, visual perception, cognitive ability and memory. For children with more complex needs it is perhaps unwise to stress sign language too early and teachers should consider whether using one of the less complex communication modes outlined earlier in the chapter, alongside or instead of sign language, will give a child access to a means of self-expression within a more reasonable timescale.

It is beyond the scope of this guide to discuss the introduction of signing in detail. Teachers will want to seek the advice of more experienced colleagues and speech and language therapists. When considering the introduction of sign to a deafblind child, a teacher should consider the following issues.

1. The child's strengths and needs:

   - Is the child's vision sufficient to allow discrimination between signs?
   - Is the child able to use any cues from lip-reading to augment sign?
   - Is the child's visual field restricted to an extent that will limit receptive understanding of signs or the understanding of signing models?
   - How close or how far should the signer be from the child?
   - Will residual hearing provide some clues to augment sign?
   - Does the child have adequate visuo-motor skills to follow signing at a reasonable speed?
   - Does the child have sufficient motor control to make signs clearly and with reasonable speed?

   Too many negative answers to these questions might cause the teacher to reconsider the use of signing at the present time, or they may indicate the need for a carefully chosen initial vocabulary to give the child the greatest chance of success.

2. The classroom environment.

Teachers using sign in classrooms need to make practical arrangements to ensure that deafblind children have access to as much of the sign around them as possible. They will consider:

- the visual environment, especially the quality of lighting;
- the arrangement of furniture and the organisation of activities – can the deafblind child see not only the signs made by the teacher but also any responses from other children?
- the role of support staff, who may function as interpreters, translating the language used in the classroom into sign at an appropriate level, as role models if other members of the class do not sign, or as intervenors, encouraging the child to attend to the teacher's signing and to respond.

3. The school policy.

Schools need an agreed policy on their signing environment to ensure that an appropriate quality and quantity of signing is available to all the children who need access to sign. Such a policy should recognise the complexity of need and leave room for a variety of approaches to introducing sign.

Perhaps the most important policy decision is the type of sign language to be used. Several options are available to teachers in the UK.

British Sign Language (BSL). This is the language of the deaf community in Britain, with its own grammar and idioms which are significantly different from that of spoken English. Using BSL gives children access to a complete language, and those children who develop a good ability in sign should certainly be exposed to BSL and encouraged to make use of some of its features. However, its complexity presents something of a challenge to adults and children alike. Like any language, BSL incorporates dialectical variations and these need to be carefully controlled in the first instance to avoid confusion.

Makaton vocabulary. This is the form of sign language most commonly used in classes for children with severe learning difficulties. It is based on a dialect of BSL but is intended to be used alongside speech, in English word order. As its name suggests, Makaton is essentially a collection of signs rather than a full language. It continues to develop within schools and the community.

Signed English. This uses the vocabulary of BSL but in spoken word order, with one sign being used for each word in the spoken language. Some additional signs have been coined to make this possible. The use of this 'hybrid' language raises some ethical concerns and for deafblind children there are additional practical difficulties. Signed English makes particular demands on visual acuity and visuo-motor skills, because of the number of individual movements, and the speed with which these have to be made to accompany the spoken word. The fine grammatical markers also place considerable demands on motor ability and on cognitive understanding, although if the child has sufficient residual hearing to pick up the pattern of speech this will be less of an issue.

Sign Supported English. This form of sign accompanies normal spoken English, but only the key words are signed. While concerns remain around changing the language of one community to fit the pattern of another, in other ways this system is a better option than Signed English. It is far easier to synchronise speech and sign while maintaining a normal speech rhythm, and the number of signs can be varied in line with the child's vocabulary and overall understanding. Adult users, however, need to monitor their language to ensure that what is conveyed in sign is clear.

Children using sign as a main language need to have access to a 'signing community' where adults and ideally many of the other children also sign to a good level, so that good models of sign language can be presented and children can learn sign in a way that parallels the development of speech. Some schools are able to appoint communicators whose main role is to provide a good signing model for the deafblind child, but the existence of these invaluable adults should not be used as an excuse for poor levels of signing elsewhere. Children using sign as an aid to spoken language or alongside other symbolic modes also need good signing models, but they may learn more effectively if a key word vocabulary is stressed, with signs being introduced in a structured way.

It is essential that schools where children will use sign have a policy on training all those staff that will be involved with the children to at least a basic competency, so that the child is enabled to use sign effectively throughout the day. Families also need encouragement to sign.

Paul's dual sensory impairment was not diagnosed until he was seven years old, by which time he had spent three years in a nursery for children with learning difficulties and been introduced to the Makaton vocabulary. On moving to a specialist deafblind group he quickly picked up a wider vocabulary using Sign Supported English and this is still his preferred means of communication. His teacher has also introduced him to BSL, which Paul now uses in more informal settings. It is hoped that he will in due course be confident enough to use BSL at the local deaf club and be able to make friends in the deaf community.

Speech

Again a full discussion of the use of speech is outside the scope of this guide, and teachers should look for advice from a speech and language therapist or a teacher of the deaf, both of whom will have specialist knowledge in developing articulation skills.

As speech is the main community language, attempts at speech will be accessible by most adults and children in the child's environment – although where the language of the child's home is not English this will need careful liaison and where possible the involvement of a speech and language therapist with a specialist knowledge of second language issues.

We should certainly try to harness any potential for developing speech, even where the most positive likely outcome is use or understanding of a few words in a social context. However, teachers need to have realistic aims. Children with a severe hearing impairment need to use their vision to back up auditory cues via lip-reading, while children with a severe visual impairment rely on listening skills to develop spoken language. Where a child has a significant impairment of both distance senses, it will be very difficult to follow spoken language. Where a child's speech is unclear, the cognitive, visual and auditory demands of a programme to teach clearer articulation will be immense. While progress can certainly be made in both the understanding and use of speech, especially if the child is well motivated towards speech, teachers need to consider carefully the efficient use of time at a particular stage in a child's development.

For many of our children, access to the 'speech envelope', i.e. the range of tone and volume which will give access to the spoken word, will only be possible if the child is wearing appropriate amplification. Teachers should do their best to liaise with medical services to ensure that children have hearing aids and where appropriate an auditory trainer. It may take some time for children to learn to tolerate amplification and time needs to be found within the child's day for an opportunity to wear aids in a distraction-free setting where there is something interesting to listen to, or in the context of a favourite activity which may encourage the child to relax and tolerate amplification. Adults should take responsibility for keeping the aids clean and in good repair and for checking batteries frequently, until the child is able to take some of this responsibility for themselves. If the child is able to work in a group setting, the use of a radio hearing aid to help him concentrate on speech as opposed to background noise should be considered. Throughout the introduction of hearing aids the involvement of an audiologist or teacher of the deaf or MSI will be very helpful.

If children are to make use of speech, either as their main receptive language or as a support to other forms of language, then the quality of the auditory environment is of course crucial. Schools are often noisy places and schools where several activities from different individual programmes may be underway in the same room are noisier than most! Classroom staff need to monitor the amount of noise throughout the day and to discuss ways of limiting background noise or separating conflicting activities. The deafblind child will need to be seated near to the adult working with him, in a place where he can also pick up speech from the other children and other important classroom sounds. It may be possible to reduce the level of reverberant sound within the classroom by using carpet on the floor or acoustic tiles on the walls or ceiling to deaden some sound.

Staff should also monitor the quality of speech used with children. An increasing group of children has hearing within the speech envelope and apparent understanding at some level but is not able to use speech in response. There is a real risk that these children will be 'flooded' with speech from well-meaning adults but not given the opportunity to respond in their own way. For them, then, speech will not be a vehicle for interaction but something that is 'done to' them and which quite possibly reduces their ability to pick up other, more useful cues from the environment. Activities with these children should be planned so that adult speech is clear and simple and serves a useful purpose, perhaps as a cue to the next step, a request for an action from the child or to give a piece of information.

William enjoys a sensory walk through the garden area of his school. His intervenor has worked with his teacher to plan the activity so as to fully involve William despite his considerable physical difficulties. The planning process has included consideration of the language she will use. William's intervenor names each part of the garden with a simple sentence, 'here's the bridge', 'this is the fountain', and comments on his actions: 'can you feel the water?', 'you can reach the fence'. In between times she is not afraid to leave periods of silence so that William can concentrate on other sensations.

Fingerspelling

Fingerspelling involves spelling out words and sentences from speech using a handshape for each letter of the alphabet. Each language has its own fingerspelling alphabet. The deafblind manual alphabet is based on the sighted code with some alterations to allow the sender to spell out words onto the left hand of the receiver. This can obviously be a very complex form of communication and it is truly impressive to see competent adult users engaged in conversation.

Children and adults may use fingerspelling to augment sign language, spelling out names or filling in the gaps in their signing vocabulary. It may also be a means of communication in its own right for those who have the tactile discrimination to receive messages and the fine motor ability to send them, used alongside spoken English or without spoken cues. In its full form, fingerspelling makes considerable demands on sequential memory and on linguistic competence. However, it can be used in one- or two-word units with children who are ready to move beyond objects of reference but whose vision is too poor for the use of pictures or signs. Because it is simple to learn and use, it allows children to be exposed relatively easily to a rich language environment in which adults communicate throughout all activities. For some children the security of this regular contact appears as important as any meaning which they extract from the code. It is more difficult for children to learn to respond but some do manage to build up a useful vocabulary.

Figure 2.2 Chatting on a sunny afternoon

Technology

Recent advances in microelectronics have allowed sophisticated communication aids to be developed at a (relatively) accessible price. Available portable aids at the time of writing vary from a switch-activated device that can be programmed to deliver one spoken message at a time to devices with complex systems of overlays that can build up whole sentences from a selection of words and then speak them.

Children who can hear speech or can understand that a machine has generated a spoken message can use augmentative aids for a range of purposes. They can allow a child to attract attention or to participate in a group activity (perhaps saying 'good morning everyone' in the greetings circle). They can give a child significant levels of independence in the community by giving voice to an order in the café or a request for a bus ticket. Children without the motor control to use sign or fingerspelling may well be able to operate a switch or press the correct section of an overlay and so have the opportunity for far more complex communication than would have been the case a few years ago.

Other devices are alphabetical and can display a written message on screen or speak a sentence which the child has typed. These obviously require the understanding and fine motor control to use a keyboard but can be accessible to some children who cannot sign, or can be used as an alternative form of communication with people who cannot use sign themselves.

Christine has cerebral palsy and although she clearly understood much of what was said to her, her signing vocabulary was limited to some 20 words, augmented by some recognisable vocalisations. She was evidently quite frustrated and this showed itself in sobs and shouts and a frequent withdrawal from the learning situation. The introduction of technology gave her access to a form of communication within her physical control and she was intrigued by the fact that the box on her tray produced speech at a level which she could hear. Two years later the Digivox aid has made it possible for Christine to join in academic lessons, putting two or three words together and making her own contribution to the morning routine by allocating classroom jobs to her peers with some degree of assertiveness.

Teaching strategies

In the course of the project 'Curriculum Access for Deafblind Children' (Porter *et al.* 1997), teachers identified 147 distinct teaching strategies which they used when working with deafblind children. It was no surprise to see that many of these strategies were closely identified with the development of communication. The main communication strategies were described by the research team as 'meta-strategies' because they were not linked to particular lessons or activities but were used throughout the day to underpin the children's developing communication or to help the children gain the maximum information within and about activities.

Objects of Reference, signing and speech, which were commonly appearing meta-strategies, have been discussed above. This section is concerned with six further strategies identified within the project, which are particularly relevant to the development of communication.

1. Intensive interaction

This approach, which was pioneered by Melanie Nind and Dave Hewett (1996) in a hospital setting where many of the students were deafblind, has had a very significant impact on the educational programmes of children in special school provision.

The approach is summarised by Melanie Nind in the article referred to above as follows:

Intensive Interaction involves the use of an optimum interactive style and exploits the range of interactive games found in caregiver–infant interaction. These interactive games form the core of the curriculum and processes that are normally intuitive are given structure and developed as deliberate progression. Intensive Interaction has the following central features drawn from caregiver–infant interaction:

- the creation of mutual pleasure and interactive games, being together with the purpose of enjoying each other;
- the teacher adjusting her/his interpersonal behaviours (gaze, voice, linguistic code, body posture, facial expression) in order to become engaging and meaningful;
- interactions flowing in time with pauses, repetitions, blended rhythms; the teacher carefully scanning and making constant micro-adjustments, thus achieving optimum levels of attention and arousal;
- the use of intentionality, that is the willingness to credit the learner with thoughts, feelings and intentions, responding to behaviours as if they are initiations with communicative significance;
- the use of contingent responding, following the learner's lead and sharing control of the activity.

Nind and Hewett might feel that describing intensive interaction as a 'strategy' fails to do it justice since they see it as an approach to the whole curriculum for children and young people at the non-symbolic stage of communication. However, intensive interaction sessions might well be seen as a context in which adults can apply several of the principles already discussed here to develop functional communication.

It is especially valuable with students using non-symbolic communication but some aspects can be used with students having a grasp of formal language, particularly where interaction remains a problem.

Intensive interaction was used with Sehar, whose enjoyment of the 'banana game' was mentioned earlier. She was initially described by her teacher, Matthew, as 'almost wholly passive, relying on smiles to engage adult attention but then having little idea of what to do with the attention and no ability to develop the "conversation" further'. During intensive interaction, Matthew gave her the opportunity to exert control using objects which she found interesting. He copied and extended her games and over time a complicated turn-taking routine evolved as Sehar came to understand that she could influence Matthew's actions.

---

2. Scripts/routines

It is generally accepted that deafblind children, whose world is likely to be a chaotic one, benefit in a number of ways from the establishment of strong routines throughout their day.

Staff at Whitefield Schools and Centre have borrowed the term 'Scripts' from the programmes carried out at Sint Michilgestel School in Holland to describe such routines when they are designed to encourage early communication.

A Script can be developed around any activity which can be carried out frequently and regularly by an adult and child in fairly close contact. It may be a care routine such as eating lunch, a sensory experience such as massage or a physical routine such as movement sequence. Ideally it will be carried out in the same place each day and at the same point in the daily timetable. At first the Script is structured by the adult. The activity will be carried out in a highly consistent way until the child appears secure and relaxed and shows some sign of anticipating some of the steps in the routine. At this point it is possible to move some control to the child, allowing them to move the activity on or to make some choices within the established structure. For example, the adult may stop part way through a rocking movement and wait for some signal to show that the child wants the movement to continue before carrying on, or the adult may be holding a spoon hand-over-hand with the child and may stop with the spoon poised halfway to the child's mouth, waiting for an indication that dinner should continue. Later the child may use particular signals to indicate a choice (perhaps between songs or between parts of the movement routine) or a wish to finish the activity.

Figure 2.3 shows part of a planning sheet for a Script, giving details of the teacher's actions and the possible participation by the child. This Script was in the early stages of development.

A Script as described above will usually exist as a self-contained entity. Alternatively, teachers working with groups or with classes with a wide ability range, often insert mini-routines into group activities, through which they aim to encourage the deafblind or MSI children in the group to communicate a preference or to lead the activity for a time. One teacher structured circle time at the end of the day to give opportunities for the verbal children to reflect on their activities but also to allow a non-verbal blind child to select an Object of Reference from her box to share with her classmates. The pupil concerned has limited comprehension of spoken language and probably does not fully understand all that is going on: however, she does relish her turn and signals eagerly for the box when her intervenor presents it to her. Another uses a scented candle at the end of the day to create a short ritual in which her pupils can signal their anticipation of the next step and ask for their turn to blow out the candle and initiate the goodbye song.

3. Resonance work

In van Dijk's approach, the first step in entering into the child's world is to **resonate** the child's movements. We reflect the child's movements back to him/herself so that an awareness of self grows. One way of doing this is to sit on the floor (or wherever the child is), close to him/her and gently and sensitively imitate his/her movements, e.g.

- the child is banging the table;
- the adult joins in the banging.

Alert to your presence.   Mark touches glasses.
Alert to activity.   Mark feels bottle (O/R).

Adult and Mark co-actively move to massage room.

Adult	**Mark**
Move Mark's hand to his shoes.	Mark touches shoes.
Mark, take off your shoes. (After a period, assist if Mark is reluctant.)	Mark removes his shoes.
Repeat above for socks.	Mark removes his socks.
"Mark remove top" (or T-shirt).	Mark removes top, (with as little assistance as possible).
Put lotion bottle in Mark's hand.	Mark holds bottle.
Co-actively squeeze lotion on Mark's hand.	Mark squeezes lotion onto his hand.
Co-actively apply lotion to Mark's feet.	Massages feet.
Ask, 'more?' or 'next?'	Mark communicates choice.
(Repeat after each body part.)	
Co-actively apply to legs.	Massages legs.
Co-actively apply to hands.	Massages hands.
Co-actively apply to arms.	Massages arms.
Co-actively apply to face.	Massages face.
Ask, 'more, Mark, or finished?'.	Mark indicates choice.
Co-actively replace top, socks and shoes.	Mark redresses.
Co-actively replace O/R.	

Figure 2.3 Massage Script – Mark

4. Co-active movement

Co-active movement is an extension of resonance, the difference being that now the child is more conscious of the adult and the turn-taking interchange/'dialogue'.

Initially the movements used will be the child's favourites. The adult and child should be in close body contact, i.e.

- the child on the adult's knee

or

- between his/her legs while sitting on the floor

or

- while walking, the child having his/her back to the adult

or

- the child lying on top of the adult (back to chest) while rolling.

The movements are done in sequence, and this is continued until the child is familiar with it.

A possible sequence of favourite movements could be (child on adult's knee facing each other):

- child and adults sway from side to side, perhaps about six times;
- adult bounces child on knee, again, about six times;
- child holding adult's hands sways backwards.

All through this sequence the adult should pick up any vocalisation the child makes, putting emphasis on the intonation, making it into a little 'song' for each separate movement. If the child remains silent the adult could initiate this, at the same time being alert to the child joining in or changing it. It is important to keep in mind that the 'songs' should remain the same for the same activities, otherwise the child will be given the incorrect clues.

After some days (or longer) of doing this, the child will have internalised the pattern and so the evoking of **signal behaviour** can begin, i.e. the adult:

- interrupts the sequence, i.e. pauses before or eliminates the child's favourite movement;
- observes the child's reaction, being alert to any signal from the child indicating his/her desire for the favourite, e.g. the child might touch the adult's hand for the backwards-movement;
- responds **immediately** to reinforce the signal.

When the child does not appear to be using a signal the adult should direct him/her into a carefully chosen one, again, reinforcing this by responding immediately with the desired movement.

Gradually the sequence can be added to, each new movement coming at the end of the familiar chain. Then the physical distance can be increased, the adult and child making contact only through hands. The sequence could look like this (child on knee to begin with):

- child and adult sway from side to side;
- child bounces on adult's knee;
- child, holding adult's hand, sways backwards;
- child and adult clap hands together;
- child is 'jumped' off adult's knee;

- holding hands, child and adult twirl together;
- child and adult crawl together,

etc.

Remember: These are only suggestions, the ideal ones are those you have noticed the child enjoying at other times and incorporated into the exercise. The child is *not imitating*, he/she and the adult are moving co-actively.

Co-active movement helps the child to communicate:

- by furthering the child's awareness of what he/she is doing;
- by isolating movements as identifiers (IDs) for activities;
- by initiating signal behaviour and thereby starting communication;
- by reinforcing memory and anticipation;

through,

- the adult moving co-actively and directing the child into the desired movements and activities;
- the adult responding immediately to signal behaviour;
- the child identifying activities through movements.

5. Calendar boxes

We have already discussed the use of 'objects of reference' for activities (see earlier in section). These objects are now used to order the child's day; in other words we create a concrete, tangible timetable.

In the early stages we simply use the same rhythm or sequence for part of each day. So, as far as is humanly possible this little sequence is adhered to during the time in school/home until the child has some idea of what it is about.

The objects of reference for the morning's activities are put into connected sequential boxes or pockets with the child each morning, so, the timetable boxes should be as shown in Figure 2.4:

(a) a spoon representing a meal;
(b) a toothbrush representing time for brushing teeth;
(c) a ball representing movement time;
(d) the child's favourite object representing time on his/her own;
(e) the spoon again representing the next meal.

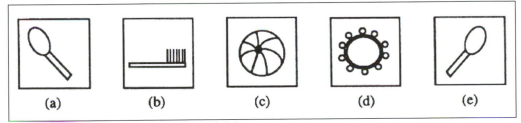

Figure 2.4 ORs for morning's activities

The next step is to help the child distinguish one day from another. So, keeping the same sequence, an object to identify a specific activity to mark the day is added to the timetable. So, the timetable boxes for Monday could be as Figure 2.5.

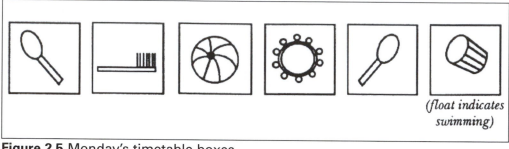

(float indicates swimming)

Figure 2.5 Monday's timetable boxes

And for Tuesday, when the child goes shopping, as Figure 2.6; and so on.

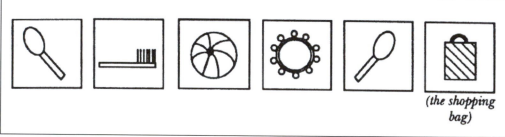

(the shopping bag)

Figure 2.6 Tuesday's timetable boxes

(*Note:* Figures 2.4, 2.5, 2.6 are from Blythman, M. and Diniz, F. A. (eds) *Contact: a resource for staff working with children who are deafblind*, Module 5, Topic 3, Sensory Series 3. Edinburgh: Moray House Publications.)

For the residential child the Friday box will hold something portable that characterises home or the child's mother or father. This could be, for example, part of the mother's identification bracelet or something the child only plays with at home. This ID for home is carried by the child on the journey home. In the same way a school ID is given by the parent to the child on his/her return to school. Gradually a concept of weekday (when he/she is in school) and weekend (when at home) builds up in the child. The simpler the pattern the easier it is for the child to grasp it. The child can only learn these concepts through experiencing them. So whatever your system, be it a day-school, weekly-boarding or term-boarding, use some means of identifying the various divisions of time. What is important is consistency. As far as is humanly possible, keep to the timetable and the activities characterising each day. If an emergency occurs and, for instance, you cannot go swimming on Mondays, go through the Monday sequence with the child, putting the ID into the appropriate box, then indicating, 'NO SWIMMING' to the child (one way of doing this is to place his/her hands each side of your head as you shake it), remove the swimming symbol from the box and put in something to characterise what is replacing it. (The child will eventually understand 'change' through this.)

At a late stage, when the child has internalised his/her basic daily timetable and has some concept of the days of the week, variations can be introduced without confusing the concepts. Simple diaries can record (using tactile symbols, or later brailled written symbols) the various different things that happen. Past events are the first to be understood but if there is some exciting event constantly happening once a month then the child will begin to look forward to birthdays, holidays, to Christmas, etc., and the year will begin to take shape.

6. Using musical cues

One of the most popular strategies identified in the Curriculum Access project was the use of musical cues. Teachers in the survey used these in two ways.

Some teachers used music to structure an activity by creating a consistent routine with different responses linked to each song. This often occurred within a music or movement session but could also be used to structure other activities, particularly those which pupils found stressful. For example, songs could be used during physiotherapy programmes, with each song cueing a different exercise, or during tactile sessions where the adult sang as the child explored different materials. In these contexts the songs sometimes appeared to be used to give structure to the adults' actions, helping them to create a consistent routine by defining the sequence and pace of the session.

Some commercially produced packages now exploit the role of music in giving structure to an activity. Teachers known to the present writer recommend 'Tacpac', where snippets of music are linked to different tactile stimuli, and 'Galaxies', which structures a multi-sensory activity around a musical story.

Other teachers used music to characterise people or activities in the same way that one might use an Object of Reference. In some classes, a song or piece of music introduced each activity, sometimes incorporating the name of the activity ('Soon it will be time for dinner, what shall we have today?') and a different song might be used as a signal that the activity was finished. In a workshop at the RNIB, Adam Ockleford describes a strategy by which each child in a class of blind children had their own instrument during music or greetings circles, which they were helped to play as a way of announcing their turn. This both focused the child's mind on the activity and served as a cue to other children, who could not see which of their classmates was in the centre of the circle.

Some tools for assessing communication

Chapter 4, which looks in detail at the process of assessing development, reminds us that school records and intelligent general observation throughout the day will usually be a more helpful source of information in planning educational programmes than published tools. Assessing communication with published tools is particularly difficult at the early stages, where the child's responses can be so idiosyncratic.

However, this is not to deny that a stock of assessment tools may be a useful resource for the teacher when used as part of a broader process of assessment. Such devices may help to structure the questions we ask and may focus our thinking. Careful use of tools is likely to highlight the gaps in a child's abilities and so suggest goals for the next year's work or indicate where the child will need support to access the curriculum.

Schools and services may find the following tools worth investigating further.

1. Pre-verbal Communication Schedule: a tool which assists in building a profile of non-symbolic and early symbolic communication, particularly helpful in identifying possible modes of communication. (Kiernan and Reid 1987)
2. Pragmatics Profile: a tool which looks at a child's use of language, applicable to both the symbolic and non-symbolic modes but most useful for children with some formal communication. (Dewart and Summers 1990)
3. Callier-Azusa Scale: a wide-ranging assessment designed for use with deafblind children, probably most useful with those who are physically able and showing some intentional communication. This schedule was designed to assist a team in pooling information. (Stillman 1978)

---

1. **For a child you know:**

   Carry out an assessment of their communication, based on your observations and perhaps using one of the tools mentioned above.

   Look at the important variables as outlined in 'Choosing appropriate methods of communication' (see page 55) and summarise your knowledge of the child's communication under these headings.

   Which communication modes are possible for this child?

   What should your next step be?

2. **Ask a colleague to video a session where you are working one to one with a deafblind child in a daily activity. Watch the video together and in discussion with your colleague:**

- identify the evidence that you have taken into account the 'instructional guidelines' on which this chapter is based;
- consider and identify some ways in which the activity could be developed further, taking these guidelines into account.

3. Self-evaluation

Record on video a teaching session with a deafblind child. Watch the video carefully and assess your use of language and communication by answering the questions below as honestly as you can. Throughout the process, try to identify what communication the child is receiving from you, which may on reflection be different from the information you thought you were giving at the time! You may wish to involve a colleague in this process.

Did the child appear relaxed and happy in your company? and vice versa? (despite the video).

What types of communication did you use?

Which of these could the child follow easily?

Which of these could the child not follow?

Did the child have your full attention?

Why and how did you use speech?

Did you try to communicate throughout the activity?

How did you use the different functions of communication (instructions, information, comment, etc.)?

What did you expect the child to do as a result of your communication?

Did they do it?

Did you pause to give the child time to respond?

What did you do well?

How could you improve the way you communicate with this child?

References

Dewart, H. and Summers, S. (1990) *The Pragmatics Profile of Early Communication Skills*. Berkshire: NFER-Nelson.

Kiernan, C. and Reid, B. (1987) *Pre-verbal Communication Schedule*. Berkshire: NFER-Nelson.

Nind, M. (1996) 'Efficacy of intensive interaction: developing sociability and communication in people with severe and complex learning difficulties using an approach based on caregiver–infant interaction', *European Journal of Special Needs Education* 11(1).

Nind, M. and Hewett, D. (1994) *Access to Communication*. London: David Fulton Publishers.

Massey, A. (1993) 'Developing Concepts', in Blythman, M. and Diniz, F. A. (eds) *Contact: a resource for staff working with children who are deafblind*. Module 5, Topic 3. Sensory Series 3. Edinburgh: Moray House Publications.

Ockleford, A. (1998) *Music Moves*. London: RNIB.

Porter, J., Miller, O. and Pease, L. (1997) *Curriculum Access for Deafblind Children*. London: DfEE.

Rowland, C. and Stremel-Campbell, K. (1987) 'Share and Share Alike: conventional gestures to emergent language for learners with sensory impairments', in Goetz, L. *et al. Innovative Program Design for Individuals with Dual Sensory Impairments*. Baltimore, MD: Paul H. Brookes.

Siegel-Causey, E. and Guess, D. (1989) *Enhancing Nonsymbolic Communication Interactions among Learners with Severe Disabilities*. Baltimore, Md.: Paul H. Brookes.

Stillman, R. (1978) *The Callier-Azusa Scale*. University of Texas.

Vygotsky, L. S. (1978) *Mind in Society*. Cambridge, Mass.: Harvard University Press.

CHAPTER 3

Personal and social development

Catherine Clark

The needs of deafblind people

Each deafblind person will have very different needs. These needs are dependent upon the amount of residual vision and hearing the deafblind person has, any additional difficulties there may be, how the senses are integrated, and the previous experience and stimulation the deafblind person has received. However, the developmental route taken by each person is generally the same.

The diversity of the impairment is so great that there is no common baseline from which to begin in the education of a deafblind child. We must therefore begin with the child. We must base our work on what the child can do and on what he enjoys doing, thus making observation and assessment essential to the ethos and culture of the educational environment.

Relationship

The development of a warm, secure and trusting relationship between child and adult is the cornerstone of the educational approach. It is only through such bonding that the deafblind child will allow the adult to become part of his world and to interact with the adult in a positive and meaningful way.

Chloe had spent most of her first few years in hospital where, because of her ill health and the medical treatment she required, she received almost no stimulation. When Chloe first arrived in school, she did not appear to recognise those closest to her, she was not yet walking and she wore a nappy throughout the day as well as at night. She spent her time lying on her back drumming her heels on the floor and resisting all contact with others. She had been diagnosed as having a profound hearing loss and no useful vision.

The first step on her developmental route was the establishing of a secure relationship between Chloe and one member of staff. This was done initially by simply being with Chloe, by being close to her, despite her loud and distressing protests, and reflecting back her movements and vocalisations. The natural touching and routine of movements which take place during the everyday activities of toileting and mobility and indeed all aspects of personal and social development helped to deepen and enhance this relationship of nurturance and resonance.

Richard's first few years of life were quite different from Chloe's. His innovative and determined mother had used every means possible to encourage Richard to make use of his extremely poor vision. However, this stimulation meant that Richard was so caught up in self-stimulating activity, movement and manipulation of objects that he had no interaction with or interest in people. Richard has a severe hearing loss as well as his visual impairment.

Again, as in Chloe's case, Richard's member of staff spent considerable time being with Richard, doing the same as him, reflecting back his movements and vocalisations. Then Richard began to take notice of the different things his member of staff was doing, realised that what she was doing was in fact quite interesting and began to imitate her! From this beginning, Richard was able to access information about the world and the people in it.

Observing the child and assessing his aptitudes, particularly at this resonance stage of development, assists us in devising the child's Individualised Educational Programme (IEP). The child's level of personal and social development will define his IEP. Therefore, the importance of *teaching* self-help skills in Personal and Social Development cannot be underestimated.

In the early stages the educator and child 'do' together co-actively. This co-active teaching and learning will only occur if child and adult have developed a relationship based on trust. Later, the child or young person will 'do' for himself independently. Each time the adult 'does for' the child, the child will be deprived of a learning experience. Thus activities such as eating and toileting are learning experiences which are taught by a trained educator and are part of the child's IEP. By enabling the child to 'do' for himself we, as educators, are empowering him to have control over his life. This empowering of the child and his right to have control over his life begins during these early stages of development. The opportunity for offering choices are constant and many in all areas of Personal and Social Development, e.g.

- snack – biscuits or crisps;
- washing – shower or bath.

By beginning in this small way the deafblind child will, as an adult, succeed in making key decisions and effect changes in his life.

Below is the morning timetable of a developmentally young deafblind pupil. Identify areas within the timetable where the concept of choice can be developed.

Timetable: Dressing, Tactile, Computer, Snack, Movement, Free play, Lunch.

The reactive environment

The environment where the deafblind child will be nurtured, educated and led out of the unpredictability of his isolation must be a reactive one.

... a reactive environment characterized by

(a) emotional bonding and, as the child grows and develops, social responsiveness;
(b) problem-solving to reinforce the development of a positive self-image;
(c) utilization of residual vision and hearing and the integration of input with that from other sensory modalities;
(d) communication, with an emphasis on dialogue.

(McInnes and Treffry 1982, p. 28)

This reactive environment, the instilling of the rights and dignity of the child, and his ability to predict and thus to control his environment are established in the development of personal and social skills. Motivating the isolated deafblind child to learn is often an arduous task. Where better to begin than in the real life settings of the bathroom, the bedroom, the kitchen which are familiar to him and where self-help skills are taught? This is where the deafblind child attaches meaning to what he is doing because he is being taught the skills in the appropriate place and at the appropriate time. Initially, he will work co-actively with his educator and later, as he develops concepts and an understanding of what he is doing and why, he will carry out the task independently. His reward is in the approval of his educator and in the successful attainment of each small step on the route to independence. He has developed the fundamental motivation to succeed, and with it a positive self-image.

Communication

Throughout all of this the deafblind child is in constant dialogue with his educator. (This dialogue may take place via objects of reference, natural gesture, signing, etc., whatever is the child's system of communication.) He comes to integrate all of his senses in the very natural and meaningful environment where personal and social development takes place. The educator, having analysed each task and broken it down into small steps, will begin the teaching process using a structured routine in the appropriate place and at an appropriate time. By establishing these procedures and routines the child will come to anticipate what is about to happen. Later, he becomes aware of choices and is then able to take control of what is happening to him. What he is doing and why, and the concept of choice are continually emphasised. The ability to make choices and decisions is vital to healthy human growth and development and must therefore begin at the very earliest possible stage in the child's life.

Everyday activities

We will now consider how building a relationship, creating a reactive environment and developing communication are key factors in enabling deafblind children to successfully engage in everyday activities.

Eating and drinking

Relationship

The basic life skills of eating and drinking have a profound impact on all areas of the curriculum, developing concepts, social skills, language and communication as well as personal development, and yet this is one area where all too often the skills are not taught by trained educators adopting a multi-disciplinary approach, but rather it is an area which is seen as simply care.

Nathan's deafblindness was caused by Maternal Rubella Syndrome. His birth was difficult and premature, resulting in him spending several months in intensive care. While there, Nathan was fed by means of a nasal gastric tube. He was allowed home when he had gained sufficient weight and was no longer needing oxygen. He was fed at home on formula milk and had progressed to accepting a little strained baby food from a spoon. Quite unexpectedly, Nathan refused to tolerate the spoon anywhere near his mouth and reverted to accepting the milk formula only from his bottle.

When he began in school at age four, Nathan still only accepted formula milk with some added nutrients from his feeding bottle, would not sit at the dining room table and had a real dislike of seeing others eat. The developing emotional bonding between Nathan and his member of staff was imperative in helping Nathan overcome his apparent fear of eating. His member of staff chewed gum, ate her lunch, drank juice all with great enthusiasm and feigned delight within the view of a very anxious Nathan. His concern for her slowly changed to interest and he was ready to begin the process of learning to enjoy the social interaction of eating a variety of foods. His educator began by:

- widening the hole in the teat;
- thickening the liquid;
- adding a variety of flavours;
- adding a few soft lumps.

When he was comfortable with one step, he progressed to the next.

Nathan was exposed to the pleasurable experience of eating by being with others as they ate and enjoyed food and was encouraged to touch and explore the food and the eating utensils.

At this stage of development the aim is to enhance the nutritional input. However in doing so, we must be aware of the dangers of too much pressure on the child to eat and drink. At every opportunity the child should be encouraged to make a choice.

Nathan's adversity to eating was seen by his family and staff to be a genuine fear. Just what had happened in his young life to cause this is not known or understood. Nathan is a clear example of the importance of emotional bonding and the close relationship between the child and his educator.

Nathan's progress, although steady in this area, was very slow and concerns were expressed by medics, family and school staff. A gastrostomy was discussed but it was felt that this was an option to be left meantime.

When Nathan was six years old he began a residential placement in school. There were many reasons for Nathan becoming a residential pupil which will be discussed later in this section, but increasing his nutritional input and lessening his apprehension were main aims.

Environment

Consistency and structure of place, time and people are essential to help the deafblind child remember and anticipate events and to become comfortable in the situation knowing what is about to happen. Nathan sat at the same place at the table with his own place mat and with the same people around him. He had breakfast, snack and lunch with his teacher, and afternoon snack, dinner and supper with his member of care staff. Limiting the number of people involved with Nathan was essential to ensure consistency of handling, of routine and of communication. Nathan's team worked very closely planning mealtimes, agreeing on strategies and keeping each other informed of progress or, indeed, lack of progress. Nathan, like so many other children, had an element of mystery and mischief. Why, for example, would he take a little creamed rice with his member of care staff but never with his teacher!

The progression through the self-help skills in the curricular area of eating and drinking will, with individual adaptations, follow the pattern of mother–child relationship where the child moves from the bottle to the cup with a spout, to strained foods from a spoon, a variety of strained foods, mashed foods and to finger feeding. Collaboration among parents and professionals is necessary, firstly, to ensure consistency and secondly, so that the independent deafblind person will not simply 'eat to live' but will enjoy the multi-faceted learning experiences of:

- eating out socially;
- eating and interacting with their family;
- shopping for food;
- preparing and cooking meals and snacks for themselves and for their guests.

Since there is no one single expert in this cross-curricular area, it will be necessary to pool the knowledge and experience of:

- parents;
- teachers;
- care staff;
- speech and language therapist;
- occupational therapist;
- physiotherapist;
- educational psychologist;
- dietician.

The learning environments where eating and drinking skills take place must be the reactive environments so well described by McInnes and Treffry (1982). These are environments where the child and young person increase their control over what is happening in their life, e.g. what to eat and when to eat it, where every step in the transition to independence is a problem to be solved and where learner and educator are in constant communication as the tasks and the required skills develop and evolve.

Communication

Just as the learning experiences surrounding eating and drinking skills are multi-faceted, so too are the means and the rationale of communication. Leah, Dipalah and Chuck (see Chapter 1) may be co-actively using natural gesture, speech and fingerspelling or deafblind manual. Communication used by the individuals will be to receive and give instructions, to develop practical signing skills, to make choices and to be part of the dynamics of the social group.

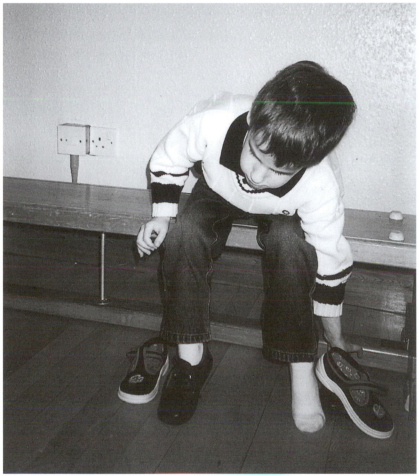

Figure 3.1 Changing my shoes

Dressing

As well as the practicalities and the necessity of dressing, it is important to remember that dressing is a means of communication for the deafblind person, of enabling him to make sense of the environment and of what is about to happen.

Richard had spent the first year or so of his education in a school for children who were hearing impaired. As well as his hearing loss, Richard also has a severe visual impairment. During this year, Richard became extremely frustrated and his behaviour reflected this. He was transferred to a school for pupils with a dual sensory impairment where the first step was to establish a trusting relationship with his member of staff in a reactive environment where he quickly displayed his ability to problem solve, his imaginative play, his sense of humour and his ability to share with others. However, during his first few months in his new school an incident occurred which had a profound effect on all members of staff.

Richard's teacher, Carol (who always wore a string of beads as her identification), and a member of the domestic team, Marie, were very similar in appearance and also shared a similar dress sense. They even had one outfit which was almost identical! Richard had just begun to form an attachment to his teacher when she was called out of school for a day. It was felt that because Richard was such a busy and energetic boy, the day would pass quickly and happily for him with the stand-in member of staff. All went well until Richard met Marie, as she hoovered in the hall. Frustration and tears followed as Richard confused Marie with his teacher Carol.

Relationship

This incident is often discussed among staff, from the abundance of communication that took place to the effect it had on:

- the developing emotional bonding between Richard and Carol;
- Richard's emotional development;
- his self-esteem;
- his interpersonal skills.

It also highlighted the importance of an identifying object for all members of staff and pupils.

When a new member of staff arrives in school, much discussion takes place about an identification for that member of staff and how we can enable our pupils who are deafblind to distinguish between one member of staff and another. The ID must have movement possibilities and this movement becomes the name sign for that person. Carol's bright orange beads can be seen by those pupils who have some residual vision, but all pupils are encouraged to touch the beads and move them from side to side. This side to side movement is Carol's name sign which she uses every time she greets or says goodbye to a child.

The reactive environment

The child who is deafblind will learn best in a real life situation where skills are taught in the appropriate place and at the appropriate time, giving the child motivation and reason for learning. We must therefore carefully plan our pupils' IEP in a way that eliminates the teaching of splintered or fragmented skills. For example, the child will learn to put on his jacket at the appropriate time, which is before going out, and therefore we must allow time for him to work co-actively, to be challenged by the activity, to achieve as much of the skill as he can independently and to be in 'constant dialogue' with his member of staff.

As our pupils approach adulthood, they will have a degree of choice as to how they will dress. They will, however, be restricted in what they wear by certain boundaries such as expense, time of day, activity, weather, as well as their use of any residual vision and hearing they may have and their understanding of the world. For many of our pupils it is likely to be a time of self-expression and of communicating their identity through their mode of dress. Before reaching this sophisticated level of expressive communication, people who are deafblind will have been using clothing and dress sense for both receptive and expressive communication in a varied and multi-tiered way.

A pupil may, while in the middle of one activity, locate and give the apron he wears at mealtimes to his member of staff, indicating that he is hungry. We must react to his communication by giving him the praise he greatly deserves, and by having a snack with him. He is increasing his communication skills and developing his concept of choice. He comes to understand that there is a 'listener' who reacts to his communication and that he has some control over his life. Another pupil may use clothing as a means of seeking-out, recognising and socialising with a peer or a member of staff.

One pupil may refuse to put on his shoes, indicating that he does not wish to go out. Does this also mean that the pupil who refuses to put on his raincoat also does not wish to go out? Not necessarily. It may simply mean that he does not like the feel of the raincoat. We must therefore 'listen' to his dialogue as we continue towards the door, utilising every opportunity for receptive and expressive communication.

Fifteen year old Martin had had a lovely summer holiday with his family. When he returned to school at the end of the summer he continued to wear the brightly coloured T-shirt and shorts which he had bought and worn almost constantly throughout the summer. Not only was he reaffirming his fashion style but he was remembering his happy family holiday. As the weather became colder, the shorts and T-shirt were put to the back of the wardrobe to be worn again the next summer, or so we thought!

One cold winter's morning when the snow was deep on the ground, Martin told his member of staff that he was ready to go out fully attired in his shorts and T-shirt. No amount of talking through, signing, graphic conversation, looking at the snow and discussing how others were dressed would dissuade Martin from wearing his favourite summer outfit. Martin picked up his bag and got as far as the bus before he decided that the clothes he was wearing, although they looked good, were not practical for a winter morning in Scotland! Martin's skin was grey-blue in colour and the hairs on his teenage arms and legs stood perpendicular on goose bumps. This experience deepened his understanding of choice. He was empowered to make reasoned choices and decisions without compromising the control he had on his life.

It can be helpful for staff to look closely at a specific area of the curriculum such as dressing to appreciate how it links and functions with other curricular areas and therefore the importance of teaching dressing as opposed to 'doing' dressing with the pupil. It also highlights the importance of staff training so that educators can make sense of 'Dressing' as an intricate part of all teaching and learning. If we classify our curriculum into four areas for example, (see Figure 3.2), we can see from the chart the significance of dressing in the curriculum.

Sex education

The importance of sex education for all children and young people is acknowledged and emphasised in recent legislation. For many people working with children and young people with physical and learning disabilities this brings a new dimension to their work. Sex education has not always been seen as an important part of the education of these children.   (Cole-Hamilton 1996)

For those working with children and young people with disabilities, sex education has two main themes:

- to enable the young person to become aware of and to cope with the physical and emotional changes which will occur;
- to empower the young person to make choices about sexuality and, in so doing, allow him a degree of protection.

Children are among the most vulnerable members of our society. So, too, are the disabled, those who have difficulty communicating and those with low self-esteem. How vulnerable therefore are our deafblind pupils, many of whom are in residential schools or residential care? How can we help them know when they are being handled in an inappropriate way and to communicate this information to caring adults?

Concept Development

Tactile training
identification of garments

Visual training
visual scanning to identify and find garments

Auditory training
perception of speech rhythms, accepting the wearing of hearing aids

Identification of activities/people/places
particular clothes worn for particular activities, e.g. swimsuit

Movement
Circuit
wearing of soft soled shoes in the gym

Diary
anticipating and noting events, deciding on appropriate clothes

Matching/sorting/sequencing/classifying
socks go on before shoes, do the socks match?

Imitation
putting on a hat just as the adult has done

Arts and crafts
locating and putting on tactile apron

Practical number
how many socks do I have?

Early number
big and small

Computer
a variety of programmes are available

'Stories'
RE   } link with theme
Topics/projects

Environmental studies
wearing a raincoat in wet weather

Play (various levels)
old clothes for rough or dirty play

Personal Development

Eating/drinking
Toileting
Dressing/undressing
Health and hygiene
Cooking
Household skills
Shopping
Mobility
Fine motor skills
Gross motor skills
Swimming
Play and leisure (PE)
Independence skills
Independent travel
Social initiative
Financial dealings

Dressing/undressing

Socialisation

Body awareness/body image
which part of the body fits into the specific part of the garment

Awareness of others/identification of people
recognition and understanding of IDs

Emotions
self-esteem
Graphic/tactile conversation

Interpersonal skills
to recognise and to behave appropriately with friends, with strangers

Sex education
appropriate dressing at all times, e.g. bathrobe

Language and Communication

Movement
Drawing

Gesture
Signing/fingerspelling
Braille
Speech training
Reading
Writing

Figure 3.2

Policy documents

The sense of touch is an important means for the deafblind person to learn about himself, and about the environment and the people in it. However, we must consider what is appropriate and inappropriate touching both for the deafblind person and for those working with them.

> For example always follow simple rules such as routinely using a flannel or sponge and never touch the child directly. Wherever possible, guide the child or young person's own hand to wash him or herself or to identify his/her own body parts. If this is done consistently by adults throughout a child's life, children will, more easily, be able to grasp the difference if touched intimately by someone not taking these familiar steps.
>
> (Cole-Hamilton 1996)

We can help staff by having a clearly structured sex education policy where staff have precise procedures and routines to follow in the care and education of the child. These precise routines may help the child differentiate between what is appropriate and inappropriate touching by others. It will be prudent to involve parents groups such as School Board, Board of Governors and Parent Teachers' Association in the drafting of the policy document but it is essential that the policy be made known to all parents. Similarly, staff must have a clear course of action to follow if they have concerns regarding these procedures and how they are being carried out by colleagues or by the child's family. Good practice in meeting the intimate care needs of the child helps promote safe learning.

The routines and the consistency of handling lay the foundations for acceptable social behaviour both for the deafblind person and the staff working with them. These routines also highlight the vulnerability of all those involved. Other self-help skills, such as toileting and dressing, which must be taught in order to lead the deafblind child towards independence, also expose the vulnerability of the adult to accusation and the young person to abuse.

For the adult, our awareness of the rights of the child to feel safe and secure, to have privacy and dignity and the constant reinforcement of our knowledge and understanding of these rights through open discussion, staff training and school policies, should ensure correct handling and correct procedures during these intimate learning experiences. For the child having an anticipation of routine, any deviation from that routine may help him grasp what is inappropriate handling and perhaps to be able to communicate this to others.

The opportunity for the deafblind person to make choices must permeate all areas of the curriculum but nowhere is it seen to be more important than in the area of personal development, and sex education in particular.

Sex education for deafblind children begins at the very early stages of social and personal development with the teaching of awareness of self, of others, of relationships and emotions. Structured body awareness, washing and body matching routines as described in Figure 3.3 will assist in achieving the following aims:

- to give the child a conscious awareness of his/her body as an entity;
- to give the child an awareness of the possibilities of his/her body;
- to give the child an awareness of self in relation to other persons;
- to aid imitation and subsequently signing and fingerspelling;

and assist in developing the emotional bond between the child and adult which is intrinsic in the education of the deafblind child. We cannot, at this early stage of development, tell him that he is cared for, but he will come to know this intuitively by the way in which he is handled and by the praise he is given.

Structured washing

Washing co-actively in the same order every time, e.g. face, neck, back, lower back, front, lower front, left arm, right arm, left leg, left foot, right leg, right foot. Look out for anticipation of the next limb or part of the body. Name the body parts as you wash and dry them co-actively.

Body matching

Sitting, facing each other, the adult guides the child's hands to feel a part of the adult's body (e.g. head) and then to feel the same part on child's body. Concentrate on principal parts only and always in the same order, e.g. (as with washing):

adult's hair	–	child's hair
adult's face	–	child's face
adult's body	–	child's body
adult's left arm	–	child's left arm
adult's right arm	–	child's right arm
adult's left leg	–	child's left leg
adult's right leg	–	child's right leg

When the child shows awareness of what is happening, allow child to touch or stroke his/her own body part.

Remove the order. Co-actively stroke different parts of adult, then allow the child to match his/her own body parts.

Return to the beginning – reintroduce the same sequence but this time the child's body is touched first and then the adult's.

Follow the same progression, gradually allowing the child to do it independently. (This is particularly difficult for the child with no usable vision.)

Child should now be able to match all major parts of his/her body to another.

(From Massey *et al.* 1993 in Blythman and Diniz)

Figure 3.3

Challenging behaviour

Many deafblind children, on beginning their school placement, present similar needs to Leah (see Chapter 1). How quickly each child moves through this early stage of development will be dependent upon the factors outlined at the beginning of this chapter and also, as in Leah's case, how we as educators can assist her in managing her difficult behaviour.

Challenging behaviour can present in a wide variety of ways. (This topic is also dealt with in Chapter 7.) Strategies and approaches in dealing with challenging behaviour are as varied and as individual as the deafblind person. However, a multi-disciplinary approach and consistency in handling the deafblind person is an essential commonality.

Charts which record the behaviours while monitoring the general health of the child, the attitude of the staff member towards the child and towards the behaviour, the environment, the activity during which the behaviour occurred, as well as other relevant categories, are also essential.

The management of her behaviour may be through Leah's limited ability to access a means of communication. Identifications for adults and objects of reference to represent activities are vital at this stage. These 'tools' will enable Leah and children like her to recognise familiar people as opposed to strangers, to anticipate and to remember and thus to make choices and ultimately to take control of what is happening.

Relationships

Perhaps, and more likely in this early stage, management of Leah's behaviour will be through the development of a secure relationship with her educator. A relationship where each individual is valued and the child's needs are recognised and understood. Once established, this relationship will enable the educator to work co-actively with Leah and begin the lifelong process of enabling her to access information, communicate with others and to move around the environment. In this early developmental stage, Leah needs to become aware of self, relationships with others and to have some understanding of emotions. As Leah comes to know and enjoy being with those individuals close to her, the circle of people in her life will, quite naturally, be widening. At this stage it will be necessary to help Leah understand the differences in relationships and how to approach and greet the variety of people she will encounter in her day to day living. In other words, how to behave in a socially acceptable way.

When Susan began her placement in a school for deafblind children she was two years and five months, although her global development could be compared to a young infant of just a few months. Given the appropriate intervention and stimulation, Susan made rapid progress. By the time she was seven years old, she recognised and named the adults and children in school, had some understanding of their roles and had the beginnings of a friendship with some of the other pupils. However, Susan greeted everyone she encountered, friend or stranger, with the same gusto and enthusiastic hug. Many adults were happy to be the recipient of such a greeting while others were decidedly uncomfortable. Susan had to be taught that there are some people who are greeted with:

- 'Hello' – when introduced to strangers;
- a warm smile, a 'hello' and perhaps a touch – when meeting a friend;
- a hug – when greeting those she loves.

Susan, given her cognitive ability, will in time come to understand the differences in relationships and how to behave towards the different people she meets. Other children will not develop this understanding and will behave in a way which is socially acceptable simply because they have been asked to do so by the adult with whom they have formed a warm, secure and trusting relationship.

Developing a secure and trusting relationship with a deafblind child will be a long and sometimes demanding task. This relationship, once established, will be the foundation for learning and progression to adulthood. Moving through childhood and approaching puberty, this bonding with another individual(s) will be fundamental in assisting the young person to understand his/her emotions and the physical changes taking place.

Physical changes

As the circle of people in Leah's life widens, so too will her understanding of communication. As stated earlier, Identifications for people are vital tools in the early stages of development. As Leah begins to understand concepts and symbolisation these Identifications will become Name Signs. For example, the member of staff who wears a beaded necklace to identify herself will, when greeting the children, always draw their attention to it by co-actively grasping the beads and moving them from side to side and at the same time saying, 'Hello, it's Carol.' The children come to learn that as well as the tangible identifying object, the beads, representing Carol, so, too, does the movement. Because of the use of Identifications, Leah will realise that there are many people in her life and, as her understanding continues to develop, that not only is their appearance or identification different but that they also have quite different personalities and different roles to play in her life.

Leah is severely hearing and visually impaired and therefore, because she can make use of her residual vision, graphic conversation in conjunction with signing will be a means of communication for her. Graphic conversation can be used to describe and discuss with Leah such changes in her body as developing breasts, pubic hair and menstruation. This task is for many members of staff and indeed for many parents a cause for concern. Planning and working collaboratively is a sound approach in a situation like this.

Leah's understanding of physical differences and changes could begin as follows:

- getting to know her member of staff – using Identifications;
- getting to know herself – Body Image Programmes;
- getting to know the differences in appearance – people who are tall or short, people who have a long ponytail or short curly hair;
- getting to know gender differences – male and female clothing, swimwear, underwear and dresses, as well as children's picture books, insert boards and jigsaw puzzles which are commercially produced for this purpose.

Sean is totally deaf and blind. He uses his fingers to spell words on other people's hands. Sean's hands and his sense of touch are his link to the world and the people in it. Sean's sense of touch, tactile conversation and fingerspelling are his means of communication. How do we help deafblind people like Sean understand puberty?

Leah and Sean must be taught about puberty and changes taking place in their own bodies; they should also be taught about differences in gender. Keeping in mind the need for privacy and dignity, plan with your pupil's team how this can be built into the Individualised Educational Programme. It may be helpful to discuss your plan with an experienced member of staff who is not a member of your pupil's team.

Emotional changes

Instilled in the deafblind child in the early stages of development is the necessity to carry out activities in the appropriate place or room. Initially this is done to aid communication and to help the child predict what is about to happen. As the child develops a degree of independence, this training may enable him to discern what is acceptable social behaviour. However, for some of our most disabled learners this may not always be possible and in such cases we must ensure that the deafblind person's rights and dignity are maintained, e.g. always closing the bathroom door, never changing clothes in a public room. To maintain the rights and dignity of the individual we must constantly question our procedures and our own attitudes and empathy towards the deafblind person and their behaviour.

Through Body Awareness and Body Image programmes the child develops an awareness of himself, the different parts of his body, the possibilities of his body, e.g. his hand to bring a glass of juice from the table to his mouth, his legs to jump, and the pleasure he receives from moving his body and from touching his body. It is at this stage that we may encounter the child who masturbates. We must decide as educators and parents how we will help the child to appreciate that this normal behaviour can only be acceptable at certain times and in certain places. The child's structured educational programme and the secure relationship developed between himself and his educator will be invaluable at this time.

Some educational establishments have a broad strategy which must be flexible to accommodate the needs of each individual:

- divert the child's attention either by a change of activity or a change of room;
- take the child to his bedroom or a quiet room where he can be safely left alone until he is willing and able to be diverted;
- if the child is tucked up in bed for the night, then this is his own private time and he should be left undisturbed.

As the deafblind child passes through puberty and continues to develop a variety of deepening relationships with others, we may see the emergence of a 'boyfriend–girlfriend' relationship. To support the deafblind person in this sensitive, delicate and extremely private relationship, we must first and always consider each individual and the relationship subjectively.

Human reproduction

Pregnancy, conception and contraception should be discussed with all young people when the individual is developmentally ready. When the deafblind person is ready to discuss these issues, his cognitive ability and communication skills will have developed in tandem with his emotional development.

Jennifer has a profound hearing loss and tunnel vision. At 15, this bright extrovert enjoyed a varied social life both with her family and with friends at the local Deaf Club which she attended with her member of staff from school. She had begun to menstruate a few years earlier and coped well with her personal hygiene and self-help skills. Although Jennifer's menstrual cycle had been discussed through graphic conversation and she had been given practical advice and demonstration from family and staff, the reason for her menstruation cycle and that of other women did not quite fit into place. This indicated to her staff that Jennifer now needed to be taught about the whole reproductive system. Her family were happy to let the school have most of the responsibility for this but to be kept informed and to give support.

The ideal opportunity to teach Jennifer about pregnancy came about when her teacher became pregnant. Jennifer was told about the impending birth as soon as the 'bump' appeared. She was involved in antenatal visits, visits to the hospital and later the buying of baby clothes and equipment in readiness for the birth. Finally, the visit to the hospital a few days after the little boy's birth where Jennifer was allowed to hold him and to watch as he was breast fed. Jennifer's interest in the baby continued. The next step was to teach her about conception and contraception. Jennifer's member of care staff had known Jennifer since she started school and over the years they had developed a deep emotional bond. She was therefore the obvious choice in being the key person in teaching this complex and extremely important part of the curriculum.

Jennifer was already aware of gender differences, friendships and emotional relationships. She was then taught about:

- arousement;
- assertiveness;
- unwanted attention;
- places where you are safe;
- places where you are in danger;
- dangerous situations.

The list is continuous and wide-ranging for Jennifer because of her cognitive ability and her social skills. For other deafblind people, their learning may go no further than awareness of physical changes in their own body.

As educators, we must be aware that sex education is the right of every person and that information and support must be given as and when the person is in need of that information. Of paramount importance is the need for privacy and dignity for the young person and as educators we must always be open to the needs of the deafblind person and accepting of those needs.

Discuss the policy or procedures followed in you school or establishment to maintain the rights and dignity of:

- the child or young person who masturbates;
- the deafblind person who wishes to form a loving relationship with a peer; this may or may not be a heterosexual relationship.

Personal hygiene

Linked closely with Body Image programmes and Sex Education is Personal Hygiene. This is an area which can cause concern because it may appear to take quite some time to achieve. When we aim to achieve independence in personal hygiene for our deafblind pupils, we are taking on board a hugely complex task both for the child and the adults involved. Therefore we must allow ourselves time to complete each small task along the way and to adopt a relaxed and confident approach.

Relationship

Children generally have an intuitive awareness of the emotions and tensions of the various adults they encounter. More so our deafblind pupils whose difficulties have necessitated a close emotional bonding with a limited number of adults in order to facilitate teaching and learning. The educator's positive attitude and approach to toilet training is important in instilling confidence and security in the child. For many months the child and his educator will have been developing a warm and trusting relationship. Once this relationship has been established, then toilet training can begin.

Collaboration

All those working with the child should be in agreement as to:

When?

- Is the child secure in his relationship with his educator?
- Is the educator confident in her knowledge of procedures, e.g. the bathroom door should always be closed, the child should always be handled appropriately, he should never be changed in a public room?
- Should the child be out of nappies throughout the day or for just a few hours each day?
- Should he continue to wear nappies while travelling to and from school or when participating in activities outwith the school or home environment?

Where?

- Which bathroom to use?
- Should he use the toilet or a potty?

Whether the child is using the toilet or a potty, toilet training should always take place in the bathroom. To do otherwise will give the child confusing messages, e.g. the child who uses his potty in the living room may interpret this to mean that it is okay to urinate in the living room. The cues in the environment will help the child understand and anticipate what is about to happen.

How?

- Which object of reference should be used?
- Should he use a step and a child's toilet seat to help him feel more comfortable and secure?
- Should he change from nappies to 'Huggies' and then into pants?
- Should a toileting routine be established, i.e. taken to the bathroom at set times during the day?
- Should he continue to use a night-time nappy?

At this early developmental stage, the number of adults working with the child should be limited to, at the most, two plus his parents (do you agree?). This is to lessen confusion and to ensure consistency of approach.

Consistency

It took Chloe many, many months to establish an emotional bond with her member of staff; once this bond was established she moved forward at a pace which was very rewarding for her member of staff, her family and for Chloe herself. The areas where her progress was most clearly seen were in her use of objects of reference and mobility.

A toileting routine was established in Chloe's timetable. She went to the bathroom when she arrived in school, immediately after her mid-morning snack, immediately after lunch, mid-afternoon and just before leaving for home. A similar routine was established at home although it was fully appreciated by Chloe's family and staff that it would be more difficult to establish a routine of any kind at home than it would be at school.

This routine suited Chloe. It will not suit every child. If the child becomes frustrated at the number of times he is being taken to the toilet, then reduce the number of visits. It is useful at this time to keep a toilet chart which records the number of times the child is taken to the toilet and the times when he is wet or soiled. We are looking for a pattern to emerge and then to plan his visits to the toilet to coincide with his pattern of wetting or soiling.

Chloe would take her object of reference (pants) from her calendar boxes and happily make her way to the bathroom, but once there she would refuse to sit on either the toilet or a potty. Chloe's team consisted of one member of staff from school and her mother. After discussion, both team members agreed that Chloe needed a reward, something tangible that could be given to her to 'ease the way' towards her understanding of what was being asked of her and also in a small way divert her attention from what was an unknown and fearful situation.

One of her favourite things was a toy mirror, which she enjoyed holding close to her face and moving back and forth on her mouth and cheeks. The mirror was to be kept in the bathroom at school and a second, identical mirror was bought and kept in her bathroom at home. The toy mirror was given to Chloe only in the bathroom and only if and when she would allow her buttocks to touch the edge of the toilet seat. Initially, this was all that Chloe would allow but gradually her desire for the mirror enabled the adult working with her to increase the time spent actually sitting on the toilet to a few minutes. Chloe's routine was kept as consistent as possible:

- co-actively closing the bathroom door;
- tactilely exploring the toilet seat;
- co-actively gesturing 'pants';
- co-actively taking down her pants;
- co-actively gesturing 'sit down'.

All these activities were carried out in the same order both at home and at school.

When we consider the minutiae of detail necessary to achieve the long-term goal of independence in toileting, the essentialness of consistency and collaboration is striking.

Task analysis

If we analyse the educational aim, 'to use the toilet to wet', we must ask ourselves, 'What are we asking Chloe to do, what teaching and learning is taking place?'

- timetabling – sequencing;
- recognise her object of reference – communication;
- anticipate what is about to happen – communication;
- carry her object of reference to the bathroom – fine motor;
- make her way to the bathroom, recognising features and cues in the environment – mobility;
- locate the bathroom door – classification;
- locate and manipulate the door handle – problem-solving;
- orientate herself around, then close the door – orientation;
- put her object of reference in the appropriate place – sorting;
- make her way to the toilet seat – gross motor;
- orientate herself into the correct position for sitting – body image;
- take down trousers/lift skirt – dressing;
- take down pants – fine motor;
- manoeuvre herself onto the toilet – gross motor;
- urinate into the toilet.

The steps are numerous and no doubt there will be more which have not been listed above.

> Video a pupil who is developmentally similar to Chloe as he washes his hands. Begin to video as he is standing by the wash basin ready to start. Write down all the steps he must learn before he can complete this task independently. This will highlight the significance of teaching as we lead the deafblind pupil towards independence.

It is the right of every person to have privacy and dignity. Therefore toileting must be systematically taught by an educator – the child's own team member – who has the skills and knowledge to enable him, as far as possible, to understand what is happening to him and to understand what is expected of him, thus allowing him the freedom to function as an integrated member of society.

Health and safety

Each school or establishment must, in collaboration with *all* staff, have detailed Health and Safety procedures and policy in place.

A child should never be left wet or soiled for reasons of:

- health and safety – his and others;
- comfort – his and others;
- dignity;

and yet if we quickly rush the child who has had a toileting 'accident' to the bathroom to clean and change him, how can we expect him to come to the realisation of what has happened and the consequences of his 'accident', that is,

- to become aware of his bodily functions;
- to become aware of his need for the toilet.

We must therefore strike a balance. We must react immediately the child wets or soils but we must also involve him as much as possible in what has happened and in how it has to be dealt with. When the child is wet:

- we must draw his attention to the urine on the floor and on his clothes – this may mean directing his hand to touch the wetness;
- we must tell him that this should have happened in the bathroom, using the language and communication which is relevant to him;
- we must take him to collect his change of clothing, giving him as much information as possible – where he is going and why;
- we must take him to the bathroom – he may be able to help by carrying his clean pants.

Once in the bathroom, he must follow his own toilet procedure. A variation may be that he needs to be washed or bathed. Again, involve him as much as possible, remembering that this is a teaching situation and not simple care. We must never at this stage:

- Scold him. He is not yet aware of his bodily function, hygiene, or of what is socially acceptable behaviour.
- Rush him. Initially the child who wets his pants will not feel discomfort. Indeed, he may derive a pleasurable warmth from the flow of urine. However, the time required to gather together his fresh clothes and make his way to the bathroom will not only allow him time to begin to process the information being imparted to him through action, gesture, sign, etc., but will also aid his awareness of bodily functions as he begins to feel discomfort as the urine becomes cold.
- Allow him to become frustrated. We are asking our deafblind pupil to carry out a large number of activities which, in these early stages, he may not understand. There are occasions when he will carry out all that is asked of him and more, even to helping clear up the wet clothes. There will also be occasions when he will not. As educators we must prioritise the teaching areas and adapt our procedures.

Each bathroom must be fully equipped with all that you as a whole-school staff believe to be indispensable for a safe and healthy environment: disposable gloves, aprons, nappies, nappy bags, disinfectant, soap, baby wipes, soft paper, towels, sanitary bin, toilet tissue, spare toilet rolls. There will be much more, depending upon individual requirements.

Ask your head teacher to set aside 15 minutes during a staff meeting for a brainstorming session. List all equipment which you as a staff deem to be essential in the children's bathrooms. This brainstorming session should include every member of staff.

All staff should know who is responsible for ensuring that each bathroom is fully stocked with the essential equipment, who is responsible for ordering the equipment and what to do if deliveries do not come on time. Staff must be supportive of one another at all times but particularly during toileting when we often find that we need at least two pairs of hands when dealing with a lively and inquisitive child. There will be occasions when we need the assistance of one or even two other adults, for example when sluicing soiled clothes. Toileting is a teaching situation and our ultimate aim is to lead the child towards independence. Therefore the people dealing with the intimate part of the toileting task are the pupil himself and his educator, who are working, communicating and problem-solving together, where the child is encouraged to make use of his residual vision and hearing and to be given as much control as possible. This is when we see cooperation at its best: when all staff from all disciplines – domestics, teachers (including the head teacher), care staff, classroom assistants, administrators – rally to support the child's educator and in so doing enable child-centred education to proceed.

Residential education

Many deafblind children will begin school confused, isolated, frustrated and often fearful. Their emotions will manifest themselves in a variety of behaviours. As educators we must lead the child from his chaos into a world which will make sense to him and offer him a degree of happiness and fulfilment. For some children, residential education is an integral part of the route to an ordered world. In child-centred education, how this is done and the time taken to achieve this will be dependent upon the individual child. However, the developmental stages the child passes through will be the same.

Resonance

This is the stage where the developmentally young child is very much in isolation, locked into his own world of self-stimulation and stereotypical behaviour. The educator must succeed in becoming part of his world. This is done by resonating or reflecting back the child's movements and vocalisations. As the educator imitates his movements and vocalisations the child will, in time, come to realise that there is someone else there. When the child stops the adult stops, when the child continues the adult continues. These are the very beginnings of interaction and communication and, of vital importance in the life of the deafblind child, the beginnings of the development of a warm, trusting and secure relationship, which is the foundation of his education.

Co-active movement

Now that the child has come to recognise and trust his member of staff, he will allow himself to be led out of his isolation and to explore the environment. Here, child and educator, two individuals, work together as one, exploring the environment and the people and objects in it.

Distancing

As the child's confidence in his educator and ultimately in himself grows, the educator begins to distance herself from the child. Instead of working hand over hand with the child as in co-active movement, the educator will now begin to move away from the child by supporting him at his wrists or elbows or shoulders as he touches, explores and forms concepts. The educator is now guiding rather than leading and the child is beginning to take some responsibility for what he is doing.

Independence

The ability to imitate, to understand symbolism and to generalise emerge and evolve as the deafblind child moves towards independence.

Assessment

When the deafblind child has developed some understanding of relationships and concepts, his multi-disciplinary team will have had extensive opportunities to assess his skills, aptitudes and cognitive ability. In other words the deafblind child and his team – which includes his parents – will have a sound knowledge of each other and it is at this time that the question of the appropriateness of residential education and the 24 hour curriculum may be discussed. Residential education need not continue throughout the whole of the child's school career. Indeed, residential education, as opposed to respite, is an option which should only be chosen when it is deemed to be of benefit to the child.

Educational aims

The reasons for residential education are wide and varied.

1. The child who, although living at home, is not an integrated member of his family. He may not yet have developed the necessary concepts to interact and grow in familial relationships. Intensive residential education may equip him with the skills to function as a family member, thus improving his emotional well-being by reducing the time spent on the periphery of family life.
2. The child whose signing skills have not kept pace with his cognitive ability and whose frustration may very well present as challenging behaviour. Focusing on developing his communication skills over a specified short-term or long-term period of time may give him a kick-start in this area of development.
3. For the child who has turned night into day and who will catnap at every opportunity, residential education will provide him with a busy and stimulating day and evening educational programme. He may be asked to assist in organising and clearing up after the evening meal, participate in a sporting or social activity, bathe and get ready for bed, organise supper for

himself and perhaps for others, and lay out his clothes for the next day before going to bed at a regular time. Consistency, routine and the support of school staff will enable him to develop a body rhythm and establish a sleeping pattern.

4. A period of residential education may be used to establish a hygiene routine.

5. Developing social skills may be the aim for a child having a residential placement.

6. Timescale, staffing and educational aims must be carefully planned. So too must the transition to residential education be planned with a gradual build up to the number of nights the child spends in school. Great care must be taken to ensure that the deafblind child has as much understanding and anticipation of the event as possible. He should spend some time in *his* bedroom in school before he actually begins his residential placement:

- exploring and playing;
- hanging pictures or posters;
- shopping for his duvet cover;
- helping to make up his bed.

When the aims have been achieved then the residential aspect of the child or young person's education may continue in the less intense environment of his family home.

Alison began her residential placement in school when she was six years old. Prior to this she had been a day pupil since she was two years and six months. Alison was a very isolated little girl and had a real fear of people she did not recognise. Although she had useful residual vision, it was very difficult to establish eye contact and she would 'block out' people by moving her fingers in front of her eyes and apparently concentrate on her moving fingers. Alison did not like change of any kind and reacted very vociferously when things did not happen exactly as she wished. She was a poor eater who refused to taste or drink anything other than her own very limited selection of food and drink. Alison's communication at this time was to display pleasure and displeasure. It was evident that Alison's understanding of the world was confused and that without intensive intervention in all areas of the curriculum, her emotional and social development would be greatly curtailed and she would not reach the potential which was so clearly displayed in her ability to problem solve.

After a very sensitive approach to her young parents and much discussion among all staff concerned with Alison it was felt that residential education was the best option for her. The transition to a residential educational placement of Monday morning until Friday afternoon was carefully graded, beginning with one overnight and gradually building up to four overnight stays in school. The speed of the transition was dictated by Alison and only when it was felt that she was comfortable with one night did it increase to two and so on. Alison's progress was such that by the time she was 12 years old, development of her communication and her personal and social skills was at a level that enabled her to be an integrated member of her family. Her residential placement in school has been reduced to three overnight stays, in the near future it should be reduced to two nights and by the time she is ready to leave school she will be a day pupil.

Richard's mother organised her day so that she could spend the evening hours with her dual sensory impaired son. She planned evening activities that would stimulate Richard and where communication was given a high priority. She had arranged to have Richard stay each Friday evening with his grandmother, which enabled her to have some time for her own leisure activities. Far from suggesting residential education for Richard, it was clear that he would lose more than he would gain from a residential placement. Much as the school staff aimed to create a warm, caring family environment, they fully appreciated that they could never replicate the love found in the family home.

Future needs assessment

In Scotland the law states that pupils with a Record of Needs (Statement) require assessment and review of their future needs within the period beginning two years before they cease to be of school age and ending nine months before that date. This Future Needs Assessment meeting (FNA) brings together all those who are involved and those who will become involved with the young person to discuss the support required to enable the young person to continue to develop and achieve throughout their adult life. The FNA for the deafblind person is not a 'one off' meeting, but is followed up by as many as is necessary to assist in the smooth transition from school life to adult life. Among the areas for discussion are:

- Education
- Employment
- Housing
- Social and leisure activities.

As far as possible the young person should be involved in these discussions. In many cases, however, this may not be possible because of the severity of the person's difficulties. In these cases the young deafblind person must have someone who will speak on their behalf.

Jennifer had been a residential pupil but because of her mastery of all that she was being taught, became a day pupil towards the last few years of her school career. Jennifer did not want to live at home with her mother when she left school. She wanted to be like her hearing and sighted older sister and live in her own flat. The feasibility of Jennifer living in a flat was discussed in great detail at her FNA meetings. Assisting her to achieve her ambition was felt to be a mammoth task both for Jennifer and for her staff. However, a bedsit was set up for Jennifer in the school. She was allowed to make mistakes and to learn from the sometimes unpleasant experiences. For example, she decided not to go shopping for her groceries in spite of being told that her provisions were running low. A missed meal and little sympathy stressed for Jennifer the importance of routine and planning. The final 18 months of Jennifer's school career were spent living in her bedsit in school. Jennifer achieved her ambition and is still living in her flat with the minimum of support. Her name is on the waiting list for a council flat and her ambition now is to live completely independently. An ambition she will undoubtedly successfully achieve.

Residential education is an option available to some deafblind pupils. As educators we must support parents in the decision they make about residential education for their child. Residential education is a means to an end, a tool to enable the child or young person achieve their potential. It must be flexible to meet the pupils' educational needs and constantly reviewed and modified to ensure that these needs are being met. At all times the emotional well-being of the pupil and his family must be emphasised and carefully monitored as the pupil makes the transition from day placement to residential placement.

Mobility

Perhaps the most important skill which enables autonomy in independent learning is the ability to travel purposefully and with confidence in the environment. The deafblind child or young person is empowered to move when and where he wishes, exploring and discovering as he goes. His confidence and self-esteem flourish. Before this can happen, however, there is much work to be done. The developmentally young deafblind child will have a degree of understanding of the environment because consistency and structure are fundamental to his educational programme. He will have an understanding of himself through such curricular areas as body image, circuit, movement programmes and motor activities. He will also have been helped to become aware of, and to make use of any residual vision he may have. He will have been enabled to develop orientation skills, the first step towards independent travel.

Figure 3.4 Skating with splints on

Greg came from an emotionally and socially deprived background. At three years old, he spent his day on his back moving his head from side to side. He had had several periods of hospitalisation and he required daily medication by means of intramuscular injection. Generally, his life had been full of inconsistencies and he was, without doubt, a frightened little boy. A medical report from hospital stated that Greg had no useful vision. His GP felt that, 'there is far more to Greg.' She was proved to be absolutely right.

Greg, now nine years old, moves around the school with great confidence, telling, when asked, where he is going and also going where he is asked. To enable Greg to achieve this skill required him firstly to view the world at the correct angle – to be enabled to orientate himself in space. He had to be encouraged to lie propped up on a cushion, then on a beanbag. Later, a small padded armchair was bought for him and soon afterwards he began to use a small straight-backed school chair. These steps progressed at Greg's own pace. Greg was developing orientation skills and independent mobility skills were soon to follow. He was also beginning to make sense of his residual vision.

During this time Greg followed a highly structured individual educational programme. His educator used musical toys to motivate him, first to reach out, then to roll towards the sound. Movement played an important part in his programme. Since Greg had missed much of the early interaction between infant and parent, many of the suggestions made by McInnes and Treffry (1982) in their chapter on Orientation and Mobility were tailored to meet Greg's needs. The gaps that had been missed in his young life had to be filled. As Greg and his educator moved around, features in the environment were brought to his attention; he was taught to 'side-step' along walls, to square off and to trail while being supported by holding one finger of his educator's hand. It was at about this stage that his educator began to suspect that Greg had, as his GP had suggested, residual vision which he could make use of as he developed mobility skills.

Today Greg has shown that he has residual vision which he can use to orientate himself and to travel independently around the school and his foster parents' home. He no longer trails in known environments but strides out confidently, using his residual vision to avoid people and objects he meets along the way. He generalises those mobility skills which he was taught and takes cognisance of cues in new or unknown environments.

Specialist input

Many schools have input from an Educational Mobility Specialist or a Mobility Officer. These visiting specialists are trained in developing orientation and mobility skills in visually impaired children and young people. Often the mobility specialist's first experience of dual sensory impairment is when they first arrive in a school for deafblind pupils. Collaboration between school staff and visiting specialist cannot be overemphasised. The pooling of skills and knowledge is essential for both pupils and adults so that the most effective educational programme is planned and there is professional development for staff.

Consultative model

A partnership between professionals leads to the establishment of practice where optimum skills are imparted to the pupil from the specialist in mobility and from the specialist in deafblind education. The mobility specialist has knowledge of:

- aids;
- long cane;
- health and safety;
- road safety;
- micromobility, which is concerned with stationary activities, e.g. dressing;
- macromobility, which is concerned with travel on foot, in a wheelchair or on public transport;
- techniques, e.g. developing reference points which help the child to where he is and to move with growing confidence.

The educator has knowledge of:

- the child;
- his residual vision;
- his residual hearing;
- his ability to integrate all of his senses;
- his understanding of the information he receives from the environment;
- his cognitive ability;
- his level of confidence;
- his family;
- deafblindness – the implications for education
                 – the implications for health and safety.

Consultation and collaboration are synonymous with good practice. The knowledge and skills of both professionals are, after observation and consultation, moulded around the pupil's needs to plan his educational programme. The programme is implemented by the educator between visits from the mobility specialist, and modified as necessary. This process is repeated as the programme is evaluated and the pupil's progress recorded. Thus, the deafblind pupil receives appropriate mobility training throughout his waking day.

As educators we strive to enable our deafblind pupils to experience all that life can offer. This includes the problems, and how to deal with them, as well as the joys.

Jennifer did not have a mobility specialist as she progressed through school. She did however have excellent staff who were committed to researching the best theory and applying it to their pupil.

As she approached the end of her school career, she knew about road safety, travelling by all kinds of public transport and was an expert in shopping. She had progressed from making her way to the local shop for her comic as a youngster, to the shopping mall for her week's supply of groceries when a bedsit was set up for her in school, to finally shopping alone in the variety of shops and department stores in the busiest street in the centre of the city. She carried with her an 'identity card' which stated her name and that she was deafblind. She also took her notebook and pen with her wherever she went so that she could introduce herself to shop assistants and then ask them to direct her to items which she wished buy.

Jennifer had often shopped in the city centre with her staff from school and with her family. Much drawing of street plans and graphic conversation had been done with Jennifer in preparation for the day when she would shop alone in the city. Her member of staff drove into the car park and told Jennifer to meet her back at the car at a certain time. As the appointed time approached, Jennifer, always a stickler for good timekeeping, had not returned. The minutes moved slowly past for Jennifer's very worried member of staff. Almost forty minutes had gone by before Jennifer appeared with a policeman. Jennifer had found herself lost but she had utilised the skills she had acquired over the years. She found someone she could trust and who would help her and communicated her problem to him.

Jennifer had exceeded all expectations. She had demonstrated independence as well as interdependency. Jennifer had succeeded in shopping in one of the busiest streets in Europe, met with a problem which she solved and returned to the car park albeit, a little late.

Jennifer was ambulant when she began school. Many deafblind pupils have the potential to be ambulant but, because of their deafblindness and the resulting poor body image, must be taught to walk as part of their educational programme. General developmental stages are:

- orientation;
- reaching out;
- rolling;
- crawling;
- walking with support – walking frame or adult support;
- becoming aware of cues in the environment;
- walking independently.

Other children however, because of physical difficulties, will be confined to wheelchairs. These pupils must be afforded as much independence as we can possibly give. For the pupil who cannot propel or activate his own wheelchair, information must always be imparted as to where he is going and why he is going there and to be given the choice, when he has that concept, of where to go and when to go there. Objects of reference may be a way of helping the child understand where he is going or the transport to be used, but how do we tell our non-ambulant deafblind pupil that we are about to go through a doorway or are about to turn right or left? We must:

- take time – to communicate who we are and where we are going;
- draw his attention to and name features and cues in the environment;
- place your hand on his right shoulder if you are about to turn right and on his left shoulder if turning left;
- keep in contact with him if you are stopped or delayed en route by placing both hands on his shoulders.

Incidental learning is infrequent, but with the development of orientation and mobility skills the deafblind person will have the freedom to move, to explore, to make changes, to understand the consequences of his actions and to learn without the intervention of another person.

How would you communicate to your deafblind pupil who uses a wheelchair that it is time to go to the swimming pool?

How can you offer him choice? (It can be something as simple as, 'Do you want your jacket fastened or left open?')

On your way through the school, you realise that you have left your towel behind. What will you do and how will your actions affect your pupil?

Religious education

Children who are deafblind have difficulty in forming concepts. They are taught through real life experiences. Experiences and activities which are tangible and meaningful to them. The ability to problem solve, to understand cause and effect, to remember and to anticipate evolves from these experiences. The ability to imagine or assume may come later in the development of the deafblind child. Religious education and the idea of a deity or a higher existence often relies on the ability to think in abstract terms. Children who are deafblind have difficulty in forming relationships, even with those closest to them, the family, who have loved them dearly since before their birth. The deafblind child's emotional development is stilted. How then can we 'tell' the deafblind child of the belief that there is a deity, a spirit, a supernatural person who also loves and cares for them?

Of all the religions in the world, the common element is love. The deafblind person will have difficulty, just as a high percentage of the population will have difficulty, in explaining or defining the emotion 'love'. How do we know that we are loved? Someone might tell us and we might believe them! However, it is so much more than that. It is communicated to us through body language, kindness, care, respect, sharing, giving, empathy, comforting, praising, helping. It would not be possible to list all the elements that make up this single emotion, but it is on this emotion, love, that we must build our religious education programme.

Ethos

We must begin by creating an ethos of care and respect throughout our establishment where every child, family, staff member and visitor is fully accepted. We must be empathetic to our pupils, their families and our colleagues, affording them the respect, dignity, privacy and support which their needs dictate.

Emotional bonding

How does the deafblind person know that he is loved? In exactly the same way as every other person. By the way we care for our pupil, by the way we handle him, empathise with him, praise him, share joyful experiences with him, comfort him and by sharing and helping him. Again the list is endless and is personal and distinct to the individuals. Many would contend that our deafblind pupils meet God or Allah or Jesus or Jehovah through the people who work with them. We develop an emotional attachment to our pupil as we work with him and, in the early developmental stages 'do for' him. Later, we will 'do with' him (co-active) and it is often at this stage in the child's development that we see our emotional care being reciprocated as our pupil recognises and is happy to be with us, responds to requests we make of him and is secure when we are close by. This is not the first time you will have read of the importance of emotional bonding in deafblind education. It is the cornerstone, the foundation for all learning throughout the deafblind person's life.

Damien's mother had always said a night-time prayer with her son. She held him close and said a few simple sentences which she felt were relevant to Damien and herself. After Damien had been attending school for a few years, his mum asked that he should begin and end his school day with a prayer. This caused much discussion among the staff. Some of the issues were:

- How relevant is prayer to Damien?
- Would valuable teaching time be lost?
- Could saying, 'God bless Papa in heaven' cause confusion for Damien?

All very important and pertinent questions. Some responses were:

- A close relationship with Damien can only be strengthened by spending a few quiet moments alone with him.
- The valuable teaching time spent in prayer would hopefully strengthen the relationship between Damien and staff.
- The prayer to be said may be, for Damien, a meaningful link between family and school.

Damien's mum and staff prepared the prayer which was used each day: 'Dear God, thank you for bringing me to school today and seeing Judith again. God bless Mummy, Granny, Grandad in heaven and all my friends at school.' As with all good practice, this was monitored and evaluated. Damien's prayer time has evolved and his staff would now like to develop his understanding of love, helping and sharing. 'Christopher went to the shops with me. Christopher held my hand. We bought strawberry yoghurt. Thank you, God, for Christopher.'

This is a brief synopsis of one child's religious education programme. However, all of what is termed 'Damien's RE' must permeate throughout the school and cultivate our ethos of care and nurture. All deafblind pupils have, for example, as part of their IEP, Auditory Training. It is part of the pupil's timetable but Auditory Training does not only take place during this timetabled slot when child and educator are working together in the Sound Perception/Auditory Training Room surrounded by musical instruments. It permeates throughout the whole of the pupil's curriculum, e.g. when his attention is drawn to sounds in the environment. So too with Religious Education. The deafblind pupil is encouraged at all times to share, to show kindness and to be courteous. As he grows and matures, he will be encouraged to help others, to empathise with others, to be accepting of others and to respect their need for privacy.

Atmosphere

How can we focus on teaching Religious and Moral Education and so perhaps impart to our deafblind pupils the realisation that there can be something or someone existing outwith our tactile, visual or hearing perception?

One way may be to establish regular Children's Services, when we endeavour to create an atmosphere of peace and tranquillity. A room, not normally used by the children, is set up in preparation for the service. Incense is burned, the overhead lights are replaced by soft lighting from table lamps and favourite music is played in the background. A theme is chosen which may be pertaining to a child, the school as a whole or the season of the year and the service is based on this. Alison *gives* her favourite sweets to everyone. We thank her and enjoy the treat. As well as the usual preparations in the room for the service, we have a bowl of beautiful spring flowers. Each person is *given* a flower to keep and 'look at'. Who *gave* us this treat? Each child will take from this what his stage of development will enable him to receive.

Many of our pupils may never be able to form an opinion about the existence of a deity, but just as we strive to enable them to experience as much as life can offer, we must also strive to enable them to experience a spiritual dimension in their lives.

Conclusion

Education is a lifelong experience developing and evolving as the person grows from infancy through childhood and adolescence and into the various stages of adulthood. When we speak of independence we are aware that total independence in our society must also mean isolation. We must therefore think of independence and interdependency as going hand in hand with each other.

Being independent conjures up images of living and caring for ourselves in our own home. The ultimate aim for those educators in schools for pupils who are deafblind is to lead the young person towards their full potential. This may be measured against the ability to draw together and apply the skills they have acquired which enable the young person to live independently.

Does living independently then mean that the young person is able 'to do' as much as he can for himself given his difficulties, and is able to allow others 'to do for him' without feelings of failure or developing learned helplessness? Is he able 'to do for others' without feeling used or put upon, is he able to enjoy 'doing for others' and to enjoy 'others doing for him'? If the answer is 'Yes', then we must consider him to be an integrated independent member of society.

At this stage in the young person's life, they are reminiscent of the lacemakers of Bruges who sit in the sun by their front door tatting the strands of bobbened threads, designing the intricate lace patterns which leave the tourists in awe of their skills. Our young deafblind pupils confidently weave the strands of the skills they have acquired to design something equally spectacular as the lacemakers. They take their skills and the relationships they have developed to weave and mould, to interact and adapt these skills to form the patterns of their lives.

References

Cole-Hamilton, I. (1996) *Sex Education for Visually Impaired Children with Additional Disabilities: Developing school policies and programmes.* London: RNIB.

McInnes, J. M. and Treffry, J. A. (1982) *Deafblind Infants and Children. A developmental guide.* Toronto: University of Toronto Press.

Massey, A. *et al.* (1993) 'Dressing/undressing', in Blythman, M. and Diniz, F. A. (eds) *Contact: A resource for staff working with children who are deafblind.* Sensory Series 3. Edinburgh: Moray House Publications.

CHAPTER 4

Holistic assessment

Jane T. Eyre

What is assessment and why do we assess?

Educational assessment is a broad term used to describe various activities which attempt to gather information about a child. The reason for gathering information is in order to answer certain questions about the child and her learning so, depending upon the questions we wish to answer, we may assess for a variety of different reasons.

Gathering information

In the early stages of working with a child who is new to us, our assessments may be concerned with gathering as much information as possible about the learner. We want to 'get to know' the child and we set about gathering all of the information available from a variety of different sources. This information will help us to establish a baseline of skills so that, together with our knowledge of the curriculum, we can plan an Individualised Educational Programme (IEP) for the child.

Assessing progress

Another reason might be to assess the amount of progress that has been made by the learner over a given period. This may be in one or in many subject areas, depending on what we wanted to find out. We may also be looking at areas where there has been little progress and trying to find out why. In both of these cases, it may be important to look at factors outwith as well as within the school and the learning that takes place there to find answers. Health factors for example, and emotional factors, may play an important part here, as may the teacher's skills and methods, and the resources used.

Specific assessment

At times we may want to look very closely at a specific feature of the learner and the way she acts. For example, if a child was displaying challenging behaviour, we may want to assess when, where and with whom the behaviour occurs, what seems to precede the occurrence, how it is dealt with and what the results of this are. In this case, we may want to devise our own tool – a behaviour log or specific observation chart. Assessing our own and others' management of these situations would be an important consideration in this kind of assessment.

Educational review

We may also be asked to provide written assessments for a child's educational review. In most special schools, these are held once or twice per school year. As the key worker for a deafblind child, our contribution will be an important one, recording and reporting on progress across the curriculum. Our ability to **summarise** progress will be crucial here – this will be discussed in more detail later on in this chapter.

Standardised tests

We can also assess in order to compare the child's results to the average results for children of a similar age. National testing attempts to do just this. Other standardised tests (i.e. tests which have been carried out on a sample population of the children being assessed), also aim to compare children's results to others with similar learning difficulties. These types of assessments may have little place in our work with deafblind children. The uniqueness of each individual deafblind child's learning difficulties does not bear comparison with any other child or group of children. If used at all, the results of these types of assessment should be viewed with caution.

Assessment then, can have many purposes. It is important that we are clear about *why* we are assessing and *what* we are assessing, as these factors will determine *how* we assess – what questions we ask, what tools we use, which methods we employ and what we do with our answers.

Assessment of deafblind learners

A positive approach

The first, and perhaps the most important, thing to keep in mind when assessing deafblind learners is that we must be *positive* about their achievements and their abilities. We must focus on what the child *can* do. Parents and families of deafblind children know only too well what their deafblind child *cannot* do. They have often spent many years trying to come to terms with the devastating information about their child's impairments and difficulties and the implications of these for their child's future.

Recently, the present writer met with a group of parents of deafblind children who discussed their experiences, thoughts and feelings on learning that their child was deafblind. Listening to them recount the trauma surrounding the weeks and months following their child's birth was a very revealing, and at times shocking, experience. In several cases, neither surgeons nor paediatricians were able to give any clear indication about what exactly was wrong with their new and very ill baby. Breathing difficulties, heart surgery, cataract treatment, tube-feeding, incubation, infection and a whole host of other medical and life-threatening problems were often faced and overcome by the child and also therefore, by the parents. Later, they found out that their child would be visually impaired, or blind. Later again, they found out that their child had a hearing impairment. Later still, that there could be learning difficulties, developmental delays and perhaps health problems that would need ongoing treatment.

The last thing that parents and families want, or need, when their child comes to school, is a list of 'can't do's'.

Our assessments should profile the strengths and abilities of the child, should focus on the positive achievements and, where there are difficulties, should suggest practical and resourceful ways of overcoming these.

It's important also to be ambitious about what the child may be able to achieve, to have high expectations. Recent literature suggests that for too long, children with special needs have been victims of the low expectations of their teachers and carers – the 'I don't think he can really manage this, so I'll just do it for him' syndrome. This philosophy can and does lead to a growing passivity in the learner. Coupe-O'Kane *et al.* (1994) illustrate this well:

> Somewhere along the line pupils have been publicly recognised as having learning difficulties as opposed to teachers who have not. The concept of 'knowing better' would thus seem to have official recognition. This attitude may translate into a variety of different responses by the adult, not least the desire to protect the individual from the outcome of his learning difficulty. The teacher may be less willing to expose the pupil to risk, to the possibility of 'failing'. Baker (1991) has argued that there is an 'unwitting conspiracy' by both professionals and parents which serves to promote continuing dependence rather than the development of autonomy. (Coupe-O'Kane *et al.* 1994, p. 15)

High expectations will in turn lead to higher achievements. This does not mean that we exaggerate the accomplishments or the capabilities of the learner. We must at all times be honest and realistic, but we can aim high rather than low, and in doing so, we will stretch the learner's abilities and raise their self-esteem.

How do we assess a child who is deafblind?

In Chapter 1, we considered what it means to be deafblind. From this you will understand that deafblind children may have the most severe and complex of learning difficulties. Their routes towards a particular goal may differ radically from those of any other child and, almost certainly, from the 'norm'. McInnes and Treffry (1982) state that these children will 'be forced to develop unique learning styles to compensate for their multiple handicaps'.

The reasons why they succeed or have difficulties in reaching goals may be affected by a whole range of factors – sensory, cognitive, communicational, personal, emotional, etc., and may be obscured by even more. This makes assessment of the deafblind child a very complex process.

Three common threads of difficulty began to emerge from the profiles in Chapter 1 and from the activities which followed. These indicated that deafblind people experience difficulties in:

- finding out information;
- communicating with others; and
- moving around the environment.

These three areas of difficulty begin to point the direction for our work in the area of assessment of children who are deafblind. Later on we will take each of these broad areas and break them down to look at the kinds of skills, knowledge and understanding required for each, and at the difficulties that deafblind learners may experience in trying to acquire them.

Observation

One of the most important tools we will use when assessing deafblind children is observation. We have already looked in some detail at observation (Chapter 1), at how important it is to acquire an 'observational attitude' in our work with deafblind children, and at some of the skills we can learn to help us. It may be useful to reread this section at this stage. Our skills as an efficient observer, our ability to record and to use our observations to enhance the teaching and learning that takes place, will be invaluable to us.

A multi-disciplinary, holistic approach

Assessing deafblind learners requires a multi-professional approach. Because of the complexity of the child's difficulties, it is likely that a number of professionals will be involved in assessing the child. Ophthalmologists, audiologists, speech and language therapists, physiotherapists and educational psychologists are just some of these. If the pupil is residential, there may be care staff involved too. Parents have a valuable role to play in any assessment of their child and, if the child attends a respite centre, staff there will have a contribution to make also.

As the key worker for a deafblind pupil, one of our crucial roles within an educational establishment is to coordinate the work of the 'educational team'.

In terms of assessment, this means gathering reports and collating information from all other professionals and individuals involved with the child and *putting this together with our own knowledge of the child and how that child learns.* (Figure 4.1)

It cannot be over-emphasised that all of the information we can gain from other professionals about the cause and effects of the child's impairments will be of great value to us. Initially, this may be the only information we have on which to base our work with the child. But deafblind

Figure 4.1 And how does it work?

children are extremely difficult to assess, not just by us, but by all other professionals who attempt to assess their abilities in any area, so we should not take ophthalmological, audiological, physical, cognitive, or any other assessments of the child as the full and complete story about what they can see, hear or do. What we need to reflect on and assess is what they do with what they've got – how they make use of their residual vision, residual hearing, how they compensate with other senses, how they can be helped to move around because of, or despite, their physical difficulties, and so on. How often have we read reports of a child with 'no usable sight', 'no response to sound', or '70db loss, right ear' – and six months later, the same child – '50db loss, right ear' and wondered if we had the correct report in our hands?

A deafblind child may not respond to pure tones, or indeed any other sounds, for a variety of reasons, one of which may be because he does not hear them. He might not appear to respond because his visual impairment means that he doesn't turn to sound; he may not respond because he doesn't understand what the noise he is hearing is, or what he is expected to do when he hears it; he might not respond because he 'blocks' all sound, having learned that it only confuses him when he's trying hard to see his world, and he may not respond for a hundred other different reasons, most of which we know nothing about because we're not deafblind.

And the picture can change radically over the years, as deafblind children begin to make more sense of their world, begin to learn how to use their limited sight or vision and begin to integrate information from their senses in order to better understand their world and the objects and people in it.

Chun-Li, a congenitally deafblind young adult, with very little sight, learned to say and understand the word 'Mum' at the age of fourteen. Hearing assessments had always been difficult and she had been assessed as 'profoundly deaf', 'with severe hearing loss', and 'moderate to severe hearing loss', at different times during her young and later years. Yet Mum and Dad maintained that she could hear a sweetie paper rustle across the length of a room! She was preparing to learn braille and one of the first brailled words she learned to read was 'Mum'. Staff felt that her understanding of this word and her ability to reproduce the word verbally were connected. Chun-Li could 'hear' when the sounds *meant something* to her. The sound of sweetie papers had been mastered long ago!

Samna was dual sensory impaired and had cerebral palsy affecting movement on her right side. She used a rolater to move around and doctors had told her Mum that she would not be able to walk unaided. But Samna was a feisty, determined and single-minded young character who had enough sight to see that other children didn't use rolaters. Despite the falls and the bruised knees, despite a very awkward gait, Samna now walks with a splint on her right leg. She doesn't like this very much either, for the same reason, and she removes the splint at every opportunity to walk in an even more awkward, but unaided, way.

Deafblind learners can change radically over a period of time, particularly where there is *early* and *appropriate* educational intervention. This is one of the reasons why we should be positive and ambitious at all times in our work with them. It also means that our own and others' assessments should be reviewed and updated regularly.

Because of the complex, multi-faceted nature of the difficulties faced by the deafblind child, any assessment we carry out must take into account all other factors which have implications for that particular area. In this way, our assessments become *holistic* – they match information about the child's visible achievements to existing information about the individual deafblind learner as a whole.

For example, imagine we were assessing a child's ability to drink from a cup independently. We place the child on a seat at a table, put the cup on the table and ask him to have a drink. The child appears to reach out for the cup, then draws back and rocks backwards and forwards for several minutes, without attempting to reach for the cup again. What does this tell us about the child's ability to drink from a cup? What factors might we have to take into account in order to assess this ability accurately? Consider some of the following.

1. Sight – Can the child see the cup and its position on the table? If not very well, have we used good contrast to help her? Is the position helpful? If the child has no sight, have we informed them that there is a cup there? Have we placed the cup appropriately for easy location?

2. Hearing – Did the child hear and process accurately our verbal instruction to drink? Was the child distracted by, for example, music coming from the next room? Is this, in fact, the reason for the rhythmical rocking?

3. Movement – Can the child reach for the cup independently? Can she lift the cup on location of it? Is this the best cup to use, or does she need a two-handled variety, a lid or spout? Can she transfer it from table to mouth without help? Have we used the right amount of liquid or will this amount spill?

4. Cognitive ability – Does the child recognise the object, a cup? Has the child picked up on the cues – sitting at a table, in the dining room, a cup in front of her?

5. Communication – Does the child understand what we have said, signed, communicated about having a drink?

6. Personal factors – Does the child want a drink? Does the child like the drink we have chosen? Does the child usually lift and drink from a cup, or is this unusual? Is the child in particularly poor health and is this affecting the present assessment?

7. Environmental factors – Is the child familiar with the room, the table, this particular place at the table, this cup? Will the child lift and drink from a cup anywhere or only in familiar surroundings?

These and many other factors may play an important part in assessing the child's ability to drink independently from a cup.

Our task, as coordinator of the multi-disciplinary team, is to weave together the information from other professionals with our own knowledge and understanding of the child to create a richer, fuller picture of the child and how he learns – a holistic profile. As the person who works most closely with the child, on a day to day basis, we are best placed to do this.

Think of a young/developmentally young deafblind child you know – imagine you were assessing their ability to (a) wash their hands independently, (b) use a switch or a touch screen on the computer, or (c) find their way to the school bus parked outside the door (choose the most appropriate of these or devise another, more appropriate task). What factors might you have to take into account when assessing their ability to carry out the task?

A familiar and trusted assessor

From the above, it will be clear that the person assessing the deafblind child must be one who knows the child well. Only then could all of the implications which may affect the assessment be taken into account. Similarly, it is important that the child is relaxed and at ease with the assessor so that a true reflection of their ability can be obtained. Any child may become disconcerted when asked to 'perform' for a stranger. For a deafblind child, this could be most distressing, particularly when explanations of who they are, what they are doing and why, are impossible.

Functional assessment

For the same reasons, our assessments must be functional. Extracting a deafblind child from the normal, routine situation to assess her ability to drink from a cup will cause confusion and frustration and results are likely to be no reflection of true ability.

> Instead of abstracting tasks from settings, functional assessment tries to structure the environment to offer opportunities for observing skills in practical use. Functional assessment approaches assume it is not possible to prescribe for each and every possible situation that may arise with a learner. (Aitken 1995, p. 9)

Three year old Neil was deafblind due to Maternal Rubella Sydrome. Despite a cataract in one eye, he made excellent use of his residual sight, visually exploring his environment and finding one thing after another to interest him. At his yearly paediatric check, the doctor was unsuccessfully trying to assess his visual memory by putting a toy car under a series of containers, to see if he could remember which one concealed the car. Neil was having none of this, and flitted from eye chart, to stethoscope, to angle-poise lamp in a flurry of excitement, sucking furiously at his dummy. His exasperated father eventually pulled the dummy from Neil's mouth, put it under a container, mixed them around and signed, 'Where's the dummy?' Neil recovered it in seconds!

This approach to assessment, of observing the learner's skills in practical use, lends itself to a much more reflective style of assessment. When a child's learning is assessed in a particular situation, with a particular educator, using particular resources, in a particular environment, then all of this criteria comes under observation and can be assessed. This promotes the holistic view of assessment discussed above, by encouraging the assessor to look closely at every aspect of the learning situation and to ask questions about how and why the child learns.

Video

The use of video can be invaluable here. Not only does it capture in a (fairly) unobtrusive way, the child as she puts skills into practical use, but also it captures all of the other criteria mentioned above and it can be played and replayed, analysed and discussed as often as required.

Another advantage of the video camera is that it allows the educator to move round in front of the child and view what is happening from this position instead, as is so often common when using the co-active or 'hands on' method, of constantly being positioned behind the child.

The writer had an uncomfortable, but valuable experience of this only a few months ago. Watching myself on video working co-actively with a child, it became apparent that the child was signing 'finished' over and over again. To my horror I heard myself say, 'Mark, is your hand itchy, will we give it a scratch and then we can get on?'! Not only was his signing as clear as day when viewed from the front, but his face registered his growing frustration with me as I misunderstood him time and time again!

The video camera, and the person operating the video camera, can provide an excellent opportunity for 'triangulation' – the process of comparing different views to reach a consensus of opinion about the skills and abilities of the child, where doubt exists. Clearly, this is desirable, but by no means always possible in a busy educational establishment. What is essential, is that our assessments are functional, that we create situations in which the deafblind learner can be assessed as he puts skills into practical use, in a familiar environment, and that we do not pluck the learner out of the normal routine situation in order to 'do' an assessment.

What do we assess?

Assessment and curriculum

Earlier in this section we looked at a number of reasons why we may wish to assess a child. All of these reasons were connected to the need to plan the teaching and learning that will take place with the deafblind child. Assessment goes hand in hand with curriculum. Our assessments will be used to inform our curriculum planning. The Scottish Education Department (SED) document, *Curriculum and Assessment in Scotland: a policy for the 90s* (1990) emphasises that clear planning creates the conditions for effective assessment. 'Planning provides a framework for building attainment outcomes and targets into existing processes of long term planning.'

We need to gather as much information as we can about the child and how the child learns, and then we need to relate this to the curriculum, to find out where the child is in each of the curricular areas and to plan our aims and objectives for our future work with her. It could be said, then, that there are two broad strands to assessment:

1. Factors relating to the child and how she attempts to:
   • find out information;
   • communicate with others;
   • move around the environment;

and,

2. Relating the outcomes of our assessment to the curriculum – planning next steps.

Factors relating to the child

Initial assessment

Initially, our assessments of a deafblind learner will be based on existing information on the child, from records and files completed by other professionals, and on our own observations of them. Parents and families will have a wealth of valuable information on the child, and it is a good idea to meet with and talk to them at this time.

Observing and assessing how deafblind children set about gathering information, how they move around their environment and how they communicate, will tell us a great deal about the deafblind child, will point us towards areas where more questions need to be asked about how they learn, and will reveal those areas where our intervention needs to be focused.

Individualised Educational Programme (IEP)

Seeking answers to the questions posed by our observations will inevitably lead to further and deeper questioning. This is what holistic assessment is all about. The answers will also begin to tell us what areas we, as educators, need to 'home in' on. Areas where the child has difficulties; areas where answers to the questions we ask are unclear; areas of social and self-help skills which are vital to the child's future independence; areas on which communication depends; areas of obvious interest and enjoyment to the child, will all be included in the child's IEP. Our knowledge and understanding of the child as an individual learner as well as our knowledge of the curriculum is vital if our educational programme is to be truly individualised.

The need for a framework

Working with and assessing deafblind children can often be an intuitive task. Establishing a warm and trusting relationship demands emotional input; methods and strategies used with the children, such as resonance and co-active movement, involve close (at times, maternal) contact; pupil–teacher ratios are low; involvement with the child's family is common, and relationships tend to go far beyond the usual pupil–teacher model. All of this means that, as educators, we carry around in our heads much more information about the child than we ever put down on paper. How often, after working with a child for some time, have we just 'felt' that they were not quite well? or just 'known' that they would thoroughly enjoy this? or just 'thought' that they were going to make the very move they just made?

This intuitive knowledge is both natural and understandable, given the relationship we must have with the deafblind child, but nevertheless we must attempt to find efficient ways of gathering together and recording as much information about the child as we can for our own use in curriculum planning, in reflection and analysis and for passing on to other professionals and to future educators.

In many establishments for deafblind children, files and records on the child abound! Because of their complex difficulties, deafblind children have usually been identified at an early age as having special educational needs. So professionals have been working with, assessing and recording information about the child, often for years, before we come to meet them. Medical reports, peripatetic and preschool reports, educational psychologist's reports, ophthalmological, audiological, speech and language, physiotherapy reports, Record of Needs or Statements may all exist on the child, each in their own named file, in their own locked drawer, in the locked filing cabinet, in the office, in the school, where no-one can get to them easily! Even when we can get to them, there are so many and we have so little time, that two days after reading them we've forgotten much of what they contained.

An assessment framework, designed specifically to focus on the type of information we need to have in order to assess deafblind children effectively, can greatly help here. A framework such as this, which can vary according to the needs of the school, and indeed, of the individual child, can help us to gather together in one document all of the pertinent information we require on the child, and can be held in the best place for such a document – in the hands of the key educator. In this way, it can readily be used for continuous assessment, for curriculum planning, for reference, for liaising with other professionals and, most importantly, to increase our own knowledge and understanding of the deafblind child and how that child learns.

So what type of information do we need to have about the deafblind child? What shape would this assessment framework take?

An assessment framework for deafblind learners

Let's think about those three areas of difficulty that we discussed earlier – finding out information, moving around the environment and communicating. What sensory, cognitive, physical, social and other skills and abilities do we use for each of these?

> Make three lists – finding out information, moving around and
> communicating – and jot down under each some of the sensory,
> cognitive, physical, social and other skills and abilities we use in order to
> carry out these functions.

It may be that sight and hearing were top of your list for all three. As babies and
young children, we gain most of our information about the world through these two
major distance senses. In deafblind children, there may be loss of or damage to both
of these senses, severely affecting how they gain information, communicate and
move around, and we must look very carefully not only at what the problems with
these senses are and how they make use of any residual sight or hearing that they may
have, but also how they use the other senses of touch, taste, smell and proprioception
(the sense by which we understand our body and its position and movement in space)
to compensate for any loss or damage to the major distance senses.

So, our assessment framework will look very closely at **vision, hearing and at
other senses**.

Vision
Ophthalmological reports will contain important information about the child's
sight, including the cause of the child's visual impairment, so this may be a good
place to start. Knowing about the cause of the child's visual impairment may help
us to place their difficulties with sight alongside the other difficulties they face and
give us a fuller picture of how they can be helped towards using their sight to access
information, move around and communicate.

We will need to know whether the child has a cortical visual impairment (CVI
– a problem resulting from damage to the visual cortex and/or the pathways to the
cortex) or an ocular visual loss (a sight problem resulting from damage to the eye
itself) as each of these may require quite different intervention approaches and
strategies. Knowing, for example, that a child has CVI will alert us to the
probability of the presence of additional disabilities (about 80 per cent of children
with CVI have additional difficulties).

We will need to know whether spectacles or other **low vision aids** have been
prescribed and whether these are used by the learner. Many deafblind children need
help in tolerating and accepting these, before they realise how much help they gain
from them.

The child's **functional vision** will need to be carefully assessed. We will want
to look in detail at their:

- visual field;
- visual acuity;

- contrast-sensitivity;
- binocular coordination;
- light/darkness adaptation;
- colour vision;

so that we have as full a picture as possible about what they are able to see and so that our intervention plans, the materials, equipment and resources we use, will help them to maximise their use of any residual sight.

Figure 4.2 I think I saw something right here!

Hearing

Here again, and for the same reasons as for vision, information on the *cause* of the hearing impairment will be important to have, as will any **audiological reports**. We will want to know whether the hearing impairment is due to a diagnosed hearing loss (a conductive or sensori-neural loss), or whether the problem is one of processing auditory information, as this will affect the teaching strategies and methods we use with the learner.

We will need to know about **hearing aids**, whether these are tolerated or used, what type of aid is used and what settings the child is comfortable with on the aid.

We will want to look at their **functional hearing**, assessing, for example, their

- awareness of sound;
- response to sound;
- location of sound;
- recognition of sound;
- understanding of sound;
- reproduction of sound.

We will want to look at **other senses** too, at touch, taste, smell and proprioception to find out how much information the child gains from these and how well these senses could be used *to compensate* for their difficulties with sight or hearing or both.

This sensory information, however, is not enough on its own. We must then put this information against our growing knowledge of the child as an individual to create a fuller picture of what all of this information means in terms of each unique learner.

> For example, Peter is visually impaired. He has good close vision for fine detail, and glasses improve this ability. He has problems with peripheral vision, though, and with distance vision, so he uses a cane for mobility. Peter is quick and curious by nature, he darts around and suffers many bumps and bangs as he does so.

> Mick on the other hand, is blind. He, too, uses a cane for mobility. He has neither close, peripheral nor distance vision. Yet Mick can move around his environment more safely and more efficiently than his sighted peer. He has learned to use his sense of touch to translate information about his environment from his cane. He has learned about rails on stairs, about doorways and how they can be dangerous, about echo-location and the information that a stamped foot or a clapped hand can give, and he has learned that moving slowly and deliberately is the safest way to go.

Gathering information about the child's sensory abilities is crucial, the amount of residual sight and hearing that the child has will greatly affect their abilities across the curriculum. But we must match this information to our knowledge of the child as an individual learner if our assessments are to be holistic.

Cognitive ability

Cognitive ability will probably have been high on each of our three lists too. We need to have some ability to *retain* the information we gain and to *use* this if we are to move around our environment and communicate. So we will want to assess the child's

- awareness – of people, objects, events, places;
- attention – ability to attend to/concentrate on a task;

- memory – ability to anticipate, predict, store information in the short term/long term;
- recognition – of people/places/objects;
- curiosity – ability to explore, awareness of cause and effect, problem-solving skills;
- imitation – ability to imitate, copy, turn-take;
- classification – ability to organise information, sort or match;
- symbolic understanding – ability to understand symbols, object symbols, tactile symbols, drawings, signs, written words, spoken words;
- number concepts – understanding of number concepts.

When assessing a child's cognitive skills it is important to keep in mind the effects that a dual or multi-sensory impairment will have, both on her intellectual growth and on her ability to demonstrate what she knows. Blind children, for example, may only really know and understand those objects which they have actually experienced, used, touched, tasted, smelled, heard. If additional disabilities are present, and the child can perhaps neither listen to, hear about nor successfully explore the object through touch, their concept of the object will be severely limited. Lack of understanding about objects and people in their world may often have more to do with sensory deprivation than with intellectual problems. They may also have difficulty in showing their understanding. Lack of, or 'inappropriate', response to stimuli need not mean that the child has no awareness or understanding of it. The problem may be that we do not recognise their response as such.

Communication

An ability to communicate will obviously be important in finding out information, and communicating with others will be a strong motivational factor in moving around our environment.

Given the importance of communication in the education of deafblind learners, we have devoted a complete chapter to communication (see Chapter 2).

Generally speaking, in assessing the communication of deafblind learners, it may be helpful to view communication as a spectrum of movements, behaviours and codes spanning two broad areas: **functional communication** (including pre-intentional and intentional communication) and **linguistic communication** (the use of formal or standardised modes of communication).

In functional communication we will be concerned with assessing:

- if and how the child **expresses emotions, needs and wants**;
- if and how the child **attempts to get the attention of others**;
- whether the child is **interested in**, or **takes part in** any form of **reciprocal interaction**;

- whether the child **initiates** communication, or only **responds to another's attempts** at communication;
- whether the child **associates** any gestures, signs, pictures, objects or words with an activity or person.

As we assess their functional communication, we may be thinking about future communication systems for the child, assessing which systems might possibly be open to them. This will mean looking at their functional communication alongside their other abilities and their difficulties. Will they have enough vision to see signs, for example, and would their movement potential allow for forming them? Might they see pictures or the written word, do they appear to have the intellectual ability to understand these? Is their hearing acute enough to hear the spoken word, are their vocalisations intentional and appropriate? Will tactile methods be the most likely route for them? Might they eventually be able to access Moon or braille?

Asking these kinds of questions will help us to shape the form of our future teaching and learning in the area of communication.

In assessing functional communication it is important also to bear in mind that our ability to interpret behaviour as communication will have a significant influence on our assessment of the child's communication skills. Much more is said about this in Chapter 2.

In linguistic communication, we will be looking at the *forms* of communication used, the *functions that language serves* for the child and the *level of language* used by the child. We will want to assess, for example, *whether* and *how* he can:

- express wants and needs;
- carry out instructions;
- answer questions;
- give information;
- have events, situations explained to him;
- explain what he is doing;
- refer back to previous events;
- 'talk about' forthcoming events;
- seek information by asking questions;
- express emotions.

Communication permeates every aspect of the teaching and learning of deafblind pupils. It is crucial that an in-depth assessment of the problems and possibilities of communication facing the deafblind learner is undertaken.

Physical difficulties
The ability to move will have a significant effect on gaining information, communicating and, obviously, on moving around our environment.

Physiotherapy reports may contain important information about the child's potential for movement, about dangers to the child associated to certain movements and about medical factors relating to the management of their physical impairments, so our assessment of their physical impairments may begin here. We will want to look at the difficulties they have and how we can increase their potential for movement through the use of specialised resources such as switches, adaptations to wheelchairs, specialised furniture and equipment. We will want to look at the limitations and the possibilities for communication associated to their physical impairments and the impact this may have on other areas of learning, such as eating, dressing and other self-help skills.

Again, our information in this area must be looked at in the light of all of the other information on the child.

Socialisation

The child's awareness of and ability to socialise with others will impact directly on communication, will have a strong influence on her will to move around and will certainly affect her ability to access information, so this will no doubt have featured on your lists too.

In assessing socialisation skills we will want to look at:

* the child's **awareness** of **self** and of **others**;
* what form **the child's interaction with others** takes;
* whether they prefer interaction **with adults or other children**;
* whether they display **attachments** to others;
* their level of **independence** or **dependence** on others.

Again, our assessments will take into consideration information from many other areas. A child who cannot communicate effectively, for example, will clearly have problems socialising. If the child is wheelchair-bound, opportunities for socialising will be limited and dependent upon others. Their ability to see and hear others will greatly affect their motivation to socialise, as will their intellectual ability, their awareness of and ability to understand attempts at social interaction.

Personal factors

As well as this, we will want to have some **personal information** about the learner, their likes and dislikes, strengths and areas where development is required. We may want to look at what is helpful to learning, for example, music or rhyme, a favourite toy close to hand. Other things may be unhelpful, bright lights for example, or too much background noise. We will want to know something about the **character** or **personality** of the child, what motivates them, what frightens them, what makes them laugh. We will need to have some idea of where they are in their **self-help skills**, whether they can eat and drink, toilet, wash and dress themselves.

Until we can add our own knowledge of them to our profile, much of this information will come from **parents**. Identifying parents as valuable members of a deafblind child's team is crucial. In most cases, it is parents who have been the **key educators** for their child for years before they come to school, and recognising the knowledge and understanding which they can bring is fundamental to good teamwork.

As well as from parents, we can gain much critical background information from **medical reports** and from other **school reports**.

Medical history

The **cause of the child's impairments** will give us some insights into the difficulties that the child is likely to face (e.g. in CHARGE association, medical problems, including feeding difficulties, may feature largely; in rubella, cataracts are likely, as are heart and respiratory problems, etc.). It would be very important to know about any **medical problems** the child may have and how these are to be managed in school.

Knowing about **extended periods of illness or hospitalisation** may help us to understand emotional problems and/or eating problems in children who have been, for example, tube-fed.

Educational history

It will be important to look at **reports from other schools**, preschool reports, educational psychologists' reports and those of any peripatetic teachers. If there is a **Record** or **Statement of Needs**, this will be important too. Brief, pertinent statements from, or summaries of these reports could be included in the framework.

Environmental factors

An important feature of any assessment of deafblind learners will be to look at how the child copes in different environments. Deafblind children often have great difficulty in generalising skills and abilities. Skills learned at school may not automatically be transferred to home, residential or respite centres, and vice-versa. Our assessments will need to look closely at this aspect of their learning to discover what features of the environment appear to aid or inhibit learning. We will want to know, for example:

- whether they are **aware** of different environments;
- if they seem to have **preferences** for particular environments, and why this might be so;
- whether particular environments appear to **suit their learning needs** (e.g. an active, highly stimulating environment; a quiet, subdued atmosphere);
- how they respond to **changes** in a familiar environment.

School-based factors

Factors relating to the **school**, where much intensive learning will take place, need to be assessed also for their impact and suitability to the learner:

- the **ethos, character** of the school may be important (an informal, friendly atmosphere may suit the needs of some children; a more formal, highly-structured environment may suit others);
- factors relating to the **attitudes, skills and training of staff** will be important (the learner may need a skilled signer, for example, or someone with knowledge of Moon or braille; personalities of staff, their attitudes and how these impact on the learner may be very important);
- how the child responds to **changes in staff** and to **changes in curriculum** may need to be considered;
- whether the child needs **specific resources**, and if these are available in the school.

Monitoring progress

Having gathered together all of the pertinent information as suggested above, we should have an in-depth, holistic profile of the learner. From this we can plan our teaching and learning to ensure that the educational intervention and interaction taking place with the child are of the highest quality.

Our next task is to ensure that this quality is maintained by monitoring the progress being made by the child. This leads us on to look at the second broad strand to assessment, that of 'Relating this to the curriculum – Planning next steps'.

Relating the outcomes of our assessment to the curriculum – Planning next steps

An intrinsic part of all of our assessments will be gauging where the child is in each of the curricular areas. We need to have a good idea of where they are if we are to plan appropriate next steps in teaching and learning.

Curricular guidelines

In Chapter 5 we will be looking more closely at curricular guidelines and frameworks, both in Scotland and in England and Wales, but for the purposes of this chapter, we can take a very general look at them.

In Scotland, the '5–14 Guidelines on Curriculum and Assessment' is the framework used for curriculum planning, development and assessment in schools across the country. Most deafblind children will follow an elaborated 5–14 curriculum (SCCC 1992–94) – a curriculum based on the principles of the national guidelines, but elaborated to suit the very different needs of children with such complex learning difficulties.

In England and Wales, the National Curriculum is the vehicle used to plan teaching and learning across the educational spectrum. This system is often viewed as a much more prescriptive, and therefore less flexible one, although recent revisions have introduced some greater flexibility.

The shared philosophy behind the introduction of national curricula was to ensure breadth and balance for all in the planning, delivery and evaluation of the curriculum. Whether a national curriculum does (or indeed could) achieve this aim for children with special educational needs, continues to be a matter for debate both north and south of the border.

However, whether in Scotland, using an elaborated 5–14 curriculum, or in England and Wales, using the revised National Curriculum, the individual needs of the children with whom we work will be met within the context of a planned curriculum.

Our assessments will reveal the stages they have reached in each of the areas within this curriculum and from there, we can plan next steps to take with them. In most schools, long-term aims or goals and short-term objectives or steps are used to plan this future work with the child. Generally speaking, this means that we set for the child a list of realistic goals, based on our knowledge of their ability, and then plan a series of learning steps which will lead them towards achieving these goals.

Developmental guides and checklists

In planning next steps to take with the child, it is often helpful to use developmental guides and checklists. These may point the direction we should take, but they must be used sensitively and with a good amount of reflection on the part of the educator. They will include many of the hierarchical skills and knowledge that young children will acquire but, as stated earlier, deafblind children may differ radically in their routes towards a particular goal, so individual adaptations as well as further breakdown of steps to achieve a goal will often be required.

Developmental guides such as 'The Oregon Project' (Brown et al. 1978), the 'Portage Early Education Programme' (White and Cameron 1987) and the 'Callier Azusa Scale' (Stillman 1978) are, however, excellent tools for reference in planning aims. Each of these divide early development into five or six different categories – in Oregon, for example, these are: cognitive; language; self-help; socialisation; fine motor and gross motor. Skills are listed in a hierarchical order, giving educators a good idea of the developmental route taken by most children. The Oregon Project is designed for visually impaired and blind preschool children, the Portage Programme for preschool children with learning difficulties and, although the Callier Azusa Scale is designed with deafblind learners in mind, the author stresses that it should not be used as a teaching curriculum, but rather as a guide for assessment purposes.

These types of developmental checklists can often create an oversimplification of the skills involved. It is up to educators to stand back and assess how useful, appropriate and functional these skills are. Real life tasks are very complex. Skills need to be practised in many different situations as deafblind children may not automatically transfer skills they have learned in one situation to another.

Alana was a young deafblind adult who was nearing the end of her school career. Parents, the school, Sense (The National Deafblind and Rubella Organisation), social workers and other agencies had worked collaboratively to ensure that Alana's future needs were being met in an exciting and innovatory way. A self-contained flat was built for Alana by extending her parent's home to include a bedsit, containing kitchen, working and relaxing facilities and a bathroom. Alana would have the best of both worlds – a good measure of independence, with her parents close-at-hand. Staff at the school had worked for several years to prepare Alana for this. Daily living skills had formed a large part of her curriculum. But these were skills that could be achieved in school, using the school microwave, the school washing machine, travelling and shopping in the school area. During her final year, staff travelled down to Alana's home, one day per week, to ensure that these skills could be successfully transferred to her new home. And it took the best part of that year to do this.

Self-help skills can be at a very high level within the familiar routine of school, but the crucial question is – can the same skills be used appropriately in real life settings? Meeting a new person, going into a new building, going away for the weekend, buying new shoes, going to a brother's engagement party – all make demands on children's concepts and skills. This is real life and as such is always the final assessment of what a child has or has not learned.

Summarising progress

Using aims and objectives is a good way of monitoring short-term progress. If the child we are working with is mastering the carefully planned and graded steps leading towards our stated aims, we can be fairly confident that some progress is being made.

But we need to look also at the wider picture. In many special schools, educational reviews are held once or twice per school year. A good way of monitoring long-term progress is to summarise what has been achieved by the child over the course of several reviews. By summarising, we mean using brief, but critical statements which illustrate what has been achieved by the child in each of the curricular areas over an extended period. This long-term monitoring will hopefully give us a clearer picture of areas where consistent progress is made or where there are clear difficulties. We can then begin to ask crucial questions about why this may be.

The reflective practitioner

Throughout this section on assessment, we have tried to impress on the reader the importance of being a reflective and analytical practitioner. This is important in every area of education – in the education of deafblind learners it is crucial. There are no easy answers. For each individual deafblind learner, we must build up a bank of knowledge about how and why they learn, and then we must *use* that knowledge to make learning more effective. To do this, we must enter the world of the deafblind child. We must try to see the world as they do by constantly asking *why?* and *how?*

A 'good' assessment tool can help us to seek answers to these questions, but it can only help, it will not assess for us. We have tried to outline what form an assessment framework for deafblind learners might take and we hope that it may be of some value to those working with deafblind children. But it is important to remember that it is our skills as thoughtful and reflective educators that will ultimately make the difference between a good and a not-so-good assessment.

References

Aitken, S. (1995) 'Assessment of Deafblind Learners', in Etheridge, D. (ed.) *The Education of Dual Sensory Impaired Children: Recognising and developing ability*. London: David Fulton Publishers.

Brown, D., Simmons, V. and Methvin, J. (1978) *The Oregon Project for Visually Impaired and Blind Preschool Children*. Jackson County Education Service.

Coupe-O'Kane, J., Porter, J. and Taylor, A. (1994) 'Meaningful Content and Contexts for Learning', in Coupe-O'Kane, J. and Smith, B. (eds) *Taking Control: Enabling people with learning difficulties*. London: David Fulton Publishers.

McInnes, J. M. and Treffry, J. A. (1982) *Deafblind Infants and Children: A developmental guide*. Toronto: University of Toronto Press.

Scottish Consultative Council on the Curriculum (1992-94) *Special Educational Needs within the 5–14 Curriculum: Support for learning*. Dundee: SCCC.

SED (1990) *Curriculum and Assessment in Scotland: A policy for the 90s. Assessment 5–14*. Edinburgh: Scottish Education Department.

Stillman, R. (1978) *Callier Azusa Scale*. University of Texas.

White, M. and Cameron, R. J. (1987) *Portage Early Education Programme: A practical manual*. Berkshire: NFER-Nelson.

CHAPTER 5

Curricular frameworks

Olga Miller and Marion McClarty

PART 1: ENGLAND AND WALES

Introduction

This section is based on the outcomes of a research project jointly funded by the Department for Education and Employment (DfEE) and Sense (a voluntary organisation representing the interests of adults and children who are deafblind). The project team comprised Dr Jill Porter, Laura Pease and Olga Miller. The project focused on curriculum access for pupils who are deafblind and grew out of the follow-up to a three-year DfEE-funded national programme which aimed to improve provision for this group of pupils. Fifty-seven teachers and a total of 82 pupils took part in the project. Although the project finished in 1997, I have attempted to relate its findings to the current context by cross-referencing them to recent developments.

During the course of the DfEE programme Local Education Authorities (LEAs) in England were encouraged to form consortia in order set up regional provision for pupils considered deafblind. Thus, a wide range of initiatives was developed over the three years. While some regions built on existing good practice, many developments were totally new. Specialist training became a core area of activity in a large number of these new developments. One of the main aims of the research was, therefore, to draw on the training and experience of teachers who had been involved in the national programme. The objectives of the research were to:

- gather information on the range of strategies employed by teachers providing specifically for pupils who are considered deafblind;
- identify how teachers make decisions about the type of strategy to use with a particular pupil or group of pupils, with reference to modifications and adaptations, including the parents and pupils in the process;

- examine the effectiveness of the range of different strategies used with different pupil groups on the basis of criteria identified by teachers in their decision-making.

Context

The introduction of a National Curriculum in 1988 and the expectation that it would apply to all school age children introduced a variety of dilemmas. There was much scepticism about the value of what initially seemed an over-prescriptive and bureaucratic model. Many professionals were suspicious about the intentions behind its introduction. It was felt that a National Curriculum was little more than a political tool devised to undermine professionalism and exert control. However, there was also a long tradition of debate around the merits of such a system as a means of reducing inequalities and as a way of ensuring coherence and progression for an increasingly mobile population of pupils. From the beginning there were difficulties in the reality of providing access to the National Curriculum for all pupils. In the main these difficulties arose from the linear progression conceptualised through the levels of the curriculum and encapsulated within the Attainment Targets. Because the curriculum was founded on the basis of age related norms and took its starting point as a chronological/developmental age of five many pupils with special educational needs were immediately disadvantaged. The majority of these pupils were being educated in special schools. A tension therefore emerged which was particularly acute in the special school sector: on the one hand schools saw access to the National Curriculum as a basic right for their pupils but on the other hand felt its starting point bore no relation to the needs of their pupils (it also has to remembered that there were fears of a return to pre 1971 when many such pupils were considered ineducable). The debate became especially tense when these schools were inspected by the new Office for Standards in Education (OFSTED) and criticised for failing to implement the National Curriculum.

In the decade since the introduction of the National Curriculum major changes have occurred (not least a change in government). However, the new government is strongly committed to inclusion and sees the presence of a National Curriculum as an important force in the pursuance of an inclusive society. There have also been modifications to the curriculum and more promised in the future. But at the time we began our research there was an unclear picture of what individual teachers were doing to enable their pupils to access the National Curriculum. Some of the early discussions taking place in special schools suggested that teachers felt the process was largely tokenistic. In the beginning these seemed lone voices but gradually there has been some response from the policy-makers, albeit more of a compromise than a rethink. Bearing this in mind it was heartening to hear a definition of an inclusive curriculum given at a talk at London University in 1999 by an official of the Qualifications and Curriculum Authority (QCA), Judith Wade: 'A total curriculum framework (of statutory and non-statutory provision) which allows each school to plan and provide a programme appropriate to the needs of its pupils.'

In response to the concerns of the special school sector, QCA commissioned the National Foundation for Education Research (NFER) to carry out a study which looked at assessment and target-setting. This provided the opportunity for schools taking part in the pilot to exert some influence over ensuing guidance. In general there began to be evidence of more awareness of special needs in documentation from statutory bodies (though it has to be said that such awareness was limited in the case of the literacy and numeracy hours). This awareness had not been a feature of official publications from the late 1980s and early 1990s. A broader acknowledgement now exists that learning for pupils extends beyond the classroom environment. There is also evidence of understanding based on more ecological foundations, which has helped to establish the place of what are now considered essential skills and activities. Personal and Social Education was thus recognised as a vital component of the special school curriculum (while being squeezed out of the mainstream curriculum) and positively viewed within the more inclusive context of citizenship. However, some fundamental dilemmas remain unresolved. How do we reconcile individual needs and education programmes with whole-school target setting (and get data worth having)? Can meaningful comparisons be made across schools? How can value added components be calculated? What will help teachers to provide successfully for deafblind pupils within the context of inclusion?

The pupils

Although the research project focused on deafblindness it was soon obvious that there was little consensus about the needs of pupils considered deafblind. Many pupils described as deafblind were also described as multi-sensory impaired. No one condition or factor was common to all children with the exception of a need to develop or enhance communication. All pupils required individual attention to meet their specific communication needs (for some pupils this meant the development of a sense of self and other, while those with less complex needs perhaps required a specific software package for transcription of braille or production of large print). Many pupils also required support for their physical disabilities. The population of children who are deafblind is disparate and difficult to quantify. For this reason the research team worked to the following definitions (based on a definition provided by the New England Center for Deaf-Blind Services):

1. Individuals who are both peripherally deaf or severely hearing impaired and peripherally blind or severely visually impaired according to definitions of 'legal' blindness and deafness; acuity to be measured or estimated in conjunction with a recognition of level of cognitive development supported by medical description of pathology.
2. Individuals who have sensory impairments of both vision and hearing, one of which is severe and the other moderate to severe.
3. Individuals who have impairments of both vision and hearing, one of which is severe, and additional learning and/or language disabilities which result in need for special services.
4. Individuals who have impairments of both vision and hearing of a relatively mild to moderate degree and additional learning and/or language disabilities, which result in need for special services or who have been diagnosed as having impairments which are progressive in nature.
5. Individuals who are severely multiply handicapped due to generalised central nervous system dysfunction, who also exhibit measurable impairments of both vision and hearing.

Provision

Although increasing numbers of children who are considered deafblind are included within mainstream provision the majority is still to be found in schools providing for learning disabilities or physical disability. Some are also placed in specialist provision for sensory impairments. In the main, the population identified by the research were deafblind but with additional, profound and complex needs. At a time of uncertainty for many small, specialist schools there is a growing tendency for LEAs to conflate provision in order to provide some economy of scale. Specialist provision is therefore increasingly focused on complex needs. This has significant implications for the teachers involved. Since the research was carried out there has been a pattern of subsuming a wide range of special needs under the label of learning disabilities.

What can we learn from research?

Educationalists are being faced by greater and greater challenges. Accountability and the need to be explicit about expectation and methods can sometimes stifle a more instinctive approach. Greater emphasis on the measurement of outcomes has made teachers wary about what they write in reports or review notes. However, for pupils with more complex needs we require a balance between the instinctive and prescriptive. This is largely inspiration backed up by strong evidence. Although research is sometimes considered as an impenetrable collection of statistics it can also offer lessons from practice. A sharing of ideas can lessen the isolation of many specialists. The research project hoped to link theory and practice by building on the daily work of teachers. To this end, teachers kept a teaching log on their work with two deafblind pupils during the course of a week. This obviously placed a considerable burden on already pressured individuals but barring accident and illness all managed to log a week's work.

Teachers' logs

Teachers' logs provided a fascinating insight into the complex decision-making which lies behind even the most instinctive approach. All over the country we saw examples of how teachers were tackling the implementation of a National Curriculum. What was particularly fascinating was the diversity of what was happening. Because no consensus existed about what should be taught at levels below the first level of the curriculum, teachers found ingenious ways of grouping activities under subject headings. Therefore, when one looked across the country it seemed that for those teachers working in levels below the range predicted for a typical five-year-old, the subject focus of the National Curriculum was open to much interpretation. The end result was a lack of coherence nationally. While it is likely that students benefited from this individualisation of the curriculum, charting progress was often difficult.

Key components of the curriculum

Teachers were asked by the researchers to identify what they felt were key components of the curriculum for children who are deafblind. Responses reflected the variety of settings in which the children were educated but also the delicate balance which has to be struck between individual entitlement and whole-school planning and management. Some teachers took what could be described as a bottom-up approach, which focused on individual needs such as the development of autonomy and motivation. Other teachers took a more system-orientated focus with particular reference being given to the organisation of the curriculum. Overall, analysis of teachers' planning documentation revealed a two-tiered structure, which recognised the need for distinctiveness at different levels. These levels included the need for specificity in relation to content, organisation and delivery. These aspects can be seen to relate to the five key strategies identified in 'Support for Learning' (SCCC 1993): Differentiation, Individualisation, Adaptation, Elaboration and Enhancement. The three main approaches centred on:

- National Curriculum + support (e.g. braille, signing);
- Modified National Curriculum (working at levels below his/her key stage + some additional curriculum subjects such as independent living skills, mobility, etc.);
- Developmental Curriculum (or other curricula) and/or working within the National Curriculum within or below level 1.

The range of additional subject areas which teachers use are largely aimed at helping the child develop specific developmental areas such as fine motor or mobility skills. School timetables differ enormously in how they delineate subject areas. Because many pupils who are deafblind follow individual timetables it is often difficult to gain a broader perspective. However, the following case histories illustrate what the different approaches to the curriculum meant when put in practice.

The National Curriculum and support

Hazel attends her local mainstream school. This is a large, single sex comprehensive set in its own grounds. Until recently it was Grant Maintained. The school caters for a wide catchment area and has a high percentage of pupils from ethnic minorities. It is a few minutes from the centre of a large city and has many of the problems associated with inner city provision. There is a large special needs department that is managed by the school Special Educational Needs Coordinator (SENCO). The special needs department is housed in three classrooms and pupils attend for specific help to support their in-class work. Good facilities are available for the production of large print versions of teaching materials. Recording and computer equipment is also available to provide visual and auditory enhancement. Hazel is developing good keyboard skills. All pupils follow the National Curriculum and there are no disapplications. Hazel is at Key Stage 3 and works within the expected range of the curriculum for her Key Stage. She has a specially trained individual support teacher and support from her local sensory service. Hazel's visual and hearing loss is considerable although she uses speech and is able to access large print. Hazel is given support within the classroom with her peers for the majority of the week. However, she is withdrawn for individual sessions when the visual tasks are difficult and she needs more time to look at specially produced large print maps or diagrams.

Hazel says that she is happy attending a mainstream school. Her elder sister is also a pupil. Hazel feels that she has to work harder than her peers do because it takes her longer to look at things. She sometimes finds it difficult to hear if the lesson is too noisy and teachers vary in how much they prepare the work in advance.

There is good communication between the SENCO and Hazel's individual support teacher. This means that most difficulties are dealt with promptly. Although Hazel would like to be more independent this seems to be more a problem at home rather than at school. Hazel is the youngest of four siblings and her older brothers and sisters are very protective of her. This means that she does not go out much at home and she does complain of feeling bored at weekends. Hazel's family is very supportive of the school and is very involved with Hazel's schoolwork. Hazel's ambition is to become a teacher. She particularly enjoyed taking part in training sessions organised to help teachers and pupils understand her needs.

Modified national curriculum

Steven attends a special school for pupils who have a physical disability and associated learning difficulties. The school is on the edge of a large city and has a roll of 70 pupils and covers all key stages. There is a unit for pupils who have multi-sensory impairments. The unit caters for pupils who have a combination of visual and hearing loss. Steven is one of eight pupils. Staffing for the unit includes two teachers, two full-time assistants and two part-time assistants. The unit is separate from the main body of the school but shares some facilities. One of the unit teachers also works in the main school so there are strong links. Steven's teacher describes the specific aim of the unit as being to give pupils their entitlement to the National Curriculum at their own level and correct Key Stage differentiated to provide access. The organisation of the curriculum is much as a mainstream school. Steven, like Hazel, is at Key Stage 3 although operationally he works at level 1–2 at Key Stage 2. Steven is able to read print but has a profound hearing loss. Steven's Individual Education Programme (IEP) covers National Curriculum programmes of study and targets are set which are negotiated with Steven. In addition to the National Curriculum subjects Steven follows two supplementary areas. These areas are augmentative communication and study skills. The overall balance of Steven's programme is weighted towards English, which gives scope for increased work on communication. Steven uses total communication, which includes gesture, British Sign Language and fingerspelling and some limited oral response. Environmental adaptations include task lighting and large print. To support Steven's communication a range of picture symbols are also used. Steven is a keen football fan and is particularly interested in following the progress of his favourite football team. He is very sociable and outgoing and is happy to work with others in the group who may need more help. Sometimes Steven does become frustrated when he has been concentrating for long periods without a break. Part of the work on study skills is to enable Steven to know when he needs to take a break and switch from one activity to another. Steven's teacher has a carefully planned range of activities, which allow him choice and variety in method and approach but which are differentiated to support the same learning outcome. She has also been careful to reduce distraction and discourages over-reliance on adult support.

Steven is happy in the Unit but does indicate he would like more contact with peers of the same age. Links have been established with a local mainstream school and Steven attends some practical sessions such as Art. Steven is an only child and his parents are particularly worried about post-school provision. Steven has indicated he would like to go to college when he leaves school but is not sure what his ultimate ambition is.

Figure 5.1 Learning within the National Curriculum

A developmental curriculum

Emma attends a special school for pupils with learning difficulties. The school is situated in a pleasant, leafy suburb. There are around 80 pupils in all and the school is additionally resourced to cater for a small number of pupils considered to require specialist approaches to meet their sensory needs. Like Hazel and Steven, Emma is at Key Stage 3. However, Emma is working at a level well below the (expected) National Curriculum level for her chronological age. Emma is congenitally deafblind and suffers from a moderate physical disability that to some extent limits her independent mobility. Emma is taught by a teacher trained to work with pupils who are deafblind. There are six other pupils in the group. In addition to the teacher there are two support workers. The main emphasis of the curriculum for Emma is the development of communication. A total communication approach is used with the emphasis on signing and fingerspelling. A simple vocabulary is the focus of each activity and is context based. The class teacher is sensitive to Emma's need for security and consistency and is very experienced in work with pupils who are deafblind. Emma's individual programme emphasises the need for a balance between challenge and security. Emma is happy to explore her environment and uses her personalised corner of the classroom as her reference point. In this specifically dedicated space Emma has a large box (big enough for her to crawl into) and a range of familiar objects which she organises. Emma retreats into the box if she is tired or feeling confused or stressed. The majority of her time is spent within the general environment but knowing that her defensible space is available gives Emma the confidence to face challenges. The teacher wanted to upgrade the box but Emma resisted and made it clear that the old cardboard box was her preferred option. Emma's orientation is excellent and her general approach to tasks indicates a high level of problem solving. Emma has good relationships with key staff members and is able to anticipate routines and explore new objects with interest and purpose.

Emma's teacher recognises that Emma is far more advanced in her symbolic communication than the other pupils in the class and has recommended that Emma transfer to specialist provision, which can offer a residential component. Emma's family finds it difficult to deal with her needs at home. The summer holidays are particularly troublesome for the whole family. Some respite care is available but only on a limited basis. When left at home Emma reverts to self-stimulation and has little interaction with others. This regression to self-stimulation means that Emma's progress overall is limited by the effect of holidays. Emma's parents are aware of the problem but do not feel they have the emotional resources to do more at home. Emma is the eldest of three children (the youngest is not yet two years of age). Emma does not use any adapted equipment beyond what would normally be available within a special school environment for learning disabilities. This means that there is a wide range of everyday and 'found' objects such as stones from the beach. Emma spends time exploring these objects which are changed to suit the theme of each particular activity.

Target-setting

In 1998 QCA and the DfEE published guidance on target-setting for schools. This was followed by more specific guidance on curriculum access published in 1999.

There is now more explicit guidance on the underpinning levels of the curriculum. These levels include a more developmental baseline with three levels common to all subject areas. The other change is the inclusion of Personal and Social Development as a core element of the curriculum. In Scotland the additional special needs guidance on the 5–14 Curriculum Framework takes a similar developmental approach. There is still much left to the skills of individual teachers and much discussion to be had about the relative starting points of the new guidance. Of major concern is that neither Scottish nor English descriptors recognise the possible implications of a sensory loss (although well over 50 per cent of children in specialist provision for learning disabilities are likely to have some form of sensory loss or processing problem). A further examination of such developmental models highlights other inconsistencies. On the positive side such documents arise out of a wish to provide a route for pupils with complex needs and do try to address some of the concerns raised by teachers and carers. However, the issues raised by the research are still unresolved. While the developmental model offers a rough guide for schools to give a general view about the baseline functioning of their general population it does not resolve the difficulties of a curriculum model which assumes a linear hierarchy leading to subject-specific outcomes.

Teaching strategies

Although teaching strategies have been the focus of much study over many years, the introduction of Individual Education Programmes has emphasised the need for teachers to be explicit about the strategies they use. The research defined a strategy as a specific teaching approach or approaches used with deafblind pupils. In order to gain an overview of the range of strategies involved, the research team devised a system of coding strategies. Firstly, strategies were grouped into two major strands, 'on the one hand those strategies which could be seen to be related primarily to the process of pedagogy and, on the other hand, those which underpinned the process of the organisation of learning' (Porter *et al.* 1997, p. 18). From these two main strands a further 11 sub-groups were identified. Within the pedagogic range were strategies which:

- promoted successful task outcome such as fading, errorless discrimination, physical prompts;
- provided access to tasks and task completion such as joint action routines, massage, sensory stimulation;
- concerned formal communication such as writing, the use of questions and signing.

Those strategies primarily concerned with the organisation of learning were those which:

- were concerned with auditory or visual access such as particular lighting, aids, physical positioning;
- related to structure such as musical prompts, objects of reference, pupil grouping, the use of scripts;
- facilitated access through alternative modalities such as tactile modification or enhancement.

Teachers used a large number of strategies; the project identified a total of 145. Individual teachers used around 30 during the period logged. Strategies came from a variety of sources. A lot depended on the initial training of teachers and where they currently worked. For instance, teachers working in specialist settings for sensory impairment used more strategies which focused on the presentation of a task and formal systems of communication. Strategy use also obviously depended on the level of functioning of the child and also on the levels of staffing available. Many strategies required one to one support, particularly when pupils were operating at developmental levels (pre-level 1). The most frequently used strategies across all settings included: objects of reference, co-active movement, hand over hand, structured routines and smell cues.

Those strategies which teachers identified as being most effective varied according to the functional levels of the child concerned, as well as their sensory impairments. What was surprising was the popularity of music both as a means of structuring the day and as scaffolding for other strategies such as co-active movement. After close examination of such dual-purpose strategies it became clear that some strategies were overarching. These were termed meta-strategies. Objects of reference would also be considered a meta-strategy because their use facilitated the use of other strategies.

It is important that teachers are able to draw on a wide range of strategies, from the more generic to the highly specialised. Teachers are required to adapt or develop an approach to meet the needs of an individual pupil within the context of a particular setting. A successful IEP is likely to be clear about how strategies relate to the teaching activity and to the individual targets set. Knowledge of a wide range of strategies has to be underpinned by an understanding of relevant theory to ensure that teachers are able to make adaptations in accordance with a child's developmental and other needs.

Thoughts for the new millennium

In the short time since the completion of the research project I have been lucky enough to visit many schools catering for children considered deafblind/multi-sensory impaired. The level of staffing required to implement particular strategies has often not been available. Teachers have to try to find other approaches. Because, as we identified in the research, teachers mainly learn about strategies by word of mouth, there is sometimes a lack of understanding about underpinning theory. Recently I have seen teachers keenly developing standardised objects of reference for a whole school, thus completely missing the link between pre-symbolic and symbolic levels of communication (see Chapter 2). On the surface, being able to apply a strategy across a whole school seems an attractive thing to do. It cuts down staff time and gives staff the opportunity to use these objects as part of circle time, etc. In the light of such basic confusion perhaps it is opportune to reflect on the reality of the population currently in specialist provision and access for staff to training and development. It is also to be hoped that there will be more emphasis on links between special needs and the whole school improvement movement. At the moment such links are flimsy to say the least.

Teaching environment

It is now rare to find specific provision for children considered deafblind. Most are to be found in integrated classrooms within schools for severe and complex needs. Because, overall, the population of specialist provision is highly dependent it is likely that nearly all pupils require one to one support. Indeed, many pupils will not have developed a basic concept of self and other. Stress levels among staff are often high. Staff shortages are common. The specialist classroom of the 1990s bears little relation to the specialist deafblind provision in Holland and Canada in the 1970s and 1980s, which evolved many of the strategies in use today. Those pupils able to use formal signing who were the bedrock of earlier provision are more often included within mainstream provision and ironically more easily obtain one to one support than their peers in special schools.

What is now commonplace in most specialist provision is a teaching environment where a staff is faced with highly dependent pupils who require extensive support for medical and other needs. The relationship between clinical and other types of input is often part of an uneasy alliance with education. Specialist training is expensive and under new types of devolved funding many small special schools struggle to afford to train teachers except in out of school hours.

There is often little opportunity to visit other schools. Yet it remains just as important (if not more so) that teachers have the opportunity to exchange ideas and explore new approaches to the education of deafblind children with such complex needs. A growing army of support staff is a key resource. Often outnumbering a teaching staff by at least three to one, they undertake much of the daily work on individual programmes. They, too, need professional leadership. In spite of such difficulties much innovative and dedicated work still goes on.

Specialist training

Staff development is therefore increasingly important. If deafblind pupils with complex needs are to be successfully included within a mainstream environment the role of the specialist is crucial. The research illustrated the positive impact of training. More responsibility is now being placed with individual schools to identify their staff development needs. A tension between the flexibility required by staff working in a variety of roles, addressing a wide range of pupil needs and the specific skills of the specialist is emerging. Ultimately there may need to be a new definition of a specialist. It is an exciting prospect that knowledge gained from the work with pupils who are deafblind can inform others. What is vital, however, is not to lose this body of expertise built up over many years and lodged on solid foundations of theory. The challenge at the beginning of the new millennium is going to be one of keeping the best from special school provision and ensuring a level of resourcing to support both flexibility and specialist expertise in the move towards greater inclusion.

PART 2: SCOTLAND

Introduction

Views as to what might usefully be included in the curriculum for pupils who are deafblind or multi-sensory impaired are discussed at length in other chapters. Most teachers, and most schools, however, are not free agents, able to make unilateral decisions as to the content and balance of the curriculum they deliver. The main concern for most teachers working with pupils with disabilities therefore, is to achieve a balance between the requirements of the educational system within which they work and the very individual needs of their pupils. The former states an official requirement for a broad, balanced and fairly standardised curriculum while the latter clearly calls for a highly personalised educational approach with, for those who are deafblind or multi-sensory impaired, strong focus on communication taking precedence and being regarded as fundamental to all other learning. It is important, therefore, that teachers are sufficiently well informed and confident about their knowledge, both of the pupils and the expectations of the authorities, in order that they are able to arrive at the most effective and appropriate educational plan for each pupil.

There have, perhaps, in the past, been suggestions that the education provided for children and young people with deafblindness should be completely different and totally segregated from that of the rest of the school age population. However, even if education authorities were in complete sympathy with arguments for a totally separate approach in the field of deafblind education, it would be neither necessary, nor indeed desirable, to isolate pupils from the educational context and culture within which we all live and work. To ignore prevailing thinking on educational issues is to encourage a move towards an undesirable segregation of both teachers and pupils, as well as a great deal of time and effort spent in 're-inventing the wheel'.

The Scottish context

In Scotland, the national curriculum for all children of school age is defined in two main sets of documentation, the 5–14 Guidelines and the Higher Still curriculum. The 5–14 Guidelines, as might be expected from the title, deals with the structure of the curriculum for children in the Primary sector and in the first two years of the Secondary sector. Higher Still provides a course of study leading to accreditation for most pupils in Years 5 and 6, and some pupils in Years 3 to 6 of the Secondary sector. There also exists a programme of study, used mainly in the mainstream sector, which is followed by most pupils in Years 3 and 4 in secondary schools. This particular course of study, which leads to Standard Grade accreditation, has proved to be unsuitable for most pupils with deafblindness and will not be discussed here.

It is not only in the content and delivery of the curriculum that guidance is available for teachers concerned with meeting the needs of pupils with special educational needs. At any stage from Nursery to Further Education, teachers are supported by advice contained in the documents *Effective Provision for Special Educational Needs'*, commonly known as *EPSEN* (SOED 1994), and *A Manual of Good Practice in Special Educational Needs: Information Pack for Staff* (SOEID 1999). The first of these is the report by HM Inspectors of Schools which was based on evidence from inspections and investigations carried out in mainstream and special schools and other establishments over the previous five years. The second, more recent publication is an important part of a quality initiative in Scottish education and provides guidance for all concerned with the education of children and young people with special educational needs from local authority staff, through schools and support services to the voluntary sector.

EPSEN contains chapters dedicated to each of the four educational sectors: Pre-5, Primary, Secondary and Further Education, and it is helpful if teachers are aware of their own particular section as well as of the general guidance. A major aspect of this general guidance is the statement of 'Ten Distinctive Features of Effective Provision for Special Educational Needs', these being regarded as fundamental to good practice whatever the type of educational establishment children are being educated in. These features are as important for teachers involved in the education of deafblind children as they are for those involved with all other special educational needs and will be considered before going on to look more closely at curriculum matters.

The first 'distinctive feature' is 'Understanding special educational needs' which, the document makes clear, means that all involved in providing for pupils with special educational needs must have a shared understanding of the continuum of special educational needs. This is particularly important when we consider that there is still an unfortunate tendency to regard children with SEN as somehow different and perhaps being more appropriately placed in a segregated establishment. By placing this at the head of the list, the writers of the document make an important point about the inclusiveness of effective provision; all learning abilities are on a continuum and it is important that we appreciate the potential of all learners whatever their difficulties.

The next five features refer to matters which might best be described as relating to practice in, and connected to, the classroom, these being:

- effective identification and assessment procedures;
- an appropriate curriculum;
- forms of provision suited to needs;
- effective approaches to learning and teaching;
- attainment of educational goals.

Under each of these headings are clear statements of the factors which HM Inspectors consider to be fundamental to good practice. The final four features refer to wider issues which are considered vital to supporting learning and teaching, these being:

- parental involvement;
- inter-professional cooperation;
- effective management of provision;
- full involvement of child or young person.

It is as important for the teacher of pupils with deafblindness as for those of all other pupils with special needs to think about each of these features and use them to evaluate their own practice.

5–14 Guidelines

Evidence suggests that the national curricular programmes in Scotland are less prescriptive and more flexible than their equivalent in England and Wales. The 5–14 programme for example, was designed, not to specify exactly what was to be taught, but rather to provide 'guidelines' for teachers in mainstream schools and 'guidance' for those in the special sector. Even where education towards certification is concerned, at the Access level of Higher Still, schools have been encouraged to have their own internal courses of study accredited by the Scottish Qualifications Authority (SQA) rather than switching to an equivalent which has been devised centrally. In this way, the collaborative ethos of the Scottish system is demonstrated and strengthened as teachers can be clearly seen as being regarded as independent professionals working in partnership with those at the centre of educational planning.

The official expectation explicit in the 5-14 documentation is that schools should develop their own approaches in such a way that the needs of their pupils will be effectively addressed. The national guidelines are sufficiently flexible to be modified in response to particular needs and should, therefore, always be applied with sympathetic attention to the special educational needs of individuals, taking full account of the wishes of their parents.

> Development work has shown that teachers in mainstream and special schools are more effective in applying the guidelines to the education of all pupils when they have first reconsidered their educational needs and then reviewed the content of the curriculum, approaches to learning and teaching, assessment strategies and resource organisation and deployment. ('Support for Learning', SCCC 1993)

In order to provide specific guidance for teachers working with children who have pronounced special educational needs, a document, *Special Educational Needs within the 5-14 Curriculum: Support for Learning* (SCCC 1993), was produced. This document has sections and is designed to combine information and guidance along with suggested staff development activities in such a way as to allow for optimum support for all pupils with special educational needs. The last, and longest, section is divided into seven subsections which contain specific guidance for teachers working with children with particular impairments. These are as follows:

3.1 Developing the 5–14 curriculum for pupils with physical difficulties.

3.2 Developing the 5–14 curriculum for pupils with visual impairment.

3.3 Developing the 5–14 curriculum for pupils with hearing impairment.

3.4 Developing the 5–14 curriculum for pupils with moderate learning difficulties.

3.5 Developing the 5–14 curriculum for pupils with complex learning difficulties.

3.6 Developing the 5–14 curriculum for pupils with social, emotional and behavioural difficulties.

3.7 Developing the 5–14 curriculum for pupils with communication and language difficulties.

As there is no specific subsection which considers the needs of learners who are deafblind or multi-sensory impaired, teachers will need to make themselves familiar with, and draw information from, those sections which connect most closely with the profile of each pupil whose educational plan is being devised. Indeed knowledge of the range of difficulties experienced by these pupils indicates that at different times teachers may find themselves consulting any of the seven subsections.

Personal research (unpublished) has indicated that most pupils who are deafblind or multi-sensory impaired are educated in special schools which cater for those with severe/profound and multiple/complex difficulties. When this is the case there is a strong likelihood that the school, either on its own or in conjunction with others in the area will have produced an 'elaborated curriculum'. In an endeavor to make the curriculum more appropriate to the processes and planning in schools for pupils with more pronounced learning difficulties, those involved in elaborating the 5–14 curriculum identified six key skills which were seen as fundamental to a broad and balanced curriculum for pupils at this stage. This will have been accomplished by following processes recommended in *Special Educational Needs within the 5-14 Curriculum: Support for Learning*, and will have been developed with a focus on 'pupils working within Level A'.

It is to be hoped that during the process of elaboration the needs of pupils with sensory impairments will have been recognised and addressed but unfortunately this is not always the case, as can be seen in the exemplar in Section 3.5 of *Support for Learning*:

Grid 1: Communication and Language
Section: Attending and responding (receptive)
Step 1: Tracks objects and people within a 180% arc, e.g. observes own hand movements or responds to sound-making toy.
Step 2: Eagerly attentive to everyday sounds or touch routines, e.g. tries to grasp spoon when being fed. Anticipates change of activity.
Step 3: Carries out spoken or gestural instructions, e.g. 'take it' or 'give it to me', when ball is held out.

In a case such as this, where it is obvious that the particular needs of pupils with multi-sensory impairment have not been addressed during the process of elaborating the curriculum, then individual, or groups of, teachers will require to make further elaborations and adaptations to suit particular pupils. This will require to be done in a way which is both logical and justifiable so that those in authority and parents can be assured that the changes are real improvements. The status quo is often regarded as being 'set in stone' and teachers feel less than confident in changing what has been decided at a 'higher level', however not to do so will lead to a situation where pupils are merely fitted into a curriculum rather than having their needs effectively identified and addressed.

Taking the excerpt quoted above as an example, the process of effective elaboration can be demonstrated. Firstly, it must be understood that what is noted here is a number of observable behaviours which are typically indicative of developing awareness and receptive communication skills. Behaviours such as these have been recorded and reproduced in the form of checklists (see Chapters 2 and 4) in order to provide standardised assessment which can be used by less experienced personnel. Although the behaviours listed are typical, the list is not exhaustive and there may be many other signs of the pupil's growing awareness. It is important then that the teacher of the pupil with deafblindness or multi-sensory impairment should have a clear understanding of the underlying skills/abilities/level of awareness which, it is assumed, the observable behaviours are demonstrating. The development which is signalled by the behaviour described in Steps 1, 2 and 3 above (SCCC 1993) is, as already stated, that of awareness of and interest in people and objects surrounding the child.

A pupil with multi-sensory impairment is unlikely to be able to track objects or people but may be clearly aware of the presence of objects or, more particularly, people. This awareness may be demonstrated in a positive or negative manner and it is important that the teacher recognises that this is indeed valid demonstration of the child's developmental stage and abilities.

Steps 2 and 3 (SCCC 1993) describe the behaviour of an increasingly socially responsive child displaying socially acceptable behaviour. This may cause difficulties for some teachers, not only those of deafblind pupils, as growing awareness and cooperative behaviour are not necessarily always combined. It is important then that what the teacher looks for in the child is evidence of the development of awareness rather than the development of 'good' behaviour. The main danger with all developmental checklists of this sort is that the educator using the system will look only for the described behaviour and overlook, or even ignore, equally valid communicative behaviour which a pupil might display. It is clear therefore that the teacher working with pupils with deafblindness or multi-sensory impairment must be both highly observant and able to see beyond the rather limited guidance available in this type of standardised documentation.

Although this is a weakness in the 5–14 documentation, this is not to suggest that the curriculum guidelines have no relevance for those in deafblind education; indeed there is a great deal of value, not least the emphasis on breadth and balance which is a counterbalance to any tendency to focus too narrowly (e.g. on methods of communication or self-help skills), and are a constant reminder that all learners need variety to maintain interest and increase motivation.

Teachers should find that the detail in which the curriculum is discussed and organised provides valuable support to their own thinking and planning in various areas, particularly those in which they lack confidence and/or are aware of personal limitations. For example, traditional thinking on physical education may not have included activities that make up several strands in 5–14:

- investigating and developing fitness;
- using the body;

- applying skills;
- creating and designing;
- cooperating, sharing, communicating and competing;
- observing, reflecting, describing and responding.

It is extremely important, however, that in making use of ideas contained in the 5–14 curriculum teachers remain focused on the conceptual level of the pupil. For example, the concept of fantasy or make believe which occurs before school age for most able-bodied children and which is central to the 'Awareness of Genre' strand in the Listening section of *English Language 5–14* is a concept which is highly problematic for many learning disabled pupils and particularly for those with multi-sensory impairment. While enjoyable texts such as *The BFG* by Roald Dahl or *The Lion, the Witch and the Wardrobe* by C. S. Lewis may be appropriate to the chronological age of the pupil, the ability to understand or obtain any enjoyment from such imaginative writing is unlikely to be present in most learners with pronounced difficulties. Teachers will require to be both creative and intuitive in order to provide a meaningful alternative for such pupils so that the stimulation and pleasure gained by listening to stories can be experienced in a way which suits their needs and abilities.

Higher Still

The Higher Still initiative designed to ensure 'Opportunity For All' provides curriculum guidelines, performance criteria, assessment instruments and accreditation for almost all of pupils of secondary school age, including learners who have previously been regarded as too disabled to be included in any programme of work leading to accreditation. The original planners of the programme regarded it as being developed for pupils/students in the post-16 age group, which in the mainstream school generally means those who have completed a Standard Grade course. However Standard Grade courses, which were themselves introduced to offer greater opportunity for larger numbers of pupils, proved to be too demanding for a significant number. Because of this, early in the planning process it became apparent that many teachers in special education were considering Access 2 and Access 3 as alternatives to Standard Grades. In addition to this, teachers were expressing concern over the plight of pupils 'working within level A' in 5–14 beyond the age of 14 as there was no clear progression from the 5–14 programme to anything more age appropriate. It has become increasingly clear during the development process that, for those learners for whom Standard Grades are inappropriate, work towards Higher Still accreditation will begin at Secondary 3.

Higher Still is a programme of academic and vocational studies offered in a number of differentiated levels – these are:

- Advanced Higher
- Higher
- Intermediate 2
- Intermediate 1
- Access 3
- Access 2
- Access 1.

The Higher Still programme is designed to provide clear progression between stages across subjects and consequently Access 3 has clear links to Intermediate 1 as well as to Access 2. It is an inclusive programme and the interests of all pupils/students are considered. This is very good news for teachers concerned with pupils who are deafblind or multi-sensory impaired and it is likely that these pupils will be working at Access levels 1 and 2. The programme recognises that pupils working at these levels will require highly individualised planning and an IEP, and recommends that this be designed round several key principles:

- all learning should be organised on the basis of providing equality of opportunity for all students; no student should be prevented access to learning experiences because of disability, other difficulties, race or gender;
- all students, whatever their achievements, should be offered learning opportunities which are progressive and age-appropriate;
- each student should be enabled to be actively involved in their own learning;
- the curriculum should offer relevant learning experiences for each student and, whenever possible, learning should be fun.

There will however be pupils/students whose difficulties are such that independent completion of even the single outcome units at Access 1 is likely to prove very demanding and, in order that the progress of such students is recorded and recognised it is recommended that their progress be described using the descriptors of Participation, Awareness and Experience, which are detailed as follows.

Participation: the student is almost ready to achieve, or is in the process of achieving, the Performance Criterion on which the target is based. The student, in working on a task or activity, is able to demonstrate understanding of the part she/he is playing.

Awareness: the student has some awareness of the learning target. The task or activity is designed to develop the student's level of awareness, highlighting the specific aspects of the target Performance Criterion that are directly relevant to her/him at that time.

Experience: the student is unlikely to be aware of the learning target. Through interaction, with significant support, the student is enabled to take part in the activity related to the target. The student can build up a range of experiences relevant to the subject area of the target.

(Higher Still draft documentation)

Case studies

The following case studies illustrate how the 5–14 and Higher Still curricula have been accessed by three pupils. The pupils vary in age and in academic ability and all are described as being deafblind or as having multi-sensory impairment. The relationship between the curriculum of the school which they attend and the national guidelines provides a clear example of the effective educational experience which can be provided when a collaborative partnership exists between schools, teachers and the designers of the national curricular guidelines. The school, which considers the development of communication and language skills as fundamental to all other learning, has been able to test the breadth and balance of its range of activities against the national statement of what constitutes a worthwhile curriculum. In this way they have been able to conserve all that is important to the education of deafblind children while being supported in efforts to guard against any tendency towards an over-narrow educational approach.

The descriptions of the programmes followed by the four pupils will be arranged under the headings of the 5-14 and Higher Still guidelines and an indication given as to how activities are categorised in the school's own structure.

Simon is 10 years old. He has Maternal Rubella Syndrome, which resulted in partial sight, severe hearing loss and learning difficulties. He seems not to make any obvious use of his residual hearing and staff believe that he is so focused on making sense of the visual information available to him that he blanks out any auditory information which might get in the way. Certainly, it is obvious when something has caught his attention as he will approach with his 'bad' eye closed and examine the person/object closely using only his 'good' eye.

Since entering the school at the age of four and a half he has displayed great potential in a number of areas although this is always affected by obsessive behaviours and an overwhelming desire for routine. He also presented great difficulties for his family as he was very unwilling, at night, to sleep for more than three hours at a time. Recently he has had particular problems with chest infections and a perforated eardrum.

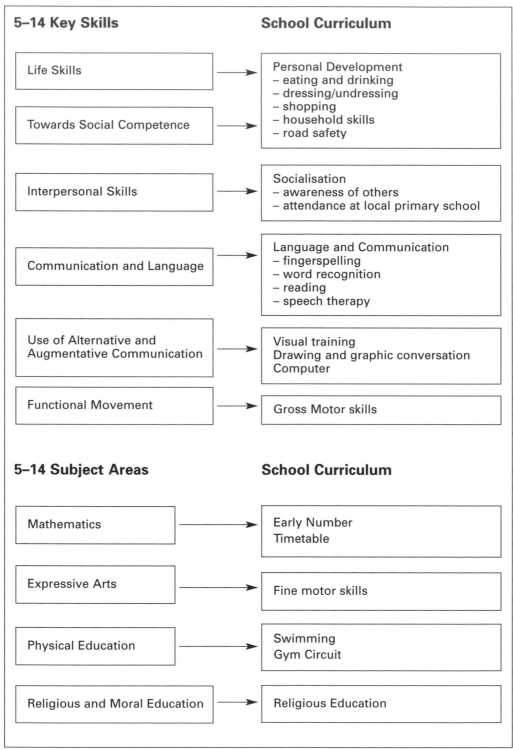

Figure 5.2 Simon's IEP

Carol is 15 years old, is deafblind and has severe learning difficulties. She uses a small number of British Sign Language (BSL) signs and also communicates through the use of her own individualised gestures and mannerisms. As a baby and infant Carol spent a great deal of time, often months on end, in hospital undergoing painful treatments and the effect that this has had on subsequent relationships and Carol's view of the world cannot be underestimated. It is considered unlikely that Carol will ever achieve accreditation under the Higher Still programme, and indeed it is perhaps somewhat irrelevant from her point of view as those who know her best believe that the concept of achievement in this way is not something which would be meaningful for her. What then is the intention when considering Carol and her educational programme within this national curriculum?

It has always been understood by those engaged in the planning of Higher Still that, for some pupils, those with the most profound learning difficulties and impairments, the awarding of certificates would be meaningless and, worse, patronising and demeaning. Accreditation and the work towards it is intended to build self-esteem and confidence as well as provide nationally accepted proof of achievement. For Carol then, the curriculum will provide a framework of activities which are age appropriate, broad and balanced and allow Carol's teachers to involve her in activities with other pupils who are working towards accreditation at Access Stage 1 which will also be meaningful and enjoyable for Carol.

It is fully understood and accepted that, for pupils like Carol there will be many activities in her programme which are highly relevant and beneficial but which are not part of the Higher Still curriculum. Aromatherapy, massage, and activities in the multi-sensory room will all be present in her programme with no need to justify their presence by creating some tenuous link to an area in the national curriculum. However the major part of her programme will be based on areas from Higher Still.

She will be involved in:

- Language and Communication
- Home Economics   Organisation in the home
                                    Living safely at home
                                    Healthy basic cookery
- Mathematics   Using money in everyday situations
- Music
- Personal and Social Education   Personal awareness and development
                                    Personal care
                                    Social awareness and development
                                    Participation in leisure time activities
                                    Using support services in the
                                    community
- Physical Education   Swimming
                                    Walking

It can be seen then, that for young people with complex learning difficulties (like Carol), there can be no justification for excluding them from the national curriculum, nor for teachers to feel pressured into limiting their experiences only to those which are contained within it. In this way Carol's best interests are served and she can enjoy a meaningful and stimulating programme of activities during her week at school.

Peter is also 15 years old and is disabled as a result of Maternal Rubella Syndrome. He is a bright active young man who displays many talents and a strong interest in everything around him. He has very limited sight and a severe hearing loss but he communicates well using BSL and can write, read and draw. One of Peter's favourite activities at present is his weekly visit to a nearby mainstream secondary school where he takes part in a woodwork class, an area in which he displays a significant amount of skill.

It is expected that Peter will achieve accreditation under the Higher Still scheme and he is already well aware of the concepts of competition and achievement. At the age of nine he won first prize in an art competition which was open to disabled and able-bodied adults and children and when he returned to school with the very grand trophy he raised it above his head in triumph, crowing with pleasure and pride. For a young man like Peter, the opportunity to work towards, and achieve, nationally recognised qualifications is both important and long overdue.

Peter's programme over the next two to three years therefore will involve him in a wide range of activities in many curricular areas (see Figure 5.3) as he achieves Access 1 and, in some areas Access 2 certificates. Although, as this is a prospective account of what Peter is likely to do, it is impossible to give an exact timescale or an accurate account of the order in which modules will be undertaken, what it is likely to include is listed in Figure 5.3. It must be stressed that completion of each separate outcome leads to a certificate at Access 1 level while completion of all outcomes in a unit, even if completed over a period of time, leads to automatic accreditation at Access 2.

In the years leading up to this stage, Peter has already experienced a range of meaningful and relevant school activities, so that the main impact of Higher Still for him is not so much to ensure a broad, balanced and relevant curriculum. What it does do is to provide an official and tangible recognition for his work, a factor which will be of immense value to Peter and his family, the self-esteem and quality of life of them all.

Subject	Access 2: (Unit title)	Outcomes (Access 1 Units)
Art and Design	Exploring Visual Images	1. Explore a range of visual images and/or artefacts. 2. Create visual images and/or artefacts of personal interest.
	Working with Materials	1. Identify a range of materials. 2. Select materials to be used and explain choices. 3. Use materials to produce visual outcomes.
Computing	Using Technological Equipment	1. Identify technological equipment in common use. 2. Perform basic operations using technological equipment in common use in the household. 3. Perform basic operations using technological equipment in common use in the office/workplace and for personal use.
English and Communication	Language Study	1. Understand simple, brief non-fiction text. 2. Convey simple, brief factual information in writing.
	Oral/Aural Communication	1. Listen/watch and respond to a simple communication. 2. Deliver a simple oral communication.

Figure 5.3 Extract from Peter's Programme

Conclusion

In considering the education of children who are deafblind and multi-sensory impaired in the context of Scottish education, primary and secondary, it is important to remember the following points:

- at the primary and early secondary stages (5–14) individualised programmes are to be planned, taking into account the needs of the learner and the wishes of parents;
- in the later secondary stage (Higher Still), individualised programmes are to be planned which take into account the interests and aptitudes of the learner;
- teachers are expected to work collaboratively with parents, other professionals and the young people themselves;
- there is no standardised programme to which every learner must adhere, or even aspire;
- the important benchmarks of any individualised programme are breadth, balance, relevance and age-appropriateness.

The teacher in Scotland is regarded as an independent, responsible professional, capable of employing all the skills required in the planning and delivery of a successful educational programme for all pupils. For the teacher of deafblind children this will require particular attention to the communicative abilities, aptitudes and interests of the pupils if this is to work well. Teachers should be confident in their abilities to work *with* the national curricula rather than merely *within* them, as the needs of a deafblind child or young person require a programme which is truly personal and individualised.

References

Porter, J., Miller, O. L. and Pease, L. (1997) *Curriculum Access for Deafblind Children*, Research Report No. 1. London: DfEE.

Scottish Consultative Council on the Curriculum (1993) *Special Educational Needs within the 5–14 Curriculum: Support for Learning*. Dundee: SCCC.

SOED (1994) *Effective Provision for Special Educational Needs*. Edinburgh: HMSO.

SOEID (1999) *A Manual of Good Practice in Special Educational Needs: Information Pack for Staff*. Edinburgh: HMSO.

CHAPTER 6

Effective teaching and learning

Liz Hodges

Introduction

Children with intact vision and hearing learn effectively from all they do and from all that happens around them. Children who cannot depend on their distance senses to provide reliable, undistorted and adequate information about their world will learn less effectively. Learning and experience are restricted in quality and quantity. Their learning is limited by what others, or chance, bring to them in a form that they can perceive. As described in Chapter 1, they do not easily learn incidentally, from events around them. Unlike that of the typically developing child, their learning must be especially arranged.

The teacher of deafblind children must make the most of every opportunity for learning. All interactions with adults and all aspects of the environment will be harnessed to help the child overcome the restrictions imposed by sensory impairments.

Although children who are deafblind will have sensory impairment in common, they will differ as learners because of the degree of sensory difficulty, and the existence of other disabilities, especially physical and movement disorders. Some will have brain injury and consequent developmental delay, others will function as slow learners because of their sensory disabilities, but will make marked progress when appropriate techniques are used.

The teacher must choose appropriate methods of teaching to meet the diverse needs of different individuals. She will consider how to arrange the learning and the physical environment to maximise each child's learning, and how to prioritise learning goals and pursue them.

Creating a successful environment for learning

People work better in an organised and pleasant environment. If the desk is tilted and the paper falls off, if other people argue constantly or if dinner time comes at a different time each day they will not work well. A pleasant and organised environment allows children, too, to make the most of every opportunity to learn, as they begin to make sense of the world and what they are able to do. A poorly organised environment restricts them further.

Stability

A sense of security is essential for successful learning. To establish basic security about their world children must discover that the world is ordered, and that they are able to use this order to make predictions about events. Structured thinking leads to learning. Structured thinking is founded on understanding of pattern in events and in responses to events. Learning follows as a child begins to understand her ability to alter and control events. Confidence in the world allows children to tackle new types of learning.

Children also need emotional security, to engender feelings of well-being and of trust in those they are working with. Insecurity causes anxiety and confusion, and makes children reluctant or unable to respond to events. Lack of trust in others prevents the child from using her faculties to learn. Security is therefore an essential feature of a successful learning environment. 'Feeling insecure drains all the energy in a person. In making a child secure, energy is released and can be spent on the capacities in the child for further development' (Jacobsen *et al.* 1993).

Children need to feel physically secure. They need to be comfortable, warm enough, and to have their other physical needs taken care of. They need comfortable positions in which to work, which may include sitting, standing (including in a supportive frame), using a wedge, sitting with an adult to provide a secure, friendly hold. They need to know that change in position is predictable, and that they will not suddenly and without warning be whisked into the air, that their chair cannot fly, and that they, in so far as they are able, are primarily responsible for their movement.

Nella sits in her supportive chair at the table. The table is at the right height for her to move her hands, the little she is able, through a low tin tray of brightly coloured balls. When Clare approaches her, she places her hands on her shoulders, and carefully moves her away from the table (so it does not just disappear). She then supports her to her feet, before lifting her gently into her wheelchair.

Nella has secure seating, and it is not suddenly moved. She is learning that her body must move to enable her to get from one place to another, even though she uses a wheelchair.

Using routines to create stability

Everyone depends on routines. Most people follow a routine on getting up, and if something unexpected happens, they may fail to leave the house on time. When on holiday, the lack of familiar routine can be tiring and frustrating.

Children with sensory impairments depend on routine to allow them to understand what is happening, and what will happen next. Routine can give them information they cannot access through their senses. As they learn to use a routine, they understand more about the world, and it seems a less hostile and frightening place.

Routines allow a child the maximum possible chance of recognising an event, and thus of feeling secure, of making responses, and of learning.

The child with sensory impairments will learn to use a variety of cues to help her understand her place in the routine. (I depend on the sensory cue of an alarm clock to start my morning routines, but others use the smell of coffee to begin getting up.)

Cues that may help children with sensory impairments to orient themselves in routines include:

- musical prompts;
- spoken words;
- touches to specific parts of the body;
- a change of position;
- a movement (being swung round);
- object 'props';
- specific places for activities (dressing in the bedroom).

Some of these cues may be deliberately introduced, and others will occur naturally during the routine.

At first, a child may only understand short, simple routines. These may involve play such as 'peek-a-boo' games, where the child starts to anticipate the cloth coming off, or singing 'round and round the garden', as the child starts to laugh before the tickle.

Simple classroom routines may also begin to have meaning.

Duwayne sits in a circle with other children, for the starting session of the day. His teacher places a light cloth to his head (touch cue) and then over his face. She sings a special song (music cue) and then pauses to allow him to pull the cloth off. He is rewarded by a raspberry blown by his teacher. They then repeat the exercise. Duwayne has the opportunity to learn the small routine, cloth on, song, cloth off, raspberry, and he has a specific part to play in it.

Cathy is having her legs massaged by a support worker (touch cue). When this is done, the support assistant will put splints on her legs, and stand her in her standing frame (position cue). Once in her standing frame, Cathy will immediately be brought her dinner.

As a child masters simple routines, more elements can gradually be included.

To allow the child to recognise and learn the routine, elements will need to be presented in the same way, and in the same order each time. One way of ensuring this is by using a script, as shown in Figure 6.1.

	Adult action	**Child action**	**Comments**
Step 1	Adult brings utensils and places them on table. Takes Jack to cupboard.	Jack opens cupboard door.	
Step 2	Adult waits for Jack to choose.	Jack chooses flat box or high box.	**Always** wheat biscuits in flat box, cornflakes in high box. Decrease assistance but continue to give at least minimal support. Sit on his right.
Step 3	Adult helps Jack carry box to table, and helps Jack to sit.	Jack assists in carrying box.	
Step 4	Adult puts Jack's hand on tab of box.	Jack opens box and puts hand in, to check contents.	Jack can change his mind at this time. If he doesn't like it, he can shut box with help, and return to choosing (Step 2). Replace box on left, so he can choose when to have more.
Step 5	Adult helps him to pour into bowl, and into her bowl.	Jack helps adult.	Switch now, quietly, if you can't stand what he has chosen for you!
Step 6	Adult pours milk on both bowls.		
Step 7	Adult shows him how she picks up spoon.	Jack follows with hands.	Let his hands rest very lightly on adult's, as she finds spoon.
Step 8		Jack picks up own spoon.	
Step 9	Adult eats.	Jack eats.	When he has finished what is in his bowl, move on to Step 10.
Step 10	Adult puts hand on box, and says 'MORE'.	Jack chooses.	Yes = opens box. No = pushes box gently away. He can have three bowls of cereal, then sign 'finished' and push box away with him.
Step 11	Adult signs and says 'finished', with his hands resting on hers. Then pauses for Jack to do it.	Jack signs 'finished', and pushes box and bowl away.	
Step 12	Adult helps him to put box away.	Jack carries box to cupboard.	

Figure 6.1 Script, Example: breakfast

Scripts can be written for simple and increasingly complex activities. A script will show what the adult will do and say, where she will pause for a response, how she will move from step to step. It will also show what the child can do, and how the child's involvement can gradually be increased.

The routine of beginning, action and finishing which underlies many activities can be emphasised by:

- beginning: taking correct equipment out of a box;
- action: placing equipment on table or tray and using it;
- finishing: returning it to the box.

This script can be used whether the activity is painting or PE. The child herself may learn to use the routine to inform adults whether she wants to start, continue or finish particular activities.

Longer, more complex routines will develop as the child learns to deal with more elements. Initially they may be routines for a part of a day, such as:

- a physiotherapy session (not enjoyed);
- a drink (enjoyed);
- playing with noisy toys.

The child may learn to tolerate the physiotherapy exercise better when she knows it will be followed by a drink.

Timetable routines for a whole day are long and complex, and initially may contain too many elements for the child to recognise. Small elements which can be predicted may be joined to create longer routines. Later the child will learn to predict the next major event from the one preceding it, and later still she will learn long sequences; for example, she may show she understands the sequence of a week's activities. She may then start to build her own routine in order to organise her own activities.

> Jeyda lives in a residential school and goes home at weekends. The last thing that happens on a Friday is that the whole school goes into the hall and sits in a circle. Jeyda often goes into the hall at other times in the week, takes out a chair, and sits on it where she sits for the circle, presumably hoping that she will soon go home. Although this does not make it Friday, it shows that Jeyda does understand the weekly routine.

> Cameron arrives in school and gives his home–school book to his teacher, gets out his favourite box of postcards and his workbook and puts them on his desk. Then he puts a can of Coke beside them. He looks through the postcards until his teacher comes over to help him with his daily diary.

Routines are an essential tool in giving the child confidence in a world that need not be alarming. They allow the child to experiment with more confidence in a predictable situation.

Helping children to feel secure with people

Like other people, children with sensory impairments prefer to work with people they know. Initially, it may be advisable to limit the number of people who work with each child. One member of staff may carry out key tasks with a child, including the teacher's programme and the physiotherapy programme, with direction. This person will also help the child at dinner times, work on interactive games, and support her in other activities. The pupil will begin to recognise that the other person is distinct from him or herself, but, at the same time is not alien or threatening. Trust in a familiar person will increase and the pupil will gradually be drawn out of an inner private world into the world outside.

When the child feels confident, another person may take on a specific task, such as helping the child with dinner, or working in music therapy. Gradually more people will be added. This helps the child to feel secure in that she works always with familiar people.

A child may develop a particularly trusting relationship with one person. Some children will do anything for a special dinner lady, but nothing for their teacher! These preferences show that the child can discriminate. At first, if possible, the child's time should be arranged so she can work with the person she trusts, while gradually widening her experience as she becomes more confident with people.

Each person should introduce themselves whenever they come to the child. This will help her to understand that people are differentiated from each other. Cues which may help a child to recognise people include:

- each having a particular touch 'game', such as ruffling the child's hair, or squeezing her shoulders;
- each having a particular item which the child can feel, such as a pair of glasses or a ring, which is always worn;
- each announcing his or her name in a different sing-song voice or rhythm.

Designing and delivering teaching programmes

Deafblind children present many challenges to the teacher, forcing her to reconsider the way she teaches in the light of children's learning. No single strategy or group of strategies will meet the needs of every child. A resourceful teacher will use various methods and resources to meet the learning needs of each child.

A strategy is not a curriculum document. Strategies help the teacher to use appropriate activities to meet curriculum goals. Strategies help to plan how and where to work on activities. Suitable and appropriate strategies cannot, however, make an inappropriate curriculum appropriate.

Teachers will also have personal characteristics which assist them. Teachers of deafblind children need to be enthusiastic, determined, flexible, creative and resilient.

Motivation

Motivation or reward is a very important part of learning. I learnt to drive a car so I could get around, and I learnt to type because my handwriting is so bad I could never get anyone to read my notes.

In designing a task, the teacher will ensure that there is appropriate motivation for the child. The most successful motivation is to complete the task itself. This is why many children are successful at learning to feed themselves! Operating a toy by using a switch, or plugging in and turning on the TV are other examples of tasks with inbuilt or intrinsic rewards.

Other tasks may be designed with specific motivating factors in the task. They become part of the task, but they are not intrinsic. A child learning to walk downstairs may learn to do this on the way to the swimming pool (if she enjoys swimming).

Sometimes a task may need additional motivation. A child getting dressed may be rewarded with a tickle each time an item is put on. A child learning to wash up may be awarded a star each time she washes up, and at the end of the day she can exchange the stars for listening to a tape recorder.

The best rewards are the child's own pleasure at success, and the teacher's. The teacher will always show pleasure, and the child will gradually learn to recognise this and find it rewarding on its own. The child may also learn to be pleased with her good work, and to enjoy getting smiling faces on her page of writing.

Children with very poor vision and hearing will find recognition of social rewards much harder, and may rely on material rewards and inbuilt rewards for longer. Deprived of the consolidating and integrating structure which our distance senses provide, activities and events may be perceived as a random set of sensory experiences. Different stimuli appear unrelated, and no pattern can be detected.

Jo sits in his chair in class. A small furry object is put into his hand, he hears an enthusiastic noise, his hand is manipulated near his face, and then another small plastic object is put into his hand. He does not recognise this as 'singing Old MacDonald had a farm'. He cannot link the sound to the objects, and the objects do not bear any relation to any animals he knows.

Jo might do better if he knew when he should make a noise, and when he should be quiet, by using a shaker or by an adult singing close to his ear and encouraging him to make sounds. This pattern is more within his conceptual understanding.

Teachers will design sensory work within activities. The work will have clear goals, such as 'looks at pictures', 'makes sounds with adult', 'handles porridge oats' and will allow the child to use her senses to gain information about the activity on a level which matches her conceptual understanding.

Small steps

Children with sensory impairments need to learn by small steps. They may be involved in complex routines, such as getting changed for swimming, but the whole routine will be too long. The teacher will need to find small, achievable goals within the whole routine.

Alexia is working on her hygiene routine after lunch. With her teacher, she fetches her toothbrush and flannel, goes to the bathroom, washes her face and hands, cleans her teeth, and then puts the equipment away. Working through the whole task gives the child context and understanding for the activity. Alexia's teacher has identified a particular part of this task for Alexia to learn, and has broken it into small steps. Alexia is learning to wash her hands. Her teacher helps her to prepare the water. She has broken the washing task into the following small steps:

- place hands in the water;
- locate soap;
- pass soap from hand to hand;
- replace soap on rack;
- rub hands together;
- place in water;
- reach for towel;
- rub hands on towel.

Breaking tasks down into smaller steps is sometimes called 'task analysis'.

Alexia's teacher works on the first step, and then joins in the second step, until she can complete the whole sequence unaided.

Some component parts of tasks need detailed instruction in a secure, low distraction environment. These may include fine motor skills, such as unscrewing bottle tops, formal/academic tasks, such as matching pictures and letters, perceptual tasks such as imitating gross body movements. In this situation an extrinsic reward may have to be devised: a smile, a tickle, a star. These skills can then be made part of routines such as making a drink, or writing a shopping list. The motivations for them will then be more obvious.

Stephanos is learning to put on his coat. His teacher has broken the task into the following steps:

- pick up coat;
- put left arm in coat;
- pull coat round behind him;
- put right arm in coat;
- pull coat on.

At first his teacher helps him to do all the steps except pull his coat on. When he can do this, she helps him only to pull the coat around his back, and he learns to put his right arm in. When he can do this, she moves on to the previous step. Starting from the last part of the task is sometimes called 'backward chaining'.

However, Stephanos cannot manage his buttons. His teacher thinks that he will need specific help and practice in doing this, and before she asks him to attempt to do up his own buttons, she works with him on doing up large buttons on doll's clothes and old dressing up clothes in a quiet, low distraction environment, to make sure he is able to learn to use this fine motor skill in a practical situation.

Pace

Children with sensory impairments may need longer than other children to use their senses to investigate an activity, and to absorb as much information about it as possible. Integrating tactile information – which is patchy, partial and sequential – to understand an object will take much longer than absorbing information with a quick glance of the eyes. They may need to examine an object or an event using first one sense, and then again with another. This too will take longer than using all their senses together. Teachers will need to be sensitive to the child's lead, and give the child the time necessary to explore.

Deafblind children may learn and act more slowly than other children. If adults are always in a hurry, act for children, intervene too quickly to help them, or solve all their difficulties, children do not learn to use their skills. They may become passive and helpless. They have learned to wait for an adult to prompt them to act, and not to act alone. An inability to act without support is a major secondary disability of children with dual sensory impairments. It is essential that teachers learn to wait for children to respond. Children must take responsibility for the things they 'can' do, even if these are very small. Of course children must be kept interested and stimulated, but they must also be given time to prepare, execute and evaluate their own responses and actions. Waiting for children is one of the most important things that a teacher does with her time.

Jeff is standing by the trailing band on the wall. He can hear the door banging as other children go out to play. He makes a sound. After some time, he moves slowly along the trailing band, and finds his coat peg at the end. He takes his coat off the peg, lifts it, and makes a sound. At this point, Edward, his teacher, comes to help him put on his coat. It would have been quicker if Edward had brought his coat to him when he had first made a sound, but if he had, Jeff would not be learning how to find his coat and that he is responsible for putting it on. He might also stop using the trailing band, because it would no longer have a purpose. As it is, he uses the band to find his coat.

A 'burst–pause activity' allows a child time to respond, while providing prompts to further activity. Many learning situations offer a natural opportunity for this approach. The adult initially leads the activity, then stops, to allow the child to take it up again. The adult then sustains it until the next pause. Many activities, such as mixing a cake, playing ball, and dancing the tango use this natural rhythm which can be exploited for learning. Teachers may need to design a burst–pause structure for other activities, such as reading or horse-riding.

Children may also pace their learning activities over longer periods. A child may be so interested in one area of development that she is not able to learn successfully in others.

Zechariah seemed to decide for himself that he was going to walk. Over the next term he spent much of his time trying to get up and walk about, and was less interested in other activities. Once he had gained independent mobility, he was ready to make gains in other areas. His teacher followed his lead, and supported his chosen activity, while continuing to provide opportunities for learning in other areas.

Repetitions

Because of the restricted information from their senses, children with sensory impairments may need more repetitions of an activity than other children. Initially, children may need the same activity repeated often in one session, such as playing 'row the boat' or splashing their legs in the swimming pool. Repetition gives time to perceive, and recognise, and respond to all the relevant parts of the activity.

A child who needs to practise the same skill many times during a day may benefit from using a 'skills matrix'. This approach is particularly useful when a child is working on only a few skills but needs many opportunities to learn in many contexts. The matrix shows how the key skill can be taught and practised throughout the day, in the classroom routine. When the skill is mastered, she will have many opportunities to put it to use.

	Gives eye contact at 15 cm	Chooses between two activities/events	Uses objects as tools	Walks 20 metres with support	Signs finished at end of activity	Rubs hands together in imitation
Welcome	to adult who greets her when she arrives			walks from the bus to waiting wheelchair		
Morning routines			uses flannel to assist in washing her face	walks to toilet area from class chair	signs finished, when helped to stand up	in prepared water, after pad change
Greeting circle	looks at teacher when given her name card (extend to child next to her)	chooses greeting song, by action	opens box to take out name/photocard		at end of circle, when cymbal is played	
Tabletop work		chooses felt pens or book to begin tabletop session	(felt pens, if chosen, to draw)	walks to work area from circle	when all work items are replaced in box	
Drink	looks at adult who brings her drink	chooses biscuits or apple	uses jug (with help) to pour drink	walks to central table from work area	when snack items are replaced in drawer	to rub crumbs off, on paper towel
Music	looks at teacher	chooses from two instruments	uses beater, if appropriate		when items are replaced in box	with some instruments, e.g. afuches, can practise
Hygiene routine	looks at adult when she brings picture			walks to bathroom from work area	when she is stood up after pad change	in prepared water, with soap
Dinner time	looks at adult who brings dinner to the table	chooses between two puddings (*after* her dinner)	uses spoon and fork	walks to wheelchair, (in chair to dining room)	when plate is empty and she has felt inside it	with paper towel, to wash 'crumbs' off

Figure 6.2 This matrix is merely an example, showing how key targets can be integrated across curriculum areas. It includes sessions which might take place everyday. It is not intended to be a curriculum sample.

Children learning through more formal tasks may need to cover content and skills several times, to ensure they have exploited all the opportunities for learning.

They may need to use different materials to check that they have understood how concepts relate across events and activities, and not just within the examples they have studied.

Nejla's group are studying body parts. They work first using their own bodies, the next week with a partner, and the following week with a doll. Then they use a model or a drawing. Finally, to ensure they have integrated the new skills within what they already know, they link their new knowledge to work on clothes.

Presentation

The teacher will design and deliver the task to make the most use of the child's sensory abilities. Materials may need to be enhanced to be more easily seen, heard, or interpreted tactilely. Some children will need tasks which they can complete using vision, others will need tasks they can complete using their hearing, and still others using primarily their tactile senses. The teacher will consider lighting, noise, colours, people distractions and other relevant factors as she decides how, when and where she will teach it.

The teacher will also consider the times of day, or of the week, when the child is most responsive, and use these for the key learning skills. She may also decide that a child will respond better with one particular adult, or with a particular, familiar piece of equipment. No unnecessary difficulties should be placed in the way of the child, for whom all learning is difficult because of her sensory impairments.

Prompts

Many children will need the support of an adult while they are learning a task. Adults may help children to start and to complete tasks by using prompts. Prompts may be:

- visual (pointing, or showing the child what to do next);
- auditory (making a sound, or telling the child what to do next);
- tactile (putting a child's hand on an object, helping them to move their hand);
- or structural (pauses, starting the next part of an activity).

The teacher will use those prompts (or combination of prompts) the child responds to best.

The child may initially need a high level of prompting, which can later be reduced. At first a child may be shown what to do, the child copying the teacher.

Later the teacher will point, hoping that this will remind the child what comes next. Then the teacher will lift her hand to point, to encourage the child to respond. At first the teacher may pause, expectantly holding the child's hand, and looking at her. Later, she may pause, but not show this level of expectation, so that the pause itself may prompt the child. Eventually the child may not need any prompting. Reducing prompting in this way is also called 'fading'. A child who is prompted too much will learn to rely on adult initiative, and not be able to complete tasks by herself. A child who is prompted throughout a task may not know which parts she is expected to achieve.

Jemima is painting. The teacher guides her hand to the paint pot, to load it with paint. The teacher then paints on the paper herself, and Jemima copies her. When Jemima has no more paint, the teacher says, 'more paint Jemima' and guides her hand back to the pot.

Several months later, the teacher now simply touches Jemima's hand to remind her to load her brush. When she has no more paint, the teacher says 'Yes?', looks at Jemima, and she returns her brush to the pot.

Working hand over hand

Some approaches may be particularly useful to children who are not able to learn efficiently from their distance senses. An adult may manipulate their hands slowly and gently to show them how to do something. This may be the only way for children whose hearing and vision are very poor indeed, but many other children will find it useful.

Taking control of the hands of a child who does not see well can frighten her and make her resentful, so that she pulls her hands away. Her hands are a primary source of information, and taking control of them is rather like having a hand placed over one's eyes. It should always be done with great care, allowing the child the opportunity to take her hands away and replace them later. It is a teaching method, and not a restraint. Some children will resist strongly, and may prefer to learn by using vision and hearing, even when these are difficult for them. Other children may be tactile-defensive and may have to learn to allow adults to use physical prompts.

Modelling

Sensory impairment prevents children from learning from the world around them. Children with sensory impairments are likely to have limited grasp of concepts which are easily grasped by other children. In many instances, they may learn best when shown what to do (visually, by speech or sound, or by touch). They may not know, for example, that toy cars travel along roads, not underneath them, or that teaspoons belong in a special compartment in the cutlery drawer. Modelling also eliminates the need for children to understand language to follow instructions.

> Adolphus attends bricklaying classes at the local college of further education. He is not able to hear or understand the instructions the teacher gives the other students. His teacher listens, and carries out the instruction near to Adolphus, so he is able to copy it. Sometimes, she puts his hand over hers, so he can follow exactly what she is doing.

Co-active to re-active learning

A valuable guide to teaching and to assessing learning is given in McInnes and Treffry's book *Deaf-blind Infants and Children* (1982). They use the terms 'co-active', 'cooperative' and 're-active' to describe three levels of response. Co-active working is when the adult leads the activity, and supports the child throughout it: 'intervenor and child act as one person during an activity'. The adult helps the child, probably hand over hand. Cooperative working is when the adult assists the child, who has some understanding of the process of the activity: 'intervenor provides the child with sufficient support and guidance to ensure success'. Re-active working is when the child manages the task alone, with the adult's presence as context: 'the child completes the task independently'.

McInnes and Treffry then describe a sequence of growing competence in a child using these working methods. At first a child resists the help of the adult in an activity, and then she will tolerate it, co-actively. Then she cooperates, passively, being part of the activity because it allows her to act with the adult. She begins to enjoy the activity for its own sake. Gradually she responds cooperatively, following the adult's lead with little direct encouragement, then she begins to take the lead in the activity, still requiring some support. The final two steps are when the child completes the task when given the initial cue or communication, and initiates the activity herself in an appropriate context.

McInnes and Treffry summarise this sequence as follows. The child will:

resist the interaction
tolerate the interaction co-actively with the intervenor
cooperate passively with the intervenor
enjoy the activity because of the intervenor
respond cooperatively with the intervenor
lead the intervenor through the activity once the initial communication has been given
imitate that action of the intervenor upon request
initiate the action independently.

Take one individual teaching goal which you are working on with a deafblind child.

Write down the whole routine.

Write down the steps the child is actually learning at this moment.

Work out the teaching methods, the senses that are used, the structure of the session, the motivations inherent in the routine.

After this analysis, think about whether changes to the way you are teaching could help the child to achieve the goals.

Making the most of the environment

The arrangement of the physical environment is especially important to the child with sensory impairments. Everyone finds it difficult to learn in noisy or badly lit spaces. Where sensory input is already restricted by impairment, the environment must allow the maximum use of remaining vision and hearing. It will also encourage development of perceptual skills.

Helping children to see

Children with sensory impairments will have different degrees of functional vision and hearing. The teacher will consider their residual senses and their ability to use them in arranging the environment to create the best possible conditions. A well organised classroom environment will be of great benefit in helping children to learn through their restricted senses.

Use of corrective lenses

Some children with visual impairments are helped by glasses or contact lenses. However, they cannot help if they are not worn. If they are dirty or scratched, they can be a more serious impairment than the visual difficulty they are supposed to be correcting! Children should learn to take responsibility, as soon as they are able, for cleaning and storing their glasses. Those who use contact lenses will continue to require attention because these are usually inserted in the morning and removed in the evening – there is often less need to attend to them in the classroom.

Organising the classroom

An ideal classroom will help the child to make the most of what she sees:

- areas for different activities are differentiated by colour of walls or floors or furniture; this will help the child to discriminate among them;
- furniture remains in the same places, to enable children to learn their way around, perhaps using furniture as cues; there is not so much furniture that the room is cluttered;
- it is well lit, by a steady light, which is even across the classroom;
- the walls are one colour, and differentiated from the floor by colour;
- important features such as the handles on doors or cupboards are picked out.
- equipment which children can use is placed where it is accessible;
- displays are well mounted, clearly discriminated from the wall behind; they use clear text and clear pictures: notices/displays for adults are placed away from those for children (and kept to a minimum);
- it is quiet, so that children can use their hearing to compensate for poor vision.

It is not always possible to work in an ideal classroom! Sometimes teachers have to make the best of what they have.

Choosing materials

Teachers will choose materials which best meet the needs of the children they work with. The following factors are likely to be significant.

1. Colour – it is generally easier to see materials of one bright colour, or two well-contrasted colours. Bright and shiny objects are easier for some children to see. Others can see some colours (often red, yellow and orange) better than others.
2. Size – many pupils will have difficulty in seeing small materials. Some small items may need to be enlarged.
3. Interest – most children will find it easier to see things which are familiar, or in which they have an interest. They will recognise a cup they know before they recognise one they do not know.
4. Integrating visual information with other senses – many children will find it easier to use their vision if they can also have clues about the object from touching it, or listening to the sound it makes.

Presenting materials and activities

The following factors need to be borne in mind when presenting materials and activities to children with visual impairment.

1. Time – children with visual impairment need more time to look at things than other children. Some children will need extra time to integrate the image into a whole, others will take time to process the image into something that has meaning for them.

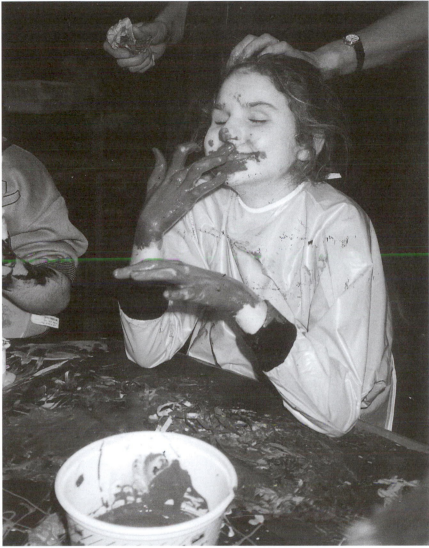

Figure 6.3 Smelling and tasting the (non-toxic) paint!

2. Distance – children may need to be much closer to materials and people in order to be able to see them properly. They may need to sit nearer to a teacher, nearer to the computer, or nearer to the table. Some children will need objects brought close to their eyes because they are not able to do this for themselves.
3. Lighting – some children will benefit from additional lighting on an object. A task light will provide extra light for a small area.
4. Contrast/clutter – most children will see objects better when they are presented singly on a contrasting background. It is particularly hard to see things against a cluttered background – for example, in a heap of objects or on a bright patterned tablecloth.

5. Glare – light reflects off most surfaces, particularly shiny and white ones, the resulting glare making it difficult to see. Table tops and trays may need to be covered with paper of a colour which will create good contrast.

Using specialist equipment

Many children will benefit from some special equipment, which may be light stimulation technology, or a piece of black card. Children who are learning to use vision may need specially designed and enhanced situations. They may use large, bright, moving equipment such as bubble tubes and projectors in order to learn to attend, to fixate and to enjoy their vision. They may use ultraviolet light to help them see objects in special conditions. Teachers will arrange programmes which help them generalise their learning to more ordinary lighting conditions.

Other children may need low vision aids (additional lenses, usually to magnify print) or closed circuit television to enlarge objects and books. A tilted desk top allows them to bring objects close to their eyes without straining their backs.

> Lydia is learning to read. Her teacher has arranged a task light to fall on her work. Her book rests on a tilt board so that to get closer to it, she does not have to lean over. She uses a book where the text is clearly discriminated from the picture, and where it is clear and black. She uses a piece of black card to help her keep her place on the line. She uses books laid out in the same format, so she is familiar with the layout and print style. She works for a short period of time before turning to other tasks requiring less visual concentration.

Computer programmes provide bright, moving, images, often interesting to children, and frequently linked with sound. The child's ability to control the image by using a touch screen, switch or mouse is likely to increase her interest in what she sees. Battery toys which flash, sound and move, such as spaceships and robots, or simple torches can be attached to a switch using an adapter. They are excellent for integrating the child's deliberate action with visual rewards and stimulation. Other computer programmes can read text on the screen for children who are learning to write, or allow children to organise and arrange music in various ways.

Simple equipment made by the teacher, such as refractive mobiles moved by the child's hands or 'beach' windmills in bright colours, can be just as motivating!

The best visual stimulation 'equipment' will always be the all-dancing, all-singing teacher, who makes herself interesting to look at, is nice to talk with and has a familiar face.

Helping children to hear

Classrooms are usually busy places, with many things going on at once. The sounds generated by turning on taps, doors opening, objects on table tops and voices make it hard to focus on sound which could give necessary information within activities. Children who do not hear well, and those who use hearing, may not be able to discriminate individual sounds from background noise.

Using hearing aids

Hearing aids can greatly benefit children for whom they are prescribed. However, they cannot help a child hear if they are not being worn, or are wrongly set. Hearing aids that are at the wrong volume or that do not have working batteries can stop children from hearing sounds that they would hear if they were not wearing them.

Organising the classroom

An ideal classroom would help the child to make the best of what she hears:

- background noise in the classroom is low, with minimum noise from movement, from equipment, from speech not related to the main activity, and from sounds outside the classroom;
- there are no interruptions into the classroom, which almost always cause noise, from movement and talk – only the most urgent messages, for example, are given during work time;
- sounds connected with the main activity are louder than background noise, clear, and close to the child;
- noise in some areas is deadened by carpets, furniture or curtains;
- there is an area of very low background noise (preferably another room) where children are able to work (temporary partitions, even curtains are a step towards this);
- the day is divided into times when there is quiet working, and the necessary times when there is moving about and organising activity – in this way the child can listen when she needs to most;
- when appropriate, children use headphones – for example, to listen to music, so that other children are not distracted.

Teachers will have to arrange their classrooms to work towards these ideals.

Presenting materials and activities

The following factors need to be borne in mind when presenting materials and activities to children with hearing impairment.

1. Distance – some children may need to be close to the sound of the activity, or face towards the principal speaker.
2. Audibility – sounds which are significant need to be particularly clear, and may need to be emphasised, for example by ensuring the background is quiet.

Children with different types of hearing loss may to some extent hear some sounds better than others. The sounds used should be chosen so that they are those easiest to hear.

3. Time/repetition – sounds are transient: they do not remain, for children to perceive and integrate. Sounds (including spoken words) may need to be repeated to give children with hearing difficulties opportunity to perceive and understand. They may need to be given longer to listen, think, and then respond.

4. Language – where spoken language is used, it should be simple, clear words in simple contexts. Speech should be specific, straightforward and relevant, to allow children to concentrate on the significance of the sounds they hear.

5. Context/using other senses – children with hearing impairment may understand better when sounds are backed up by context and by other sensory cues. They are more likely to discriminate the sound of cutlery in the familiar setting of the smell of dinner.

Using specialist equipment

Children with hearing impairment may use an auditory training unit, which helps to amplify sounds coming through a microphone with a minimum of background noise. Battery operated equipment may be linked to a sound switch, which activates when the child makes a noise. The child is then given immediate reinforcement from making sounds.

Radio microphone systems are easily wearable by teacher and pupil and reduce the effect of poor acoustic conditions common to most classrooms. They also reduce the effect of distance or barrier between teacher and pupil. In these systems a transmitter (the teacher's microphone) transduces the speech signal into radio waves. On reception by the pupil's unit these are transformed back into an amplified speech signal.

Loop systems have in recent years become of more benefit to pupils with a hearing impairment. Previously the adult had to wear a microphone attached to a trailing wire. Now the amplifier is used in connection with a radio transmitter. The 'loop' is a loop of wire running round the room or part of the room and may be built into the floor, ceiling or the walls. A magnetic field is set up by the electric circuit flowing through the loop. If the pupil's own hearing aid is set to the 'T' position, a coil in the aid picks up this field and the signal is converted back to sound. Without being attached by trailing leads the pupil can hear from any position within the loop, possibly from a short distance outside it with background noise eliminated.

Expensive equipment need not always be used. Simple equipment such as a cardboard tube or a bendy plastic tube can be used to make an adult's voice louder when talking down the tube, and can be great fun for turn-taking games. A bendy tube can also amplify the child's voice to herself, albeit only slightly.

Children who do not hear very well will find some environments very difficult. Swimming pools and large rooms, and those where they have to take out hearing aids (such as ball pools) will make hearing harder. They will need extra visual or physical support in these situations to compensate for not being able to discriminate significant sounds.

Working in a group

Deafblind children may be educated in classes with other children who have sensory impairments or who have learning difficulties or other severe disabilities, or with children in mainstream schools, or within a group of children who are also deafblind. Most deafblind children will, at least at first, need a considerable amount of one to one attention. Staffing ratios vary however, and most children will on at least some occasions, have to work in a group, perhaps without adult support. While children developing more typically are keen to get involved in group work and also interested in experimenting on their own, deafblind children will need to learn the skills involved in both.

When planning group work the teacher will need to think about where the child who has sensory impairments, and particularly the child with dual sensory impairments, will sit in relation to the group. She will need to ensure that the child can see and hear as well as is possible. This may mean the child will be near to the teacher or adult leading the session, or it may mean the child will be near the materials or equipment being used. It may mean that the child has her back to the window, and the teacher faces the window.

Compromises may have to be reached when a number of children have similar needs, because they cannot all be in the same place. The child will need to know and understand how the group functions, what the purpose of the group is, and her role within the group. The deafblind child needs to know:

- whether the group should listen or speak;
- how children and adults take turns;
- when children may pick up and handle the equipment;
- how the group will finish.

If the group has a formal structure, the child must understand these things or she will appear to be always working against the teacher. Her sensory impairments may prevent her from picking up clues from the rest of the group as to what behaviour is appropriate. The child with dual sensory impairments may, in fact, not be aware of the group around her. She may need to have opportunities to approach, to touch, to communicate with other members of the group, and to learn where they are sitting in relation to her. She may need artificial means to be kept in touch with each of the others during the session.

Some children will not understand the concept of a group. They may need direct information about how and when to respond in a session, the rest of which they may not understand.

April sits with her intervenor while the rest of the group start the morning greeting activity. The children pass a Koosh ball amongst themselves. The child holding the ball says hello to the adults and to the child who gave him the ball. When a child gives the ball to April, April recognises this object, and when the child shakes her hand and says hello close to her ear, she makes a sound. She does this for each adult who comes to see her at this time, reserving her special warmest greeting for her intervenor. Then, with the intervenor's help, she passes the ball to the next child in the circle.

Group work does to some extent have a natural burst–pause rhythm which may be very useful for the deafblind child. The child may participate in her turn, and then wait while others do so. However, it is important that when she is not taking her direct turn, she has some information about what others are doing. The deafblind child may have to work on each section of a group project, for example, because unlike children with better vision and hearing, she cannot see the contributions of others, and so cannot make sense of the fragments she is asked to do.

Serpil is making cakes with her class. Children take turns to put different ingredients in the bowl and stir them. The classroom assistant who is supporting Serpil has put aside some of each of the ingredients for Serpil to add to the bowl, and allows her to feel them, and to feel the other child hold the spoon and stir.

Working independently

Working with an adult all the time is tiring for both the child and the adult. All children will need some time to themselves. That way they can consolidate what they have done, have a break from continual stimuli and demands, and perhaps pursue their own interests. However, it is very easy for some children to resort to passive and negative behaviours when left alone, or to withdraw into themselves.

Purposeful activity should be available even if the child is working without an adult. It can, though, be difficult to find purposeful activity for a child with poor vision and hearing, who may have few skills. Each individual will be very different, and what suits a particular child will have to be worked out after various things have been tried. It is very easy for children with dual sensory impairments to lapse into passivity, and not to act on their environment without adult support, so as soon as a child can use any sort of skill, from moving her fingers to sorting coins, she should be given opportunities to practise it independently. Some children may benefit from simple sensory toys/equipment on a clothes-rail hanging over them, while others may need a box of words to copy and draw. Equipment which a child can use independently can be stored in boxes clearly marked with the child's name, so that any adults in the classroom, or ideally, the child herself can find it whenever she is working alone.

Children with dual sensory impairments can become cut off from other activity in the classroom when they are working alone. An adult, or able peer, should make some form of contact with them by word, touch or vision, regularly, so that they know they have not been left alone, and to give them the opportunity to communicate. For many children, computers and technology have enabled them to work or play with things independently, which they could not have done before. Although a child may need an adult initially to teach them to use a piece of equipment, perhaps the greatest benefit of technology is that children can use it unaided because it is able to respond.

Switch equipment such as battery operated toys, fans, vibrating equipment, and music can give a child an opportunity to practise a movement while engaging in an activity she likes. Most mains equipment can also be operated via a switch using a mains switcher. Computer programmes help to support and consolidate learning in other fields and for some children, programmes which show them the right answers will be very helpful.

Working alone may present difficulties for some children, but it will be a very important part of many children's days, and so it too must be carefully planned and structured.

Using alternative and augmentative communication

A well-organised classroom will give the child as many opportunities as possible to find out about the world. In typical classrooms most information is given and received through the medium of speech, or speech in its written form. Most children with dual sensory impairments will not learn to speak, and are therefore deprived of this significant avenue of communication. Many will need the support of other forms of communication for the whole of their lives.

The use of alternative and augmentative communication systems (AAC systems) must therefore underlie all classroom activities. Children need as much information as possible about classroom activities, and later about what ever is going on in as wide a world as they can access. This additional information may be through object and position and movement cues, through objects of reference, through a symbol system, a signing system, or through print.

Communication will provide structure to activities, as the teacher uses communication cues, presented as most appropriate to the child, to begin activities, during them and to finish them. This will in itself become one of the most basic routines, and help the children to understand that things begin, take place, and finish.

Initially, the cues used will be entirely provided by the teacher, who may also have to store the cues used – photographs, objects, symbols. As the child begins to understand the system, she will need to have access to these materials so that she can make her own contribution. Later it will be very important that the child will have all the vocabulary available so that she can express herself. Sign and touch systems are, of course, always available to the child, but those which need materials or equipment must be made available to her.

The teacher must decide what AAC system she will use. In her decision-making, she will consider how she can make the vocabulary accessible to the child. If the child is to use symbols, the teacher must consider whether the child will be best able to handle a chart or a book. She will consider the availability of a computer programme so that the child can write using the symbols system. She will consider how the child and the class will have access to symbols that are not often used, and may not be kept with her book. The teacher will also decide where the system will be stored so that the child can have access to it – in a bag by her wheelchair, in a book on a table she can reach, or perhaps there will be symbol charts on key parts of the wall at her height.

> Florence uses her symbol book to request items she wants, and to discuss with adults what will happen next. She is beginning to make choices about activities, for example, whether she should kick or throw a ball. When she goes to the swimming pool, she takes a sheet of relevant symbols, laminated to protect them from the water, into the changing room and the pool. It has to be remade fairly often, as it gets old and bent, but she is well motivated to use her communicate in a situation she thoroughly enjoys.

Maintenance and development of the system must be considered. Someone (probably the teacher, but perhaps a speech and language therapist) must be responsible for ensuring that as the child's vocabulary is ready to expand, so new vocabulary in the AAC form she uses is available if the child is using a voice output communication aid or other technological aid, someone must ensure also that it is charged, working and serviced regularly.

AAC systems will also be part of the classroom environment. Children's day charts or timetables, using objects or pictures as necessary, will be placed in the classroom so the child can find them. Certain parts of the classroom may be labelled with photographs, symbols or objects, so that the child can recognise the place, and later learn to respond to requests to go there. Furniture and equipment may also be labelled, to help children to learn that objects have names. Typical children hear words hundreds or thousands of times before they learn to use them. Children with sensory impairments may also need many chances to see words used before they are able to understand and eventually use them.

AAC systems should be used by all members of the classroom team. We do not expect typical children to learn French from adults who only know a few words of the language and use them intermittently. Adults working with children who use AAC systems must be confident users themselves. An adult working on painting with a child who uses symbols should point to her own choices of colour and use the symbols to explain what she has painted, and when she has finished. Adults should also, when close to the child, use the child's system to each other, to show it is a respected system of communication. For example, one teacher may tell another it is time for her coffee break now.

In many cases, the teacher will also use AAC systems when she is working with the whole class. She will accompany her singing with signs when she is doing a music session, and she will use symbols when she is explaining a recipe. She may need to be careful of using too many systems at once, and overloading the children. Which systems she uses, and when she uses them, will be decisions made on the basis of the needs of the children in her class.

Wherever possible, children should also be able to use their systems with other children. When children are able to use early symbolic systems, with one conventional meaning attached to one symbol, they can begin to share communication with other children using the same system. Children at very early levels of development will still use idiosyncratic and highly individual systems, whether these be touch, gesture or object based, and will not have enough abstract and general understanding to be able to use these with anyone but sophisticated communicators who are able to interpret them – probably their teachers.

AAC systems help children to communicate. Some children will use complex systems such as British Sign Language (BSL), which are not readily understood by others. Where possible, however, communication systems should be made transparent, so that more people both in the small community of the school and the wider community of the world can understand them.

Dean does not hear speech, but he uses a symbol system to communicate. He uses a communication book well. Under each symbol the word it relates to is written, so people who do not know the system can work out what he is trying to say. When he goes out to the café, he takes a voice output communication aid, so that he can order the items he wants in a voice rather like everyone else, without being dependent on a sensitive and willing helper to look at his symbols and interpret them.

Robin, who has very little hearing and sight, and communicates competently via fingerspelling, travels to Asda in a taxi. An assistant takes him round, using his typed shopping list. He was unhappy with having to give up his purse to the assistant, who could not tell him how much he had spent. Now he takes a small dial, with the prices rounded up, written on a card in print and braille. The assistant lines the pointer up to the print figure, Robin reads the braille one, and gives the right money, without having to lose his independence and trustingly give over his purse. This simple AAC system works perfectly in this situation.

There is no one answer for all children with sensory impairments. To describe a class of children who recently left or will soon be leaving a school for children with sensory impairments shows how diverse the answers may be.

Katy uses a technological device to write simple sentences. Adults write simple sentences to her. Reading and writing was Katy's first and primary means of communication.

Philip uses speech. Occasionally he will use a sign to make his meaning clear, or adults will sign to him.

Gulam signs to adults in rapid BSL and adults sign to him. Sometimes they encourage him to use his voice!

Abel uses some symbols, when he is motivated to indicate his key needs. Otherwise he goes to things he wants, or points in the direction of them.

Fayznnah uses a complex system which includes some sounds, some gestures which have become standardised, some gestures based on fingerspelling, and a few more or less standardised sounds.

Hannibal uses facial expression and a few sounds which let adults know how he feels. He is not able to express things at a more complex level.

The teacher of children with dual sensory impairments will have to work hard to find the best system for each child, and then the best way of integrating it into the child's educational programme, and her environment.

Developing concepts

Vision and hearing provide enormous amounts of information. From an early age the child perceives differences such as:

- big and little
- on and under
- far and near
- loud and quiet
- hard and soft

and many others.

These perceptual differences, ones that are noticed immediately and without thinking, offer a solid foundation on which concepts are developed. Words can be attached to these concepts and understood by very young children, even though they may mix up the words when they themselves try to speak them.

Of the concepts listed above, however, few of them are as easily understood through touch, and even fewer through taste and smell. The deafblind child needs to be introduced to these and many other concepts by having to think about them, to base them on experiences of feeling, exploring, tasting and smelling. The ease and immediacy of perception – given by vision and, to a lesser extent, hearing – is missing. Concepts have to be learned. In order to form a concept of a person, place, object or activity the child needs to:

- use all senses to acquire as much information as possible;
- experience interacting with the person, going to the place, using the object, or participating in the activity.

Only then can the child form an internal image or concept of the person or object and from that point go on to integrate it into his or her existing concepts of the world or use it to form the basis for new concepts. Some may even be able to go on to name that concept of person, place, object or activity.

In the remainder of this chapter we describe in more detail how to help make the pupil's experiences meaningful, how to help the pupil form an internal image or concept of the world around her, and how to integrate experiences.

Making experiences meaningful

If experiences are to have meaning, the activities ventured on together should either interest the pupil or be related to basic needs, for example eating, washing, dressing. New experiences should be connected with familiar interests or experiences. For example, the child who is moving reluctantly from using a bottle to a cup may go through several stages, drinking from:

- a covered plastic cup with a spout and no handle;
- a cup with half a lid and a spout;
- a cup with a slit in the half lid instead of the spout.

As far as is possible the outcome of these activities should be made clear to the pupil. The steps taken towards completion should be as simple as possible and suited to the child's abilities. Above all, the pupil needs to experience by doing, firstly with help, then moving towards independence, within the child or young person's limits. Taking short-cuts when in a hurry may well work but only in the short term. In the long term the child is confused. The aim should instead be to instil, as far as is possible, a sense of self-direction and self-worth.

The pupil should be helped to form an internal image or concept of the world around her and to integrate experiences. Reflect for a moment on how you distinguish one activity from another. You might have considered:

- what you do;
- what you use (objects);
- where you do it (places);
- when you do it (time);
- who you do it with or who is associated with it (people);
- how you feel when you do it (emotions).

If the pupil who is deafblind is to recognise an activity, cooperate with others and learn from experience, he or she needs some way of identifying and recognising an object, the activity carried out, the time when it is done, or the person it is done with. We consider these below.

Identifying and recognising objects

The pupil with dual sensory impairment will need to be helped to identify and recognise, or characterise objects, in order to form concepts. The pupil will need:

- to touch objects;
- to move objects or move his hands over them;
- to use objects;
- to be given help to identify object characteristics so that the object can be distinguished from other similar objects.

While encouraging the pupil to explore objects as fully as possible it may be helpful to limit use of some objects to appropriate situations. So, playing with cups, shoes, spoons, nappies, etc., in a playpen may help the child who is learning to explore objects – but may confuse the development of concepts associated with these objects. On these occasions it might be helpful to introduce other objects, e.g. egg boxes, balls, shiny paper or whatever is of interest.

When using an object with a pupil the features or characteristics which identify it can be emphasised. The same identifying features should be used by other staff.

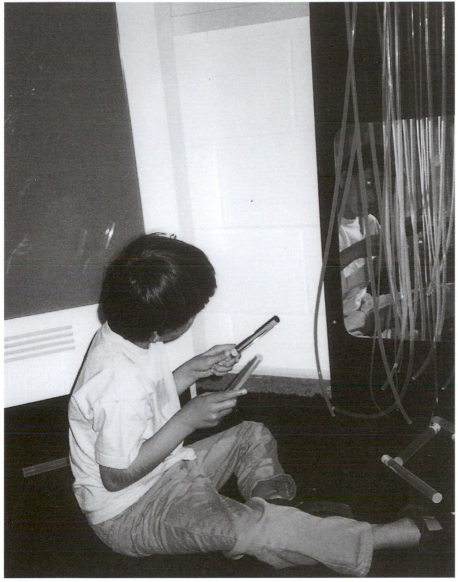

Figure 6.4 Now, what did I do with these the last time?

To identify a hairbrush to Danir the features of bristles and handle are emphasised. Co-actively, the brush is lifted with the child. Adult and child together feel the bristles and the handle. Danir's hair is then brushed.

Jodie's sweater is identified to her by together feeling the texture of the body of the sweater, then the two long sleeves. With Jodie participating to whatever extent is possible, she is helped to put it on.

> Erin's shoe is differentiated from a slipper by adult and child together exploring with their hands the space for the foot, then feeling the texture, then the laces (or straps) to distinguish the shoe, or the pom-pom to distinguish the slipper. Finally, the item is put on her foot.

These activities illustrate that it may be helpful to keep to the same or similar objects. When Erin is learning to put on shoes she may not be helped by having shoes with straps one day, shoes with laces the next and so on. After a time, however, it will be possible and indeed necessary to introduce variety – otherwise the pupil's concept of shoe and slipper would be limited to that shoe and that slipper.

Sorting

For pupils who do gain an internal representation of object, sorting activities can be introduced. At first these should take place in their natural setting.

> Sajeed is involved in putting away cutlery after washing up: spoons are matched with spoons; knives with knives; and so on. Clothes are put away in the right places after the laundry, i.e. all the socks in the top drawer, pants in the second, or whatever.

With learning taking place in the natural setting of bedroom, kitchen or bathroom and by using the appropriate objects in a structured way, the pupil is helped to internalise the qualities necessary for forming concepts. To enable this to happen, all those working with the pupil need to communicate and cooperate. The concepts being taught should be reinforced in all areas.

Identifying and recognising places

A similar approach can be taken to that for identifying objects, in order to help a pupil who cannot see or hear to identify and recognise a room or building, the playground or shops. The pupil might become aware that this is the same room by:

- moving in it;
- identifying objects peculiar to it, e.g. a bed in a bedroom;
- having particular experiences in it.

Certain activities are always carried out with John in one room and he is encouraged to identify the room by exploring its key features with him. He is also given time to explore and discover its similarities to other rooms.

He gradually internalises the idea that a bedroom is where his bed can be found; the dining-room is where he eats and so on. Over time he realises there is more than one bedroom in the house, and that some bedrooms are shared. All of these experiences broaden the concept of bedroom. Each step is based on characteristic features, building on previous knowledge.

Developing a concept of self and others

The young dual sensory impaired pupil has difficulty distinguishing other people from self and from each other. The pupil may perceive little or no difference between mother, father, school staff or travel escort. To help differentiate people each person's characteristics may be highlighted.

Sunil recognises his care assistant by her distinctive bracelet which she always wears when with him. At first, movement was always associated with this distinguishing feature and he was encouraged to spin it around the care assistant's wrist. He is being introduced to another teacher and he has already been inclined to touch this person's beard.

This teacher will use his beard to identify himself to Sunil. When beginning work he will direct Sunil's hand to the ID of 'beard'. For some time this characteristic will remain constant. Each time they come together the ID will be presented and used. No other person at school has a beard.

Developing the pupil's awareness of self

At the same time as drawing the pupil's attention to the characteristics of others he or she will begin to build up an image of self. Massage oil or aromatherapy oils may be appropriate. (It is important to ensure that guidance is available and followed on acceptable practice in the use of oils and massage. In this way the safety of the child is assured. Issues of safety and the legal context operating are discussed more fully in the next chapter.)

Identifying and recognising emotions

The pupil with dual sensory impairment needs support to understand his own and other people's emotions. A pupil with sight and hearing receives information from people's facial expressions and the tone of voice used. A pupil who is deafblind misses all these clues. She may experience the emotions of other people through the muscle tone and tension in others' bodies, and the way the she is treated.

> The pupil's attention can be drawn, in ordinary everyday activities, to other ways of characterising emotions. When her teacher is happy, Francesca's attention is directed towards the teacher's mouth, the vibration in her chest, and noise made. Signs of emotion are exaggerated by hugging her and dancing. A happy movement is identified, such as clapping hands, so helping to assign a symbol for that emotion. On another occasion when going home, Francesca is seen to be happy, and co-actively the 'happy movement' is given. In these ways the more basic emotions of happiness, sadness, anger and fear are identified to Francesca. More complex emotions such as jealousy, loneliness, frustration will probably need to await further development of formal language.

Identifying and recognising activities

The pupil can be helped to identify activities by introducing her to:

- what is used (objects);
- where the activity is done (place);
- who it is done with (persons);
- how she feels when doing it (emotions);
- when it is done (time);
- and how it is done.

Throughout, consistency is the key. The pupil recognises the activity through being physically involved in what happens. At the same time he or she begins to form concepts of objects, places, time, persons, self and emotions by having these identified within activities.

All are aspects of the activity. However, because so many possible associations exist, some means of quickly and easily referring to that activity is needed. To do this, one particular item is pinpointed to identify and label the whole activity. This ID should be:

- an intrinsic part of the activity;
- as far as possible, be identified by the pupil and/or be attractive.

> An ID is to be chosen for Jerry to refer to mealtimes. His teacher begins by observing him while involved in the activity. During mealtimes an object that is especially interesting to him and associated with mealtime, such as a spoon, plate, napkin, is identified as an ID. Jerry is given this 'label', or 'key', or object of reference just before the meal begins. He carries it to the table. Jerry begins to associate it with mealtime.

Fixing symbols in the pupil's mind

Memory lets us compare, conclude, discover, recognise similarities. We use memory to anticipate both happy and sad experiences. We rely on it to discuss, to imagine, to relive situations. It has a vital role to play in the development of language; and it is necessary for communication. One of the ways of helping to 'fix' memories is to introduce a memory box (especially if the pupil is blind), or a memory book (if partially sighted). Objects are identified as symbolising activities or events and these are stored in their own boxes.

> Ben looks forward to going home every Friday, a regularly occurring event that appeals strongly. A box is introduced that contains objects Ben needs for going home on Fridays, i.e. a bag, a favourite home toy, and a home–school diary with tactile clues in it. After using this for many months he anticipates Fridays when any one of these items is introduced. At this point one of the items becomes the identifier, representing the entire event of going home, and his 'home box' is discontinued.

Summary

The deafblind child is educationally disadvantaged by her lack of access to communication and information. The teacher of deafblind children is responsible for creating a learning environment that minimises the effects of dual sensory impairment and maximises the opportunities for learning. Initially she will enable the child to feel secure with both adults and in her environment, in order to release her potential for further learning. Routines and structure, as well as helping the child to recognise those she works with, will lay the foundations for development in all areas. She will create physical and learning settings which allow the child to use her remaining hearing and vision as well as possible, and use techniques which compensate for sensory difficulties. The right environment is essential in helping the child to learn effectively. She will choose and use appropriate alternative and augmentative communication, ensuring that this communication is available to the child at all times. She will carefully plan teaching programmes, which will assist the child to make progress. She will consider the child's extra need for motivation, and for control of the learning situation as far as possible. She will design tasks which take into account the time the child needs for learning, the styles of prompting she can best use, and which uses every opportunity to put learning into practice. The deafblind child is severely restricted in what she can learn incidentally. She is more reliant than other children on how her teacher organises, plans and delivers programmes. Good teaching, based on appropriate principles, will allow the child the opportunity for learning.

References

Jacobsen, K. *et al.* (1993) 'Communication with congenitally deafblind persons', *Deafblind Education*, January–June 1993, p. 13.

McInnes, J. M. and Treffry, J. A. (1982) *Deafblind Infants and Children. A Developmental Guide*. Toronto: University of Toronto Press.

CHAPTER 7

Deafblindness and society

Stuart Aitken

Introduction

The subject of **Challenging behaviour** (Topic 1) may seem at odds with what you have read so far. However, the discussion of challenging behaviour is set within the context of pupils who, because of deafblindness, and having few effective communication strategies, resort to what may work best for them. Dealing with challenging behaviour is one of the many instances in which practice has to take place within legally acceptable boundaries, and this legal context is one to which we return in the final topic of this chapter.

Before that, we consider approaches that help to ensure effective working relationships with others. Topic 2, **Working with people** recognises that any individual working with a pupil who is deafblind will be a part of a wider system of influence on the pupil. That system will include the child's parents or carers. It will include colleagues who may be part of a close-knit team employed on the same site, perhaps a school or other centre. In addition, practitioners based in other disciplines and in other organisations may be involved with that pupil, possibly on a frequent basis. We suggest areas in which skills can be developed that will help to ensure an effective working team, in which each member understands his or her own and others' responsibilities, and can build on the knowledge and expertise offered by parents and the wider network of practitioners.

In Topic 3, **The Legal Context**, we consider a context even wider than the network of practitioners involved directly or indirectly with the child or young person. The last few years in the UK have witnessed wide-ranging legislation reform in health, education and social services. With such a diversity of legislation and its effects, we consider areas of reform that have direct implications for those who work with children and young people who are deafblind.

Topic 1: Dealing with challenging behaviour

What is challenging behaviour?

Challenging behaviour has been defined for example as 'behaviour of such intensity, frequency or duration as to affect the physical safety of the learner or others' Phillips (1989).

Expanded to include the fact that it can be a barrier to learning opportunities:

severely challenging behaviour refers to behaviour of such an intensity, frequency or duration that the physical safety of the person or others is likely to be placed in serious jeopardy, or behaviour which is likely to seriously limit or deny access to and use of ordinary community facilities. (Emerson *et al.* 1987)

Examples of challenging behaviour include:

- stereotypic behaviour such as hand waving, rocking, eye poking and rubbing;
- self-injury such as biting or hitting oneself;
- aggression towards the environment such as breaking things, throwing or trashing things;
- aggression to others such as slapping, punching, hair-pulling;
- inappropriate social behaviour such as masturbating in public or stripping.

Why is it more frequent with people who are deafblind?

By no means all children and young people who are deafblind indicate challenging behaviour. Nevertheless it is true to say that many do. Does this demonstrate that challenging behaviour is an inevitable consequence of deafblindness? If this is true then it suggests that very little can be done to alleviate the problem. But other possible causes of challenging behaviour exist including:

- deafblindness could be just one form of damage to the brain: challenging behaviour would then be 'just' another form of brain damage;
- it could be a result of an underlying but unidentified medical condition, for instance the person could be in pain or discomfort;
- a difficulty in communicating with others – in 'getting one's message across' or misunderstanding another's intentions; challenging behaviour would be a way of communicating or, perhaps just as important, a way of withdrawing from communication;
- attitudes of others, such as not being given enough freedom, too little choice, or too much choice.

Of these suggested causes, most could be alleviated by changing the opportunities available to the person who is deafblind. This raises two important points. First, challenging behaviour often serves some function for the pupil. Second, in order to deal with it effectively, it may be possible to ascertain one or more causes and these may well be to do with what we or others do rather than a problem existing in the pupil.

We already know that one of the most important consequences of deafblindness is the difficulties it causes in communicating with others. Challenging behaviour is often an attempt to communicate a message, or a way of expressing confusion, fear or frustration. As such it is often a symptom of an underlying issue, rather than an issue in itself.

In many situations the reason we see this behaviour is because the person does not have a more appropriate and socially acceptable way of expressing him or herself. The pupil might be trying to say 'I am unhappy', 'I don't want to do this anymore', 'I've got toothache' or any one of hundreds of other things that he or she cannot express.

It can be difficult to change challenging behaviour as it is often performing a useful function for the person. It could be how the pupil is trying to tell you that he or she does not like others making decisions for him, or that he does not want beans on toast for his lunch.

Instead of saying 'no' to the pupil, one of the messages to get across is 'Don't do what you are doing – do this instead.' What might 'instead' look like? It could include for example the suggestions given in Chapter 2 on communication as well as those contained in Chapter 6 on effective teaching.

Preventing challenging behaviour

There is no single response to challenging behaviour. Both the pattern of behaviour and the particular location in which it occurs will vary from person to person. One of the difficulties in dealing with it is that most of the effective strategies for overcoming challenging behaviour are long-term. Effective strategies require positive and systematic identification and the use of methods of communication which eventually give the individual with challenging behaviour an alternative and more constructive means of self-expression. This longer-term view is proactive, and depends on sound planning within a team, sharing information and implementing strategies with consistency and continuity. After discussing this proactive approach we will describe short-term strategies. These are essentially designed to be reactive, and are used to respond quickly to events. Rather than thinking about what to do to prevent it happening, they concentrate on what to do once it has happened.

Dealing with challenging behaviour: planning for the long term

First and foremost, try to establish trusting relationships and offer experiences that are meaningful and which take place through familiar people within a safe and predictable environment. Through this the foundations for communicating with the pupil are laid down. This in turn reduces the need for her to express feelings and make requests in ways that are potentially damaging to all. In doing so instances of challenging behaviour are also reduced.

Good information

Make sure that you know as much as you can about:

- the person's likes and dislikes;
- how he or she communicates and the vocabulary used;
- methods of responding to behaviour at home and elsewhere.

It is vital to ensure a good flow of accurate information, ideas and approaches across teams and between teaching and care staff. Encourage colleagues to share information on what they have found to be successful in their interactions. Forward planning of activities should consider how to:

- identify communication strategies that will indicate what is to come next rather than having the world continually happening to the learner;
- let the pupil know how long he or she is staying;
- have a consistent approach and, if possible, a continuity of staff with a limited number of staff relating to the individual pupil;
- where appropriate, use tactile objects of reference or signs for people's names and use these consistently;
- emphasise the pupil's likes and, as far as possible, avoid dislikes;
- avoid confrontation as far as possible, instead try diverting attention to something the pupil likes;
- ensure good communication between staff, especially if there are staff changeovers;
- plan activities ahead of time and in accordance with the pupil's level of ability and interest;
- avoid a haphazard approach but remain flexible;
- agree a consistent approach to handling behaviour;
- be aware of the composition of the group of pupils – the group may be made up of some who prefer to take part in non-group activities – in this case ask yourself why activities are being planned as part of a group.

Identify the cause or causes

It is easy to convince oneself that there is a single cause but often opinion will vary among staff who know the person. If the source of the behaviour is wrongly identified then any long-term strategy for eliminating it will not work and may even make it worse. It is therefore important to use accurate record-keeping.

Common methods for recording and monitoring behaviour include:

- ABC charts (Antecedent, Behaviour, Consequence);
- frequency charts which help to identify patterns over weeks or months;
- customised charts can be designed to identify specific difficulties.

Ask yourself why you are saying 'no'

It may be worth thinking twice before saying 'no' to a request from a young person. Is your refusal really an honest response to something that is not possible? If so, what can we do to help that person to understand why it's not possible? If it is possible, perhaps we could 'go with the flow'.

The most effective way to prevent challenging behaviour is through good practice. Introducing effective strategies by which the pupil can communicate will almost always reduce difficult behaviours and will often eliminate them. Bear in mind, though, that if the pupil has had these difficulties for a long time, it may well take that length of time or even longer to eliminate them.

Non-aversive behavioural intervention

This approach is based in part on modifying the person's behaviour, reinforcing 'good' behaviour and reducing inappropriate behaviour. (The reason the word 'good' is in quotes should by now be clear. Whether a person's behaviour is thought to be good is often a value judgement. We might think a certain behaviour is not good because it involves destruction of the nearest furniture, but for the pupil that behaviour may be good because it gets what he or she wants.) In essence, if a person is rewarded in some way for a behaviour then it will be more likely to occur. The reward is something positive to that person.

There are many different approaches to non-aversive behavioural intervention. All of them incorporate certain key principles, although each method emphasises each of these elements in different ways. Below we give a simplified example of 'differential reinforcement of other behaviour'.

Differential reinforcement of other behaviour (DRO)

Reward is given when there is a certain time interval without the challenging behaviour recurring. It might be that after a half hour without the behaviour some reward that is positive to that person is given.

Care needs to be taken when choosing the time interval. It should be neither too large, nor too small. Also the reward needs to be chosen with care. It should be positive to the person and not be given more often than he or she would ordinarily seek it out when free to do so.

The idea is that over time as the behaviour reduces, the gap between rewards can be increased.

However, non-aversive behavioural intervention – dealing with the behaviour itself – should only ever be one of the elements considered in planning. It is essential that hand in hand with a programme to reduce behavioural difficulties there is an accompanying input to the curriculum. This should focus on one or more from:

- increasing the person's ability and opportunities to communicate;
- increasing the number of activities the person can do;
- substituting more desirable behaviour(s) for the undesirable one(s);
- identifying learning needs;
- identifying difficulties presented within the environment or with other people.

Reacting to challenging behaviour: short-term solutions

Despite the best intentions, there will be times when incidents of challenging behaviour cannot be prevented, where the best laid plans just do not seem to work out, perhaps because the pupil is feeling unwell. Nevertheless it may be possible to reduce the frequency, duration and intensity of any instances.

Stay calm
It is very important that when managing challenging behaviour staff should try to remain in control of the situation. If you can keep calm it may have a calming influence upon the individual experiencing difficulties.

Divert the pupil's attention
If the person builds up gradually to challenging behaviour, it may be possible to identify the early warning signs and to develop diversionary tactics. In some cases the solution may be to provide the person with the means to become more relaxed, such as playing a favourite piece of music, offering a massage or a comforting object.

Don't all rush to help
A team of workers trying to intervene when someone's behaviour becomes challenging may be perceived as threatening. The situation may become worse. It is usually more helpful for one 'key' worker to interact with the young person. Other staff members should back away if possible (but remain within calling distance).

Going out
Management of challenging behaviour instances outwith the school or other centre presents additional difficulties. There is less control over the environment outside. As a result some means of physically restraining the person may be required. This

may be needed in order to protect the client from pavements, walls, etc. It is worth considering the following questions before going outside with a pupil who has been observed exhibiting challenging behaviour on a regular basis.

1. Are there at least two people accompanying the child/young person? One person may need to call for assistance.
2. Do you have an official ID card? You may be challenged by a member of the public who may not understand what you are trying to do.

Physical restraint or intervention

From time to time it may be necessary physically to intervene and to restrain a pupil who is about to harm him or herself, others, or to damage property. Often the term 'physical restraint' is used when referring to this physical intervention. In our view the term 'physical intervention' is perhaps more appropriate than 'physical restraint'. The word 'restraint' conjures up images of straitjackets, wrist straps and the like. It is unlikely that you will have used or considered using such forms of restraint. However it is quite likely that you have used or have considered using other forms of physical intervention, which would include:

- holding fingers, hands, wrist, arms, legs or other parts of body;
- blocking movements;
- removal from a room, from a group, or removing an object;
- confining to a room, or by a duvet, blanket, a harness, a chair, or to a bed.

Some readers may be surprised to read that an intervention as simple as holding fingers or hands, or removal from a room should be considered as a form of physical intervention. Nevertheless they are. As such, staff should be aware of the need to prepare a physical intervention record.

When physical intervention may be appropriate
Physical intervention can only be justified under certain circumstances.

1. A pupil may constitute a danger to him or herself by self-mutilation, head punching, etc. Physical intervention may be needed to ensure his or her safety. This is in line with a legal 'duty of care' staff have towards that pupil. Later in this chapter we discuss the legal framework in more detail.
2. A pupil may need to be restrained to prevent harm to others or, on occasion, a member of staff. Only such effort as is needed to calm the situation should be employed. Physical punishment should not be used under any circumstances.
3. Intervention may be needed to prevent damage to property. Property must never be placed above the pupil's interests. However, if, as can happen, a pupil

sets about the destruction of training equipment or the property of others, it is in order to use such minimal physical intervention as will calm the situation, nothing more.

Physical intervention should only be used as a last resort. It is not constructive to use it on a regular basis, as this will obstruct the build-up of a trusting and valued relationship.

Minimum levels of physical intervention
In determining the 'minimum' level of physical intervention, it will be necessary to consider the following points:

- the physical frailty/strength of the pupil;
- the dual sensory impairment;
- the pupil's most effective means of communication.

Recording instances of physical intervention
The physical intervention record is a record of actions to be taken with a pupil in specific circumstances. It reflects what is agreed as part of general good practice with that pupil and is evidence that planning has taken place. It is a record which can be called upon to assess actions, review plans and chart progress.

Any physical intervention should be clearly thought out and the rationale for its use recorded. In a very real sense then the physical intervention record is where long-term planning meets the need to respond to situations that arise in the short term. Precise records should be kept about what actions to take, where, when and how. This process aims to encourage good and safe practice consistent in approach, with clear and well thought out agreed interventions.

Accountability
Staff should ensure that the pupil's parent or carer is aware of plans for dealing with specific behaviours. Plans should include the actions to be taken by staff, the intentions (both short-, medium- and long-term), the perceived advantage to the pupil and review arrangements. The pupil or his or her representatives should have the opportunity to comment on plans and any representative who has a legitimate interest in the pupil's welfare should expect to have the records made available: in the future this may include representatives of social services' registration and inspection functions.

Completing the record
A sample record of physical intervention is shown in Figure 7.1. Individual schools or other centres will most likely use a format tailored to their own purposes.

Physical Intervention Record

Date completed	
Completed by	
Agreed by	
Reviewed by	
Risk assessment by	

Pupil name

Pupil address

What the
Pupil does

What you
should do
immediately

Additional
Guidance

How the
intervention
benefits the
pupil

Risk
assessment
outcome

Comments
or
reservations

Actions to be taken
☐ record incident
☐ discuss with senior staff
☐ inform family
☐ inform social worker
☐ inform senior manager
☐ modify plan and record
☐ monitor the behaviour
☐ report on monitoring
☐ review the risk
☐ agree future actions

Figure 7.1 Physical Intervention Record

Identifying the behaviour

Behaviour is identified and described by the staff member and specific agreement with this description must be provided by senior staff. The description of the behaviour must be clear and unambiguous, brief and to the point, identifying only the physical behaviour. Someone reading this description should be able to visualise the behaviour or context and recognise the behaviour when it happens.

Taking action

Immediate specific actions are described for each behaviour. These should be clear and unambiguous, brief and to the point, identifying only the actions required to be taken by staff involved. These actions will be the least required to achieve the desired result and will aim to protect pupil safety and minimise risk or injury to the pupil or other pupils and staff. Force can only be used if it is immediately necessary and only for so long as it remains necessary to avoid serious harm to the pupil. Actions will also take into account the communication abilities of the pupil and his or her physical condition, including any health condition. Actions are agreed between the senior manager and staff and approved with the family or other representative if appropriate. Actions should be achievable and staff should be trained in their use.

Escalations

Often minor behavioural signs indicate that something will happen later if action is not taken immediately. The initial behaviour may be insignificant and may go unnoticed unless specifically identified. It is helpful to say what might happen next but it is important to avoid creating the expectation that it will happen next. While it is preferable to have one record for specific behaviours and actions, staff may want to include some step by step guidance.

Additional guidance

Additional guidance may need to be given.

Benefits for the pupil

It must be clear that taking action is for the benefit of the individual pupil concerned, be the least restrictive to achieve that benefit and that the benefit could not be achieved without the intervention. The record should state what that benefit is.

Assessment of risk

The risk associated with all physical interventions must be assessed. Such an assessment may normally be undertaken by a senior manager of staff, or delegate, along with the staff member who knows the pupil best. On occasion, it may be necessary to seek an assessment of risk from an external colleague.

Comments and reservations

In agreeing and reviewing actions taken with pupils, all staff involved in making the agreement and putting into practice the actions agreed should have the opportunity to share constructive comments or reservations about these actions – both on the record and in discussion with senior staff. Once an intervention is agreed, all staff should follow it.

Follow-on actions

Accurate and effective records should be kept on the use of restraint. Incident forms should be completed for all occasions of the use of physical intervention. These incident forms should be reviewed by senior staff.

In reviewing and monitoring the pupil's behaviour and the use of restraint, those involved in determining activities and working practices should agree future actions needed to identify the causes of the behaviour and areas for communication and other curriculum development.

Inappropriate methods of control

Challenging behaviour requires sensitive, thoughtful handling. It is very important to establish explicit boundaries. There are several methods of control which are generally not acceptable.

1. Physical restraint which exceeds the *minimum* necessary to secure the well-being of the pupil.
2. All forms of corporal and physical punishment, including smacking, pushing and striking.
3. Restrictions in social contact with family members or friends.
4. Inappropriate use of secure accommodation – rooms with locks must never be used as a place of containment or punishment.
5. The denial of food or of a meal as punishment. Food is not just physically sustaining, it is also important psychologically. Its withdrawal could lead to resentment and confusion. It may be necessary though to withdraw the pupil from the meal table, if this is where the behaviour took place. However, he or she should be allowed to finish the meal, either back at the table or elsewhere, once the problem has subsided.
6. The use of bedtime as a punishment. Instead this should ideally be a happy time. More than this, the young person's bedroom should be a personal place where he or she can go to be alone or to undertake activities alone.

Reporting back to families

It may not be necessary to report every single incidence of challenging behaviour to the family/carer, unless this is requested. When reporting, be honest about what occurred, what happened and the outcome. Document and explain to families whenever bruising or other injury has occurred.

Discussions such as these would usually be carried out by senior members of staff but all staff should be aware of the need for the sensitive disclosure of facts, making sure not to exaggerate the incident and taking care to stress positive outcomes – for example, the fact that a reason for the outburst was identified or that a new means of diverting attention was discovered.

Topic 2: Working with people

A child who is deafblind will be given various forms of help, especially in early childhood. A number of professionals or practitioners will be in contact: health workers will deal with medical care throughout the child's life; educational visitors, teachers and classroom assistants will work with the child in nursery school and beyond; social workers may offer respite care and other forms of support and will adopt an increasing role as the pupil reaches school leaving age. In this topic we discuss some of this network of support available to the child. We outline how this can be of help and describe some of the difficulties that can arise when the child, and especially the family, are on the receiving end of offers of support. We begin by thinking of the most important source of support to the child.

Working with parents and carers

A parent of a child, Jim, who has special educational needs and was due to start school next term, visited the school to discuss her older child who already attended. Making conversation, the girl's teacher asked the parent 'When will Jimmy go to school?' An innocent enough remark, or so it would seem. On her journey home, the parent worried about that remark. She interpreted it to mean that her son would have to attend a different school from his local school. Her reasoning was that the teacher had used the word 'go', instead of saying 'When will Jimmy come to school?' She continued to worry about which school her son would attend until he started school – the same school as his sister.

This story illustrates several points. First, it suggests that innocent remarks, despite the best of intentions, can unknowingly be hurtful. Second, it demonstrates that parents can and will experience heightened sensitivity, where remarks can have double meanings. Third, it suggests that certain times in a child's life are associated with parents being especially vulnerable. These times are usually during periods of transition, for example from preschool to school, or in preparation for leaving school.

What parents want from you

A great deal is often written by practitioners about what parents and families expect from an education service or, more widely, from the range of services with which both their child and themselves might come into contact. Less often, parents of children with special educational needs have been asked about their expectations. In preparation for a conference presentation in 1996, Sense Scotland invited parents to comment on their feelings of involvement in their child's education. When things felt good, what was it that had happened? The results were interesting.

Parents wanted people to take time to listen. Where they had expressed concerns it had worked well when their concerns were dealt with at the time, not left to stack up until a crisis arose. Parents did not want to be patronised. There was a general feeling that, although getting and maintaining their involvement right had taken time, in the long term it had saved those organisations involved in their child's education both money and time.

Dealing with difficulties was recognised as not being easy. However, it was found that the process of dealing with these difficulties could be a source of strength. Parents mentioned that some of their most positive experiences of education had come at the end of a difficult process of resolving some problematic issue. Respect and trust was developed because the practitioners involved were honest about these difficulties and worked through them with the parents. Some parents reported a real sense of working together, of recognising the value of each others' resources and views.

One way to think about improving your contact with parents is to consider the different sorts of contacts you have with parents and to analyse in what way things might be improved. You might want to discuss with a senior colleague whether a parent or group of parents could be consulted to discuss how approaches might be improved. (If this seems in any way threatening, either to yourself or to others, ask yourself why this might be the case. Or, if you feel that there is no need for improvement, ask yourself how you would check that this is true.)

Initiating and maintaining successful contact with parents and families is affected by many factors. First and foremost, successful contact depends on the quality of each interaction you will have with a parent. Next, by understanding the different sorts of reasons for contacts taking place with parents, ways to improve each of these contacts can be identified. Circulating information to parents, telephoning to arrange meetings, report-writing, are all examples of different sorts of reasons for contacting parents. More broadly, the structures set up by the particular service in which you work can effect successful contact. Education and other services can take actions that set a climate for successful contact. We will describe each of these briefly in turn.

Quality of interactions

1. Treat all requests for advice and support confidentially and with honesty, sensitivity and respect.
2. Work in an open and cooperative manner and involve families in planning and decision-making.
3. Recognise and respect the uniqueness of each child and his or her relatives and carers and always give information in an appropriate manner.
4. Give clear and concise information and avoid making statements which may be misleading or misunderstood.
5. Treat all relatives and carers in a way that takes account of their individual needs, including such things as ethnic origin, religious background, disability or sexual orientation.
6. Do not share personal opinions about other pupils or staff.
7. Help colleagues deal with calls and requests by ensuring that you record information accurately and promptly.
8. Always reassure callers that you will pass on information and make sure that you do.
9. Always think about the individual and their needs before you speak.
10. Make sure you put enough time aside. There is nothing worse to a parent than having someone constantly checking their watch in anticipation of the next appointment. If there is a pressing engagement, set the time limits at the outset of the meeting.
11. Do not gossip or make throw-away remarks. Especially if taken out of context, these can be very damaging and are likely to cause distress.
12. You are bound by confidentiality on matters relating to other pupils and other staff: if you find yourself in difficulties speak to a senior member of staff.
13. Avoid making statements such as: 'We never have that problem here.' This can make parents feel inadequate. It is also probably not true. If it is true that you do not experience a specific problem which parents do, this needs to be approached very carefully, and is probably best done by a senior staff member.
14. It can be painful for parents if their child suddenly achieves new goals for the first time when away from home. These occasions need to be dealt with tactfully.
15. Cultural needs are extremely important. It *does* matter if children are given the kind of food that is culturally taboo. It *does* matter for many Muslim children and their families that they be showered and *not* bathed. Things that may seem of no importance to many may make all the difference as to whether a family can trust you or not.

16. Don't make assumptions about personal care: soap may damage some types of skin, some children's hair should always be oiled, some families will want their child assisted only by a person of the same gender – or, indeed, only by females.

17. Don't make assumptions about any pupil's needs – always check through everything with families. If you are not sure whether it is worth checking something out with a family, think of all the little things that are important to you, and how you would feel if assumptions were to be made by others about you.

18. If you need to take notes, at the start of the session explain what you are doing and what will happen to this information.

Quality in contacts

By attending to each of the points mentioned above, interactions with parents and carers can be made to work more effectively and a relationship based on trust developed. Individual interactions are also affected by the nature or type of occasions for contacts taking place with parents and carers. Different types of contact include:

- circulating information to parents;
- receiving information from parents;
- planning meetings, either just with parents or with other practitioners;
- at the time of meetings;
- sending reports either written by you or colleagues, or written by other practitioners such as a speech and language therapy report.

Circulating information to parents

Information is a powerful tool and the person who provides information is in a position of power. Before circulating information care should be taken to ensure that the language used is neither derogatory nor disabling. Examples of disabling language, and to be avoided, include using terms such as: 'the deafblind', 'she is an autistic', 'he is epileptic', 'handicapped'.

Use of jargon should be avoided. For example, the meaning of the next paragraph in a letter to a parent may be clear to some of those working with the pupil concerned, but it will be less clear to others:

His expressive communication is coming on well. I thought I would bring you up to date on our achievements over the past few weeks since you last saw him. We are about to introduce objects of reference. These will help integrate development of concepts like representational understanding into his day to day communication.

(You might like to note down other points in this paragraph that would be a cause for concern, given that it appears in a letter to parents.)

Be aware that there is potentially an ambivalence when success is achieved with a pupil. On the one hand, parents will most likely be pleased about these achievements, after all they confirm any decisions they made about their child's placement. On the other hand, these very same achievements may remind parents their child is different and that they are unable to help their child in the same way. The paragraph below, a hypothetical letter to a parent, demonstrates this ambivalence:

> Can you believe that, having been here only four weeks, Ian has picked up ten new signs and he only came here knowing one sign? I have discussed this with my manager and we agreed it would be helpful if you were to be able to see these signs on video. That way you will be able to keep on using them and give him practice while he is home for the week's holiday. Give us a ring if you are not clear about how to use any of the signs or the situations to use them in.

(Other than the consolidation of ten new signs in four weeks, what else stands out in this paragraph. Hint: think about parental involvement.)

If you are sending information that is not good, consider if it might be better to phone up to discuss its contents before sending it. That way the news can be less distressing than if it appears first in black and white.

Information received from parents

Information sent by parents should never be ignored or glossed over. Always acknowledge receipt of that information. This need not be by letter; a note in a home–school diary may be enough.

Arranging meetings

Often meetings need to be arranged with parents. These might involve colleagues within your own school or centre or other practitioners might be involved. Often parents are the last to be contacted to find out if a meeting is convenient. Even worse, they are often not asked if the meeting is convenient but told the time and place of the meeting and expected to attend.

While it is not always possible to meet parental expectations for meeting times and dates, it is important to keep under review the following points:

- how arrangements are made;
- who is consulted first for dates and times;
- whether access to the building meets the needs of parents (and others) attending;
- whether arrangements are needed for child care, especially if there are preschool siblings;

- whether parents are invited to add items to the agenda;
- that minutes of previous meetings are circulated in time.

Holding meetings

Most practitioners are well used to attending meetings, taking an active part in them, know colleagues well and generally know 'the form' a meeting will take. This is by no means true for all parents, though some may well be even more used to attending and chairing meetings than other practitioners.

Note that each time you meet a parent you remind that parent that their child is different. If you do not think this is true, ask yourself this question: 'If the child had not been deafblind would the parent be attending this meeting?'

Quality services

Below we list some of the simple actions that can be taken that will help to establish a relationship with parents that is based on mutual respect, trust, openness and honesty. As will be seen, the actions that we suggest are not based on some sort of abstract theory. They are ordinary, everyday actions that most people find helpful in their interactions with other people. As such they might be called 'people skills'.

1. Ensure that information is automatically made available to parents, that it is written in an accessible form that is easily understood.
2. Provide parents with a clear point of contact. This person should be able to answer questions, make decisions and should be able to coordinate and ensure actions that are agreed are then taken.
3. Where concerns are raised by parents, ensure that early action is taken (and if a decision will take time, let parents know this and give some idea of when a decision is likely). Action taken should be sensitive, positive and helpful. Ample time should be given to allow time for people to air concerns, so that decisions are not rushed.
4. Ensure that any time-scales agreed are kept to and that the timing agreed suits parents as well as yourselves.
5. Where assessment is being carried out ensure that it takes on board parental views:
   - there should be full discussion with no hidden issues – no last-minute surprises should occur;
   - people should listen to what is being said and be open to differing views and opinions.
6. Aim to make decisions about your service or other services in agreement with the family.
7. Ensure that arrangements to use your service, or give access to other services, are straightforward.

8. Make your service open to scrutiny by parents, ensure that it is flexible and responsive to their individual needs.

9. When difficulties arise be prepared to be open to concerns and willing to hear all the issues, to work things out together and to sort things out amicably.

10. Ensure that everyone involved understands their roles, the roles of others, and make sure they know the child's or young person's details.

Figure 7.2 Enjoying fish and chips on a day out

Working with others outwith the family

Aside from close family, relatives and often neighbours, other sources of support are available to a child or young person who is deafblind. All families in the UK have contact with a range of practitioners when a baby is born. For most families, contact with health practitioners is restricted to the health visitor and GP. One or two health checks may take place prior to the child starting nursery school. But the experience of health care and the education system anticipated by most families is one of irregular contact made with a small number of familiar people (in a rural community most practitioners contacted will be known within that community). Most others in the community will be able to give information about what to expect, who they will meet and what will happen.

Contrast this situation with the birth of a child who is deafblind, especially if that child has additional complex health needs. Before the child enters school the family will have come into contact with many practitioners, possibly including:

- GP and health visitor
- paediatrician
- ear, nose and throat specialist
- ophthalmologist
- orthoptist
- audiologist
- hearing aid technician
- speech and language therapist
- occupational therapist
- physiotherapist
- social worker
- educational psychologist
- educational home visitor
- teacher of hearing impaired children
- teacher of visually impaired children.

Each of those people will be in a position to offer some sort of support to families and may have expected the families to become involved in some way in the treatment offered, activities suggested or locations to be visited. Each will no doubt be in a position to offer information to families. How should that information be given? People need information to:

- be clear but sensitively given;
- be understandable to them;
- suggest what they can do next, but recognise other commitments;
- say what others will do next;
- invite feedback, and further questioning.

So, information can be a powerful tool. As such it can do a great deal of good and, if information-giving is done wrongly or insensitively, it can do harm. One of the ways information can do harm is when a large number of people is involved with the child and where each of these people expects the parent to be involved in what they are doing with the child. For example, one might want help from the parents to introduce a system of signing. But first, that practitioner has to ask himself or herself whether he or she is making a reasonable request. There will be other priorities and pressures for that parent and these too need to be recognised.

Another of the down sides to involvement arises when there is lack of continuity. In order to be involved, pupils and parents may have to get to know and adapt to many individual styles. It is not unusual for a child, by the time he or she is eight years old, to have had the following practitioners working regularly with the child:

- four speech and language therapists;
- five physiotherapists;
- four educational psychologists;
- five auxiliaries or classroom assistants;
- five class teachers;
- one or more teacher for hearing impairment;
- one or more occupational therapist;
- eight or more doctors.

As can be seen, while the intentions of the various practitioners might be valuable and honourable, the practicalities of involvement can be tiring in the extreme.

Working in a team

One point stands out above all others when working with other people towards a common goal, of educating the pupil who is deafblind. It applies irrespective of where the other people are based, whether based on a single site or working from different sites for different employers.

The most important objective for all is that effective communication takes place between individuals who are in contact with the pupil who is deafblind. Without effective communication among colleagues, the pupil will be faced with a series of disconnected individuals, working in isolation from each other, using techniques to communicate with him or her that have no shared understanding, engaging in activities with no obvious purpose. The pupil will remain bewildered by a fragmented, unpredictable world.

Effective communication among colleagues is vital. What can be done to improve communication among colleagues? It may come as a surprise that the elements that make for effective communication with parents and carers also, for the most part, help to ensure effective communication with colleagues.

Record-keeping

In addition to developing one's interpersonal skills attention needs to be paid to the quality of record-keeping. Some of the purposes of record-keeping include:

- to share information;
- to improve awareness and understanding;
- to provide a reminder of future events;
- to provide a reminder of past events;
- to pass on instructions;
- to provide encouragement and reinforcement;
- to assist planning and review processes;
- to measure progress, identify problems and trends;
- to check and monitor effective use of resources;

- to provide evidence of meeting objectives;
- to be accountable.

These few simple rules may help to improve quality when writing records:

- be clear;
- be concise;
- be accurate;
- be objective and avoid subjectivity;
- respect the person about whom you are writing;
- avoid using slang and in-house words/phrases;
- do not use in-jokes;
- do not pass judgements;
- do not use insulting language;
- do not emotionalise and over-dramatise;
- avoid using jargon.

Working with people in other disciplines

Earlier we identified a few of the wide range of support services which a pupil who is deafblind may receive before and during his educational career. Some are based in education, others in health and others still in social services. Each of these agencies or organisations will have different skills and experiences to offer. How this various expertise is harnessed to best effect can play a vital role in ensuring that pupils receive effective educational, health and other forms of support. How can this best be achieved?

The multi-disciplinary approach

In this approach all practitioners are aware of each other's goals. In addition, each contributes to the overall objectives by:

- carrying out his or her own programmes;
- working in parallel with others;
- sharing findings and reports.

This is the most common working practice exemplified by the following: a speech and language therapist working on developing a pupil's communication, or an occupational therapist working with the pupil to improve hand function.

The inter-disciplinary approach

The term 'inter-disciplinary' is often used interchangeably with the term 'multi-disciplinary', as an approach to team work. However, they signify quite different approaches. In an inter-disciplinary approach:

- practitioners incorporate the views of other disciplines;
- practitioners incorporate other disciplines' goals in own activities.

An example of this approach would occur if an occupational therapist used literacy materials or a voice output communication aid to develop a pupil's hand function.

The trans-disciplinary approach

This approach is slightly different to the inter-disciplinary approach. In it the boundaries between one professional group and another, and between professionals and parents, are even more blurred than in the inter-disciplinary approach. In this approach:

- a small number of practitioners (and this might instead be members of the pupil's family) carry out the aims and objectives of the other disciplines involved with the pupil.

One example of putting this approach into practice would be where the teacher incorporates all the goals of occupational therapist, speech and language therapist and physiotherapist within the pupil's whole curriculum.

Each of these three approaches represents an important advance in that each offers the chance to build on the expertise of other practitioners. However, for any one of these models to work with any effectiveness there needs to be a commitment made by all concerned to ensuring that effective communication takes place. The basis of effective communication can be established by:

- being open and honest with each other;
- recognising the worth of all potential contributors (including parents and others);
- establishing and maintaining trust;
- acting on the basis of individual needs;
- being accountable.

The role of the coordinator

Finally, in our discussion of working with people, we consider the role of a coordinator. Throughout this topic we have addressed the need for effective communication with parents, carers, colleagues on site and colleague practitioners from other disciplines. We have addressed this need from different angles, including:

- what specific actions can be taken to improve interactions and communication with parents, carers and others;
- what commitments a service can make to improve working practices with parents, staff and colleagues from other disciplines;
- ways of improving report-writing and record-keeping.

The overarching theme we have taken is that, when it comes to forming and maintaining effective relationships with other people, there is, for the most part, nothing unique about children and young people who are deafblind. The skills required are present, or can be learned by all of us.

The difficulty arises when applying these principles, actions and standards with children and young people who are deafblind. Their need for effective communication is so much more pressing. The pupil depends on effective communication among other people so that he or she can access information in a consistent way, has someone to communicate with and something to communicate about, can begin to make choices, anticipate the people, objects, places, events and interactions in his physical and social world.

Often effective communication depends on someone being designated to have the role of coordinator. The coordinator should have a mixture of contact time with the pupil and be given time to coordinate input from other practitioners, including education and therapy inputs. For a coordinating role to be effective all inputs are channelled through this person. This is not to say that other practitioners should not have contact with the pupil. They should, but that education contact should be planned in advance in conjunction with the coordinator. In this approach no occasion should arise when individuals carry out isolated assessment or teaching work with the pupil. The purpose and content of that work should first be agreed with the coordinator.

This should apply to speech and language therapy intervention just as much as to the educational curriculum. For best results, speech and language therapy materials used should be consistent with the rest of the pupil's curriculum. So too for occupational therapy and physiotherapy.

The importance of the coordinator's role cannot be over-emphasised. Too often, coordination is a missing link, and parents end up having to act as go-between or link person among professionals. This is emotionally draining. There is a very real need to bring together the disparate views, practices and skills offered by each specialist area. If coordination does not take place before the pupil receives all these different practices, then he or she will have the task of integrating all these fragmented opportunities for learning: learning is made much more difficult.

The coordinator should:

- regard parents as having a real and valuable contribution to make in identifying and planning their child's curriculum;
- have a sound knowledge of special educational needs, preferably with a background in deafblindness;
- have the ability to work with other professionals, be able to integrate their views into a complete package, and be able to challenge views in a non-threatening way;

- adopt a problem-solving approach; he or she should not believe that answers will come from applying an 'off-the-shelf' assessment and/or intervention package;
- be able to work in a non-hierarchical manner; the views held or contribution to be made by a classroom auxiliary or parent should be regarded as having equal importance to those of other practitioners;
- be able to agree goals, set these, set time-scales for review and evaluate what is and is not working, and be willing to amend objectives in the light of results.

Topic 3: Delivering education and care: the legal context

Introduction

In Chapter 1 we described how deafblind children and young people require support in finding out information, in communicating with other people and in moving around their environment. This book has looked at how to offer that support. We have learned that impaired sight and hearing result in greater reliance on the person's remaining senses, having to touch others and be touched by them. Depending on the nature and extent of the child's impairments, touch may be a primary or a secondary route to learning. Touch may be needed in order to sign to the pupil or for the pupil to communicate with other people; it may be needed to carry out intimate care tasks such as continence management or washing. And, as described earlier in this chapter, touch may be required for physical intervention.

But learning through touch and being exposed to being touched by other people introduces its own concerns. Touch requires an intimacy that most often occurs only with young babies. How can the pupil's dignity, privacy and self-respect be promoted at the same time as the very techniques used to promote them might make the pupil more vulnerable? A whole host of legislation covering education, health, social work services and other areas, as well as the general legal context of civil and criminal law, has a bearing on this everyday contact with a pupil who is deafblind.

Legislative background

With such a diversity of legislation, we consider only a few which you need to take into account when providing support to the child or young person who is deafblind. The legal systems are different across the UK and, rather than presenting a rather sterile account of these differences, we acknowledge two important points. First, although the systems differ, they deal with similar matters and each takes account of the other's proceedings. Second, the United Nations Convention on the

Rights of the Child, ratified by the UK Government in December 1991, now underpins the legal systems across the UK. We therefore begin with a brief overview of the UN Convention.

The UN Convention on the Rights of the Child

The convention applies to many aspects of a child's life, including health, social welfare, education and justice. The key principles of the UN Convention are: all rights apply to all children without exception or discrimination of any kind (Article 2); the best interests of the child must be a main consideration in all actions affecting children (Article 3); children's views must be taken into account in all matters affecting them (Article 12). A sample of the 54 Articles of the Convention include the following, which are relevant to all those who work with children:

- to ensure the child's best interests are a primary consideration in any decision which may effect them either as individuals or as a group (Article 3.1);
- to ensure that all services and facilities provided for children conform to standards of safety, staffing and supervision established by competent authorities (Article 3.3);
- to ensure children are not separated from their parents or carers unless it is in their best interests (Article 9);
- to ensure that children have the opportunity to express views about their own health and treatment and have them taken into account according to their age and maturity (Article 12);
- to ensure that children from ethnic linguistic or religious minorities are able to enjoy their own cultures, religions and languages and that, in particular, their linguistic needs are taken into account (Articles 13 and 17(d));
- to respect the rights and responsibilities of parents and guardians in assisting them to bring up their children (Articles 5 and 18);
- to respect the child's right to privacy and confidentiality (Article 16);
- to ensure that examinations and treatment are necessary and in the best interests of the child and do not interfere with the child's right to physical and personal integrity (Article 19);
- to ensure children with disabilities and learning difficulties are able to achieve the fullest possible social integration and individual development (Article 23);
- the right of the child to education (Article 28);
- to respect the right to equal opportunities in education for children who are unable to attend school regularly (Articles 28 and 29);
- to ensure that there are facilities for play, recreational and cultural activities for those who are in hospital or receiving long-term treatments (Article 31).

The Children Acts

The Children Act 1989 and Children (Scotland) Act 1995 provide the main legislative framework through which the welfare of children in the UK is promoted. The Acts stipulate the local authority's duty to promote the welfare of children in need, which includes those who are disabled or affected by disability. When local authorities and others make significant decisions or provide services, the welfare of the child should be their paramount concern. When making decisions affecting children they should seek and have regard to the views and wishes of children. And in order to put this into practice, professionals involved with children should seek to work in partnership with the child's family.

Duty of care, choice and risk

Duty of care

Common law gives certain responsibilities to those who care for others in health and social care, the duty to care and ensure the safety of those in their charge, and the right to restrain to prevent harm, as long as the restraint used is the minimum necessary. The duty of care then is on you as the responsible adult to take reasonable steps to protect the welfare of a vulnerable person, in this case a deafblind pupil. The duty is to act reasonably, and the more vulnerable the person, the greater the responsibility. There is a duty of care to other pupils in the class as well as to the public.

Choice and risk

Increased understanding of how to exercise choice, and increased opportunities to exercise that choice, result in increases in the variety and quality of incidental learning experiences. It encourages independent mobility – when you can go where you want to go and leave when you want to leave. And it encourages communicative competence – making requests known to a wider circle of people.

But there are disadvantages to exercising choice. Of primary concern is the potential for increased exposure to risk. To balance this exposure to risk, it is important to try to encourage the pupil to assess risks and to take responsible risks. For example, for one pupil, chopping vegetables may involve the risk of being cut. Staff might instruct the pupil as carefully as possible how to cut vegetables. Before deciding that the pupil can be exposed to the risk of cutting himself, a risk which other people take every day, staff need to be sure that they have assessed the risk involved and have reviewed the degree of assistance required.

Risk assessment, then, is a task not only to be carried out at designated transition points, for instance when deciding if a pupil might attend a particular class or school, but also should become a routine part of lesson planning.

Figure 7.3 Gardening

Health and Safety at Work Act 1974

Employers are responsible for the health and safety of their employees and anyone else on the premises. In schools this will include head teacher and teachers, non-teaching staff, pupils and any visitors.

The employer of staff at a school must take all reasonable steps to ensure the health and safety of employees and make sure that others, including pupils and visitors, are not placed at risk. In order to comply with duties under this Act and related 1992 legislation, the employer's actions would include:

- drawing up a safety management policy;
- making sure staff are aware of the policy and their responsibilities;
- ensure appropriate safety measures are in place, including risk assessment;
- ensure staff are properly trained and receive guidance on their responsibilities as employees.

Most schools will at some time have pupils with special medical needs and many pupils who are deafblind have complex health needs. The employer must ensure that safety measures cover all pupils at the school, often requiring special arrangements for particular pupils.

Putting legislation into practice

Those working with children and young people with special educational needs, including those who are deafblind, need to know about their school or local authority guidance on procedures for:

- using escorts and transporting children;
- providing intimate care, including toileting, changing, washing and dressing;
- protecting vulnerable children from abuse;
- carrying out medical examinations;
- providing medical treatment including rectal administration of medicines.

What does this background legislation mean in practice? Consider a typical school day.

From home to school

Although the parents have a continued responsibility for their child, at what point in the school day does the parents' duty of care end and the school's duty begin? It would seem clear that once a pupil enters a school ground and the parent departs then the duty of care passes from the parent to the school. This duty would include all activities carried out by staff and others appointed by them while outwith the school grounds. The parental duty of care is taken up again on the child's return to them or when they pick up the child. If the child is transported between school and home the escort has a duty of care during that journey.

The escort should know and understand how to implement any necessary emergency procedures, have contact telephone numbers and should carry an emergency medication kit, and ideally a mobile phone. Escorts may require specialist training in carrying out emergency procedures and should have some basic understanding of how to communicate with the child.

There is no doubt that the whole question of transport between home and school is of great concern to staff in schools as well as to parents. Staff and parents perceive a risk to the child's safety because the child is away from both home and school. Moreover, routine travel arrangements can be adversely affected by many ordinary events such as traffic jams, behaviour of other drivers, mechanical failure and inclement weather. To minimise risk, cooperation is needed between school and those responsible for organising transport and guidelines drawn up for drivers and escorts who are responsible for the child's care during the journey.

Providing intimate care

Once in the school the pupil may require one or more forms of intimate care to be provided, perhaps help with undressing and dressing, washing, continence management and administration of medication. These activities are of special significance with pupils who are deafblind. Not only are they possibly required as forms of intimate care but the way these activities are carried out may be instrumental to the pupil's learning experiences (see Chapter 3). In the world of the deafblind child, boundaries between education and intimate care may become blurred. Because of this intimate care has to be given sensitively and should foster the pupil's positive image of his or her own body. Key principles should guide all practice:

- know how to communicate what is going to happen, what is happening next and when it is finished: putting intimate care into context;
- wherever possible, encourage the pupil to express a choice of who should carry out intimate care and how it should be done;
- take account and act appropriately if a pupil shows he or she does not want intimate care to be given by an individual;
- encourage the pupil to choose the sequence in which care is provided;
- ensure privacy, respecting age and the situation in which care is to be provided, especially if being carried out away from the school;
- encourage as far as possible the pupil to take responsibility in caring for himself or herself.

If these principles are borne in mind in all intimate care actions, the pupil's self-esteem is enhanced and important life skills and independence are acquired. Each school should, in consultation with the local authority, have drawn up procedural guidance for staff. For example, guidance might cover:

- the need to consult with parents on how best to deliver intimate care;
- what is and is not considered to be intimate care;
- individual children's perceptions: the need to discover what they regard as intimate;
- how to encourage the child to take responsibility for intimate care;
- instructions on which staff are allowed to deliver intimate care;
- what skills staff must acquire before engaging in intimate care and how supervision will be managed;
- where to find a record of staff allowed to provide intimate care (preferably in each child's file);
- how senior staff will assess suitability of staff for carrying out intimate care;
- what information staff need to carry out intimate care, where to find it and who is responsible for ensuring that it is kept up to date.

These statements show that it is vital that schools consult with parents on how it is most appropriate to deliver intimate care.

Administering medication

Like all children, disabled children have a legal right to consent to or refuse medical examination or treatment, provided they can understand the nature and effects of the treatment. In practice, the decision on whether a child is capable of understanding their right to consent to or refuse treatment usually rests with a qualified medical practitioner. At the time of writing there is a move towards decisions being based on consultation between doctors, carers and the child. Teachers and other school staff are excluded from giving consent to a child's treatment and it is important to be aware of the specific guidance on consent to treatment applied within each local authority. For example, one authority may direct that staff need to work out how to deal with treatment in an emergency directly with parents.

There is no statutory obligation on local authorities to provide medical treatment for pupils but they are required to cooperate with health services to make provision. Education authorities are therefore expected to take reasonable steps to assist health services to make medical treatment available to pupils, as appropriate.

At the time of writing, teachers' contracts also do not oblige them to administer medicines to pupils. Therefore any arrangements education authorities make for teachers, or other staff, to administer medicines normally given by parents, are voluntary. The documents *Supporting Children with Medical Needs: A Good Practice Guide* (DfEE 1996) and *Helping Hands* (The Scottish Office 1999) provide detailed guidance on administering medical treatment.

Invasive procedures

Some pupils with epilepsy are prescribed rectal medication to reduce the frequency of seizures or to alleviate the effects of seizures. Other pupils may require other invasive forms of treatment. Some schools have the support of a school nurse, others do not and need to make other arrangements.

Where staff agree to administer these more invasive forms of treatment they need to know how to do it before undertaking the task and so should expect to be given support and training from management, education authorities and health care personnel. Parents are most often happy to be involved in this.

While a consistent policy needs to be issued to all concerned and staff made aware that they will be indemnified provided they follow agreed procedures, it is important that guidance is tailored to take account of each pupil's individual needs. Personal Communication Passports are a way of providing personalised, practical information about how to ensure that experiences are safely carried out in a way that is sensitive to a pupil's privacy and dignity (Millar and McEwen 1993).

Each passport is designed to establish a positive view of the child and his or her strengths. Specific information and instructions can be provided through the passport, not just about how to administer rectal medication and other forms of intimate care, but to reflect the whole child: how she communicates; the style of learning that is best suited; who she knows and what each person means to her in a practical sense. Personal Passports help others to understand how to interact with the pupil in all aspects of everyday life.

Child protection

Suppose that while administering medication you notice bruising on the pupil's legs and upper arms. What do you do?

The Children Act 1989 and Children (Scotland) Act 1995 revamped measures to be taken to prevent or (if it had taken place) to deal with child abuse. The education service does not have an investigative or intervention role in child protection but it does have an important role to play in recognising and referring abuse and suspected abuse. Teachers and classroom assistants have day to day extended contact with children. They are in a position to spot changes in behaviour, failure to develop and other signs of child abuse.

You should know in what circumstances to alert social services or the police if you suspect child abuse, and how to alert them. Children's Services Plans and local arrangements stemming from them will describe procedures to be followed if abuse is suspected. Schools, including nursery schools, should be notified if a child's name is included on the child protection register. This helps to prompt observation of that child's pattern of attendance and development. Staff should be aware of local arrangements on child protection and reporting of abuse that apply to them.

Schools can help prevent child abuse by setting objectives within the curriculum. At the time of writing, indications are that child protection issues will be included in the national curriculum for initial teacher training (England and Wales). As yet it is unclear how this will be implemented and it does not address the issue for teachers who have already qualified.

Deafblindness is associated with particular difficulties regarding child protection and abuse. Because of difficulties in accessing information, communicating with others and moving around abuse can take place and go unsuspected and unreported. With other pupils who are deafblind abuse may be suspected or reported when it has not in fact take place. Consider the categories used for the purposes of registering a child on the local authority Child Protection Register: physical injury; sexual abuse; neglect or non-organic failure to thrive; emotional abuse. How might deafblindness be associated with under-, or indeed, over-reporting of abuse?

Physical injury

At what point does dealing with difficulties in feeding become force-feeding? If a child with feeding difficulties is not fed, you or the parents may be accused of neglect. However, efforts to feed the child may appear as force feeding.

Sexual abuse

Sex education is an aspect of education and personal and social development that is routinely accepted within the curriculum (see Chapter 3). We know that learning by touch and physical contact is a method for learning used in every other area of a deafblind child's education (e.g. massage to increase body awareness). However, sex education through physical contact can appear to others as abuse.

Neglect or non-organic failure to thrive

The deafblind child has limited opportunities to control his or her world. One effective way of doing so is to reject food. If there is no clear organic basis for failing to thrive does this constitute abuse or is it the child's way of controlling the world?

Emotional abuse

A deafblind child might exercise control by withdrawing from social contact. How can you help a pupil access community resources if he or she is distressed by increased contact with other people?

The child protection process emphasises the benefits of being able to consult with the child. But severe communication impairment will make consultation difficult at all levels of the protection process: from identifying that physical or other forms of abuse may have taken place through to being consulted at review case conferences. How might your work on improving communication assist social services to consult with the pupil? Throughout this book we have emphasised the importance of approaches to communication that promote choice, encourage self-esteem, can be applied outwith the classroom setting and encourage the pupil to take control of his or her own learning.

The curriculum

The ways in which intimate care needs are met and medication is administered are two of the more obvious concerns for educators with the duty of care. Although traditionally more associated with care and welfare, administration of medication can be integral to the child learning new skills, improving communication and exploring the world. What about those activities that are thought of as more within the province of educators? Do learning activities have to be monitored to ensure they comply with legislation usually associated with care?

Each and every contact with the pupil, whether arising from attending to the welfare of the child or associated with learning, is subject to the same legislation designed to promote the welfare of the child. Below we discuss a few examples.

Attending to the task

When trying to attract a child's attention to focus on a task, how might this be done? One method might be to place one's own hand or hands on the child's head and turn it so that his or her eyes are turned towards the object or task. Perhaps the child's attention is attracted quickly, perhaps in the short term this technique is effective, but it may not be on firm legislative grounds. To comply with legislation, other ways of gaining attention than physically holding and turning the child's head may have to be devised. These might include investigating:

- if the pupil uses eccentric viewing, if so the poorest area of attention may be in the midline;
- the type of activity being undertaken, is it sufficiently motivating?
- whether there are other means to the same end, i.e. can we do this differently and still get the child's attention.

Going swimming

To many pupils swimming can offer a relaxing environment in which to learn or consolidate new skills, develop gross motor skills and generally to have fun. In order to achieve these ends, however, clear procedures are needed to ensure that swimming can take place in a safe environment, elements of which would include:

- ensuring transport to and from the swimming pool is safe and sufficient support staff are available;
- checking that water is warm enough for children who are less able to regulate their own body temperature;
- understanding if any special risks exist for individual pupils, e.g. due to medication, reduced immunity to infection;
- devising procedures to ensure that privacy and dignity are respected during dressing and undressing, for example that no staff member is unsupervised with a child.

Moving and handling

European Commission regulations on moving and handling are generally interpreted solely in terms of physical characteristics, e.g. hoist requirements above a certain weight, what to do if lifting from floor level, and so on. As such it may seem inappropriate to discuss this topic in the context of education and learning. However, the consistency of contact required for successful moving and handling can reap benefits for pupils who are deafblind. Specific touch cues can be agreed and used consistently before, during and on completion of each instance of moving and handling.

Massage

Massage is often used with pupils who are uncertain of touching and exploring objects and being touched by others. If the pupil's main route to communicating will be signing, and he or she dislikes being touched or touching, then awareness and tolerance of touch will be an important step towards learning to communicate.

In these circumstances, massage is often considered as a means of relaxation and of experiencing touch in a positive context. When using massage, staff need to understand that the child becomes more vulnerable. Massage should therefore be carried out within a relationship of trust, built up gradually with staff who already know the child and who can interpret and respond appropriately to what the pupil does. Most guidance recommends that massage be restricted to areas of the body such as the hands, feet and face.

Conclusion

Legislation has moved in the past ten or twenty years to clarify and update what it means to have a duty of care to the child, to ensure his or her best interests and to provide a safe environment. One major influence has been that of the UN Convention on the Rights of the Child. We can anticipate further developments which will affect contact and communication with children and the curriculum delivered to them. For example, the trend will continue of whole-school policies being developed with pupils themselves making a meaningful contribution to their own development.

The principles driving current legislation share much in common with successful efforts to educate pupils who are deafblind, that is to:

- be open to how the pupil communicates, about what and with whom;
- focus on learning that is rooted in experience;
- understand what motivates and interests the pupil;
- give information that, in both form and content, encourages choice;
- encourage exploration.

With these in place contact, communication and the curriculum will be enhanced.

Summary

The deafblind child is educationally disadvantaged by her lack of access to communication and information. The teacher of deafblind children is responsible for creating a learning environment that minimises the effects of dual sensory impairment and maximises the opportunities for learning.

Initially she will enable the child to feel secure, both with adults and in her environment, in order to release her potential for further learning. Routines and structure as well as helping the child to recognise those she works with will lay the foundations for development in all areas.

She will create physical and learning settings which allow the child to use her remaining hearing and vision as well as possible, and use techniques which compensate for sensory difficulties. The right environment is essential in helping the child to learn effectively.

She will choose and use appropriate alternative and augmentative communication, ensuring that this communication is available to the child at all times.

She will carefully plan teaching programmes, which will assist the child to make progress. She will consider the child's extra need for motivation, and for control of the learning situation as far as possible. She will design tasks which take into account the time the child needs for learning, the styles of prompting she can best use, and which use every opportunity to put learning into practice.

The deafblind child is severely restricted in what she can learn incidentally. She is more reliant than other children on how her teacher organises, plans and delivers programmes. Good teaching, based on appropriate principles, will allow the child the opportunity for learning.

References

DfEE (1996) *Supporting Children with Medical Needs: A good practice guide*. London: DfEE.

Emerson, E. *et al.* (1987) 'Developing services for people with severe learning difficulties and challenging behaviours'. Institute of Applied and Social Psychology, University of Kent, Canterbury.

HMSO *Children Act 1989*. London: HMSO.

HMSO *Children (Scotland) Act 1995*. London: HMSO.

HMSO *Health and Safety at Work Act 1974*. London: HMSO.

HMSO *Health and Safety at Work Act (as amended 1992)*. London: HMSO.

Millar, S. and McEwen, G. (1993) 'Passports to Communication', in Wilson, A. and Millar, S. (eds) *Augmentative Communication in Practice: Scotland*. Edinburgh: CALL Centre.

Phillips, G. (1989) *Challenging Behaviour: Severe behaviour problems of children who have learning difficulties*. Report to Scottish Education Department.

The Scottish Office (1999) *Helping Hands: Guidelines for staff who provide intimate care for children and young people with disabilities*. Edinburgh: The Scottish Office.

United Nations (1991) *Convention on the Rights of the Child*. New York: United Nations.

Further reading

Ackerman, D. and Mount, H. (1991) *Literacy for All: a whole language approach to the national curriculum for pupils with severe and complex learning difficulties*. London: David Fulton Publishers.

Aitken, S. and Buultjens, M. (1992) *Vision for Doing. Assessing Functional Vision in Learners who are Multiply Disabled. Sensory Series No. 2*. Edinburgh: Moray House Publications.

Anderson, S., Boigon, S. and Davis, K. (1991) *Oregon Project for Visually Impaired and Blind Preschool Children*, 5th edn. Oregon: Jackson Education Service District.

Best, A. B. (1987) *Steps to Independence: practical guidance on teaching people with mental and sensory handicaps*. Kidderminster: BIMH Publications.

Best, A. B. (1992) *Teaching Children with Visual Impairments*. Milton Keynes: Open University Press.

Bloom, Y. (1990) *Object Symbols: A communication option*. North Rocks, Australia: North Rocks Press.

Blythman, M. and Diniz, F. A. (eds) *Contact: a resource for staff working with children who are deafblind*. Sensory Series 3. Edinburgh: Moray House Publications.

Bradley, H. and Snow, R. (1994) *Making Sense of the World: a guide for carers working with people who have combined sensory and learning disabilities*. Scotland: Sense.

CNEFEI (1997) *Communication and Congenital Deafblindness: development of communication: what is new?* Suresnes: Editions du centre national de Suresnes.

Creemers, B. P. M. (1994) *The Effective Classroom*. London: Cassell.

Cunningham, C. and Davis, H. (1985) *Working with Parents: frameworks for collaboration*. Milton Keynes: Open University Press.

Etheridge, D. (ed.) (1995) *The Education of Dual Sensory Impaired Children: recognising and developing ability*. London: David Fulton Publishers.

Freeman, P. (1985) *The Deaf-blind Baby: a programme of care*. London: Heinemann.

Goetz, L., Guess, D. and Stremel-Campbell, K. (eds) (1987) *Innovative Program Design for Individuals with Dual Sensory Impairments*. Baltimore, Md.: Paul H. Brookes.

Goodrich, J. A. and Kinney, P. G. (1985) *Curriculum Adaptations for the Deaf-Blind: the sensorimotor period*. Kentucky: The University of Kentucky.

Hyvärinen, L. and Lindstedt, E. (1981) *Assessment of Vision in Children*. Stockholm: Tal and Punkt.

LaVigna, G. and Donellan, W. (1986) *Alternatives to Punishment: solving behaviour problems with non-aversive strategies*. New York: Irvington Press.

Longhorn, F. (1988) *A Sensory Curriculum for Very Special People: a practical approach to curriculum planning*. Human Horizon Series. London: Souvenir Press.

McConnell, A. (1994) *The Massage and Aromatherapy Guidelines: working with children and adults with learning difficulties*. (The Jade College of Natural Therapy, 12 Jenkyn Road, Bedford MK43 9HE. Tel: 01234 767619.)

McConnell, A. (1994) *The Massage and Aromatherapy Workbook*. (See above.)

MacFarland, S. Z. C. (1995) 'Teaching Strategies of the van Dijk Curricular Approach', *Journal of Visual Impairment and Blindness* 89(3), 222–28.

McGee, J. J. *et al.* (1987) *Gentle Teaching: a non-aversive approach to helping people with mental retardation*. New York: Human Sciences Press.

Miller, O. (1995) *One of the Family*. London: RNIB videos.

National Curriculum Council (1989) *From Policy to Practice*. York: NCC.

National Curriculum Council (1989) *The National Curriculum and Pupils with Severe Learning Difficulties*. York: NCC.

National Curriculum Council (1992) *Special Needs and the National Curriculum, Opportunity and Challenge*. York: NCC.

Nielsen, L. (1992) *Educational Approaches for Visually Impaired Children*. Denmark: Sikon.

Nottinghamshire SLD Sex Education Project (1991) *Living Your Life*. A Sex Education and Personal Development Programme for Students with Severe Learning Difficulties developed by Ann Craft and members of the Nottinghamshire SLD Sex Education Project, LDA.

Ockleford, A. (1993) *Objects of Reference*. London: RNIB.

Qualifications and Curriculum Authority (1998) *Supporting the Target Setting Process*. London: DfEE.

RNIB (1996) *Taking the Time: telling parents their child is blind or partially sighted*. London: RNIB.

RNIB and VITAL (1998) *Approaches... to working with children with multiple disabilities and a visual impairment*. London: RNIB.

Sacks, S. Z. and Silberman, R. K. (1998) *Educating Students Who Have Visual Impairments with Other Disabilities*. Baltimore, Md.: Paul H. Brookes.

Scott, E. P. (1972) *Can't your Child See?* London: University Park Press.

Siegel-Causey, E. and Downing, J. (1989) 'Nonsymbolic communication development. Theoretical concepts and educational strategies', in Goetz, L. *et al.*, *Innovative Program Design for Individuals with Dual Sensory Impairments*. Baltimore, Md.: Paul H. Brookes.

SEN Policy Unit (1998) *Special Educational Needs in Scotland*. Edinburgh: The Scottish Office.

SOED (1991–93) *Curriculum and Assessment in Scotland: 5-14 Guidelines*. Edinburgh: SOED.

Scottish Office (1997) *A Commitment to Protect*. Edinburgh: The Scottish Office.

SOEID (1994) *Health Education in Scottish Schools: Meeting special educational needs*. Edinburgh: SOEID.

SOEID (1994) *The Education of Pupils with Language and Communication Disorders*. Edinburgh: SOEID.

SOEID (1996) *How Good is our School? Self evaluation using performance indicators.* Edinburgh: SOEID.

SOEID (1998) *Improving the Care and Welfare of Residential Pupils: self-evaluation using performance indicators.* Edinburgh: SOEID.

Social Services Inspectorate/Department of Health (1994) *Inspecting for Quality: standards for residential child care services.* London: HMSO.

Thomas, M. (1991) 'Vision, motivation and movement', *Focus* 3, 12–15.

University of Strathclyde (1997) *Clear Expectations, Consistent Limits.* Glasgow: The Centre for Residential Care.

van Dijk, J. (1982) *Rubella Handicapped Children.* London: Swets and Zeitlinger.

van Dijk, J. (1986) 'An educational curriculum for deaf-blind multiply handicapped persons', in Ellis, D. (ed.) *Sensory Impairments in Mentally Handicapped People.* London: Croom Helm.

van Dijk, J. (1989) 'The Sint Michilsgestel approach to diagnosis and education of multisensory impaired persons', in Best, A. B. (ed.) *Sensory Impairment with Multi-handicap: current philosophies and new approaches.* A European conference, Warwick University, 6–11 August 1989: Papers on the Education of the Deaf-Blind. International Assocation for the Education of the Deaf-Blind.

van Dijk, J. (1991) *Persons Handicapped by Rubella: victors and victims*, Chapter 6. Amsterdam: Swets and Zeitlinger.

van Uden, A (1970) *A World of Language for Deaf Children. Part 1. Basic Principles: a maternal reflective method.* Rotterdam: Rotterdam University Press.

Wyman, R. (1986) *Multiply Handicapped Children.* London: Souvenir Press.

Glossary

Accommodation: the ability of the lens of the eye to vary in thickness (focus) so that a sharper image falls on the retina.

Acuity: clarity or sharpness of vision. Also visual acuity.

Amblyopia: is a condition where central visual acuity of an apparently healthy eye is reduced because of lack of use during early childhood (0–7 years). Often it occurs because the 'good' eye is preferred. Sometimes known as lazy eye it is usually due to a squint. It may be treated by patching the good eye and exercising the amblyopic or lazy eye.

Anophthalmia: the absence of one or both eyeballs.

Astigmatism: impaired eyesight resulting usually from an irregular shape of the cornea.

Audiological physician: a GP who has had further training in Audiology. They can diagnose and treat ear and hearing disorders.

Audiological scientist: is non-medical and has a postgraduate qualification in Audiology. They are also trained to perform hearing assessments of all kinds and fit and monitor hearing aids.

Audiology technician: is non-medical and is trained to perform hearing assessments of all kinds and to fit and monitor hearing aids.

Auditory nerve: group of nerve fibres that carry impulses from the cochlea to the hearing centre of the brain.

Binocular coordination: use of both eyes together so that the separate images (which are slightly different) are interpreted by the brain as a single image.

Blindness: the statutory definition for the purposes of registration as a blind person is 'so blind as to be unable to perform any work for which eyesight is essential'.

A person with visual acuity below 3/60 Snellen may be regarded as blind.

A person with visual acuity of 3/60 but less than 6/60 Snellen may be regarded as blind if the field of vision is considerably contracted, but should not be regarded as blind if the visual defect is of long standing and is unaccompanied by any material contraction of the field of vision, e.g. in cases of congenital nystagmus, albinism, myopia, etc.

Cataract: means the lens of the eye is cloudy or opalescent and the result is a loss of vision for detail. Caused by congenital anomalies such as rubella, Down's syndrome or by infection, drugs or severe malnutrition during pregnancy. Nowadays surgery is carried out as soon as possible after birth to minimise the risk of severe visual impairment. After surgery the lens which is removed is usually replaced with spectacles, contact lenses, or implant lenses.

Cerebral: to do with the brain.

CHARGE Syndrome or **Choanal Atresia**: this is an acronym for Coloboma of the eye; Heart disease; Choanal Atresia; Retarded growth; Genital hypoplasia; Ear abnormalities. Medical treatment of all aspects of this syndrome and appropriate educational provision are essential.

Closed Circuit TV (CCTV): device that electronically enlarges print material on a TV screen. Choice of brightness, foreground/background colour and magnification are usually available.

Conductive hearing loss: is caused by anything which prevents sound waves reaching the inner ear, i.e. by problems in the outer and/or middle ear.

Cones and rods: two types of cells that form the photoreceptor layer of the retina and act as light-receiving media. Cones are concerned with visual acuity and colour discrimination while rods perceive motion and vision at low degrees of illumination (night vision).

Congenital: present at birth or shortly after; (of blindness) occurring before visual memory is established.

Congenital deafness: or deafness at birth, can be caused by premature birth, jaundice or use of drugs for very sick babies. Such occurrences are few; often the reasons for deafness cannot be pinpointed.

Conjunctiva: mucous membrane that forms the posterior layer of the eyelids and covers the front part of the eyeball, ending at the corneal limbus.

Contact (corneal) lens: lens made to fit directly on the eyeball; used for correction of keratoconus (cone-shaped cornea), retinal image, after cataract extraction and for cosmetic reasons.

Contrast sensitivity: ability to see where one surface edge ends and another begins. A measure of this may give good indication of ability to see objects rather than measuring acuity.

Convergence: process of directing the visual axes of the two eyes to a near point, resulting in the eyes turning inwards and facilitating the ability to focus on objects, etc.

Cornea: clear, transparent portion of the outer coat of the eyeball, forming the front of the aqueous chamber and serving as eye's major refracting medium.

Corneal scarring: a lack of transparency of the ordinarily clear corneal tissue.

Corneal transplant: see keratoplasty.

Count fingers (CF): method of recording vision with people who cannot see well enough to read Snellen chart. Examiner records the distance at which the person can count their fingers.

Cryo: treatment by freezing.

Damage to auditory pathways: the auditory pathways can be damaged through infection, shock or growth of a tumour, although such causes of deafness are rare.

Dark adaptation: ability of the pupils and retina of the eye to adjust to dim light.

Depth perception (ability to judge distance): can be affected when one eye can see much better than the other, or if one eye has no sight at all. Difficulty in judging distances can lead to problems in moving around safely.

Diffused light: light spread widely (by a diffuser) to cover a large area, to prevent glare.

Diopter: unit of measurement of lens power.

Diplopia: double vision or seeing one object as if it were two.

Direct light: light with no shield, so that it creates glare.

Dislocation of the lens: the lens is not in its normal position. Caused by a defect in the suspensory ligament and results in difficulties with accommodation (focus).

Distance vision: ability to see objects clearly when removed in space.

Ear, Nose and Throat Surgeon (ENT): a medically qualified consultant who specialises in the ear, nose and throat. They are usually responsible for the diagnosis and treatment of ear and hearing disorders.

Eardrum: the outer ear gathers sound and passes sound along the auditory canal to the eardrum (the tympanic membrane) which is a very thin layer of skin.

Eccentric viewing: is a method of enhancing the vision of people with central vision loss, using their peripheral vision. This method has to be learned with professional assistance because of the natural tendency to look straight at an object.

Educational Audiologist: is a teacher, trained in audiology, who may support and work out programmes for speech and general educational development. They often visit the homes of under 5-year-old children and work with the parents and families.

Electroretinogram (ERG): method of recording the movements of the eye, usually to assess the functioning of the retina; records the changes of potential in the retina by assessing the electrical response of the retina when stimulated by light.

Enucleation: complete surgical removal of the eyeball.

Eustachian tube: The middle ear contains a small tube (eustachian tube) which runs from the middle ear to the back of the throat.

Evoked Response Audiometry: is an electrophysiological hearing test used for children under three years and people with poor visible responses. Electrodes are place on the skull to record electrical signals produced in response to sound.

Extraocular muscles: the muscles which move the eyeball.

Eye specialist: licensed ophthalmologist or optometrist.

Field of vision: the space within which an object can be seen while the eye remains fixed upon one (central) point including the limits of peripheral or indirect vision.

Fixation ability: ability of the eyes to direct gaze on an object and hold it steadily in view.

Focus: point to which rays of light are converged after passing through a lens.

Fovea: small depression on the retina; the part of the macula adapted for the clearest vision.

Functional vision: presence of enough usable vision that the person has the ability to use sight as a primary channel for learning or living. Relates to the total act of seeing and how the person uses sight to function.

Functionally blind: person whose primary channels for learning and receiving information are tactual and/or auditory.

Fusion: power of coordinating images received by two eyes into a single mental image.

Glare: quality of light that causes discomfort in the eye. It may result from a direct light source within the field of vision or from a reflection of a light source not in the field of vision.

Hearing Therapist: is not involved with the fitting and monitoring of hearing aids but works alongside other professionals to counsel, advise and help with any problems which may arise after a hearing aid has been fitted.

Hereditary deafness: in a relatively small number of families deafness can be transmitted genetically. A child may be born deaf, become deaf early in life, perhaps before learning to speak (prelingually), or be born hearing and gradually develop a hearing loss.

Hypotonia: diminished muscle tone.

Inattention/Neglect: if the part of the brain responsible for knowing that a target is present is deficient, then inattention may occur. Usually it occurs on one side or the other and is present when both sides are being simultaneously stimulated, for example when walking down a corridor which is symmetrical, one side of the corridor may not be seen. In an asymmetrical environment vision may be more normal.

Inner ear: the inner ear contains the cochlea which is a snail-shaped structure which lies deep inside the skull. The fluid in the cochlea is also shared with the organ of balance (three semi-circular canals).

Interocular/intraocular: within or inside the eye.

Iris: coloured, circular membrane suspended between the eye's cornea and immediately in front of the crystalline lens. It separates the anterior (front) and posterior (rear) chambers and it controls the size of the aperture of the pupil, thus controlling the amount of light allowed into the eye.

Keratoplasty: using a disc of corneal tissue from a donor cadaver to graft onto the eye of patient with an irreparably damaged cornea.

Large print or type: print that is larger than type commonly found in magazines, newspapers and books. Ordinary print is 9–12 points in height. Large type is 14–18 points or larger.

Lens: a transparent disc of highly specialised cells, suspended from the ciliary body in the eye. The lens changes shape to focus on near, middle distance or distance.

Light adaptation: power of the eye to adjust itself to variations in the amount of light.

Light preference: choosing a specific type of light and/or degree of illumination to accommodate for a visual impairment, such as direct light to indirect light or dim light to bright light.

Light projection perception (LPP): ability to determine the direction of light. Light perception (LP) alone is the ability to determine if a light is on or off, but unable to identify projection. No light perception (NLP) is the inability to distinguish light from dark.

Low vision: partial sight or subnormal vision which nevertheless allows vision to be used as a primary channel for learning or receiving information.

Low vision aids (LVA): optical devices of various types such as magnifiers, monoculars, lenses, hand-held telescopes or prism lenses, which are useful to people with visual impairments.

Low vision assessment: comprehensive assessment of a person's visual impairment, visual potentials and capabilities.

Low vision clinic: facility that gives eye examinations, provides low vision assessments, prescribes low vision aids and offers instruction on how to use these aids.

Macula: the central part of the retina and the area of most acute vision. The nerve endings of the macula are sensitive to fine detail and enable reading and close work.

Microphthalmos: an abnormally small eyeball.

Middle ear: the middle ear is air-filled and contains three small bones: the hammer (malleus), the anvil (incus) and the stirrup (stapes).

Mobility: term used to denote the ability to navigate from one's present fixed position to one's desired position in another part of the environment (also orientation).

Monocular: pertaining to one eye.

Multiply impaired: having two or more concomitant disabilities that have a direct effect on learning ability.

Muscle balance: ability of the six muscles surrounding each eye to pull together to allow binocular vision to occur in all directions; horizontal, vertical, oblique and circular.

Myringotomy: treatment for glue ear performed, usually under a general anaesthetic, where a ventilation tube (grommet) is inserted in the eardrum.

Near vision: ability to see objects distinctly at the required reading distance.

Night blindness: condition in which rod function is diminished to cause deficient acuity at night and in dim light. Often a side effect of retinitis pigmentosa (RP).

Noise induced deafness: sustained noise can lead to permanent damage of hearing. It is not necessarily the level of noise but the length of time the ears are subjected to it.

Nystagmus: is a rapid, involuntary to-and-fro movement of the eyes. In Primary nystagmus near vision is good or about normal and there may be a head posture which controls the nystagmus and improves vision. Secondary nystagmus may be caused by problems with the eye movement control centre or be due to poor vision in interior visual pathways, e.g. cataract.

Ocular: pertaining to the eye. Ocular disorder is an abnormality of structure and function of the eyes.

Ocular pursuit: act of tracking a moving object in all cardinal directions; vertical, horizontal, oblique and circular.

Ophthalmologist: doctor who specialises in diagnosis and treatments of defects and diseases of the eye, performing surgery when necessary or prescribing other types of treatment, including spectacles or other optical devices.

Ophthalmoscopy: examination of the interior of the eye by means of an ophthalmoscope.

Optic atrophy: nerve fibres (optic nerve) transmitting information from the eye to the brain are affected by wasting. Vision can be helped by bright illumination of objects and high contrast of materials.

Optic disc: the head of the optic nerve (see below) in the eyeball.

Optic nerve: group of nerve fibres that carry impulses from the retina to the visual cortex.

Optician (Optometrist): person trained to carry out sight testing, including the motor coordination of the eyes, prescribes, dispenses and adjusts glasses or other optical devices to correct refractive errors and anomalies of binocular function.

Orientation: process in which a blind or visually impaired person uses remaining senses to establish his or her position and relationship to all other significant objects in the environment (see Mobility).

Orthoptist: non-medical technician who provides scientifically planned exercises for developing or restoring the normal teamwork of the eye system.

Otosclerosis: the stirrup can become gradually immobilised by a build up of bony growth. Various surgical procedures have been developed and typically a stapedectomy can be performed to replace the stapes.

Otoxic drugs: drugs which can cause deafness or damage hearing. Examples include Streptomycin used for treating TB and meningitis.

Partial sight: there is no statutory definition of partial sight but for registration purposes, and the provision of welfare services the following guidance is given.

(a) those with visual acuity of:
   (i)   3/60 to 6/60 and a full field of vision;
   (ii) up to 6/24 with moderate contraction of the field, opacities in media, or aphakia;
   (iii) 6/18 or even better if there is a gross field defect; e.g. hemianopia, or there is marked contraction of the field as in pigmentary degeneration, glaucoma, etc.;

(b) for children whose visual acuity will have a bearing on the appropriate method of education:
   (i)   severe visual disabilities 3/60 to 6/24 with glasses;
   (ii) visual impairment better than 6/24 with glasses.

Perforation (of the eardrum): can be caused by disease or sudden blast of noise, etc. A small hole in the ear drum may not alter the hearing significantly but large ruptures of the eardrum can cause noticeable hearing loss.

Peripheral vision: perception of objects, motion or colour by any part of the retina, excluding the macula.

Photophobia: when light hurts the eyes and the person keeps her eyes away from bright lights. In extreme forms the person performs best in very low light levels.

Prelingual: the early part of life before a child learns to speak.

Prosthesis: visually speaking, an artifical eye.

Pupil: the round opening or black area in the centre of the iris that corresponds roughly with the shutter opening of a camera and permits light to enter the eye.

Pure Tone Testing and Tympanometry: instruments which produce different kinds of sound. The results of a pure tone test are plotted on an audiogram while the results of tympanometry are plotted on a tympanogram. Since these tests require responses from those being tested they are not suitable for very young children.

Refraction: bending or deviation of rays of light in passing obliquely from one medium to another of different density; the determination of the refractive errors of the eye and their correction by prescription of lenses.

Refractive error: defect in the eye that prevents light rays from being brought to a single focus on the retina.

Retina: made up of specialised cells called cones and rods (around 120 million rods and 7 million cones) this acts a bit like the film of a camera. The most sensitive part of the retina is the fovea, which is used for seeing close detail.

Retinitis: inflammation of the retina.

Retinoscopy: observation of the pupil under a beam of light projected into the eye, as a means of determining refractive errors.

Rubella (German measles) is considered the single greatest cause of deafblindness. When contracted by a pregnant mother, particularly in the first trimester, it can cause deafness, blindness, heart defects, brain damage and any combination of these in the foetus. This is preventable by vaccination. Support group: Sense.

Saccades: rapid paired eye movements, fixation and refixation movements, e.g. eye movements used in reading.

Scotoma: blind spots caused by retinal scarring in most instances.

Sensori-neural (perceptive/nerve) hearing loss: in most cases is due to damage in the cochlea in the inner ear or in the neural pathways which transmit the electrical impulses to the brain.

Serous otitis media (glue ear): the eustachian tube can become blocked and fluid gathers in the middle ear which is unable to drain away. It becomes thick and 'glue' like.

Smooth pursuit: smooth following eye movements.

Snellen Chart: a chart for testing distance central visual acuity. Letters or symbols are drawn to a measured scale in such a way that a normal eye sees the largest at 60 metres and the smallest at 4 metres. The measure of a person's visual acuity is given by the fraction indicating the smallest row he or she is able to read at a given distance, e.g. 6/60. This means that the person has to be as near as 6 metres to see letters which someone with normal vision can see at 60 metres distance.

Speech and Language Therapist: a person trained to correct problems in speech production, use of language and general communication procedures.

Strabismus (squint): muscle imbalance, squint, crossed eyes, the failure of the two eyes simultaneously to direct their gaze at the same object and work in unison; due to muscle imbalance.

Suppression: ignoring one of the two images which appear as a result of a squint or double vision. Central vision decreases through non-use. Amblyopia is usually diagnosed (see Amblyopia).

Tonometry: checking intraocular eye pressure.

Tunnel vision: tubular vision; a contraction of the visual field to such an extent that only a small area of central visual acuity remains. This is common in the condition retinitis pigmentosa (RP).

Visual cortex/cortical: to do with the part of the brain which receives and interprets visual signals.

Wax: all healthy ears produce wax which stops dust from entering the ear canal and generally keeps the ear clean. Excessive build up of wax can reduce the input of sound into the middle ear.

Adapted from the Sensory Information Service (SIS) database, produced by the Scottish Sensory Centre; http://www.ssc.mhie.ac.uk

Index